Advance Praise for *Keys to the Corner Office*

"*Keys to the Corner Office* [illegible] ead about the journey to the C-suite. It is a how-to guide from a wise, compassionate trailblazer who is committed to mentoring a new generation of women who want to lead. This book is infused with powerful advice and Rhonda's personal insights. Grab the *Keys,* and get going!"

—Lorraine Herr, Marketing Showroom Director, Sub-Zero Group Midwest, LLC

"Rhonda's professional coaching has had a profound effect on my career trajectory and success. Her no-nonsense, respectful, and empowering advice was one of the key factors in me obtaining my current role as president of an innovative, fast-growing clean tech company. This book will transform your life and accelerate your career."

—Rebecca Boudreaux, PhD, President, Oberon Fuels

"*Keys to the Corner Office* is a take-action book empowering you to make changes in your career. It's an ideal 'how-to-achieve' success manual for anyone—women or men. It maps the business terrain and points you in the direction of the corner office."

—Teresa Daggett, Founder and Principal, Quantum Law

"Highly successful in the male-dominated industries of medical devices and biotechnology, Rhonda Rhyne knows what it takes to survive and thrive. Having significantly benefited from her wisdom, guidance, and leadership, I am excited that she has written *Keys to the Corner Office.* It's a must read for any woman wanting to successfully rise through the ranks of business with grace, respect, and joie de vivre."

—*Bonnie Dupuis Ortega, Vice President, Investor Relations and Corporate Communications, Cardium Therapeutics*

"Rhonda's visionary leadership, inspired confidence, and respectful support taught me I could achieve successes I never thought possible. The principles she shares in *Keys to the Corner Office* made *the* difference in my career success. Do yourself a favor... read this book, implement the advice, and watch your career soar!"

—*Celine Peters, Vice President, Patient Safety and Clinical Development, CRISI Medical Systems*

"Corporate headhunters search for well-rounded executives, beyond their track record of achievements. We monitor people's careers over years. *Keys to the Corner Office* provides value-added tips to help women develop leadership as they advance toward pinnacle career goals—C-suite and corporate board service."

— *Betsy Berkhemer-Credaire, President, Berkhemer Clayton, Inc., Executive Search, Author* The Board Game: How Smart Women Become Corporate Directors

"Whether you are just starting your career or are well on your way, your path to the corner office will be more direct if you follow the road map provided in *Keys to the Corner Office*. Rhonda offers candid advice and actionable tips based upon extensive research and personal experiences."

Karin Eastham, Independent Director, Biotechnology Industry, Author Cook the Part: Delicious, Interactive and Fun Team Cooking

Amanda, 7/14

Thank you for the UC Davis 2013-14 study of CA Women Business Leaders. I look forward to meeting you & hope you enjoy Keys to the Corner Office.

Much Respect,
Rhonda

KEYS *to the* CORNER OFFICE

Success Strategies for Women by Women

RHONDA RHYNE

Keys to the Corner Office: Success Strategies for Women by Women

Published by Crosswalk Press®
PO Box 3772
Rancho Santa Fe, California 92067 USA
www.crosswalkpress.com

ISBN: 978-0-9845563-4-2
LCCN: 2014907107

Cataloging-in-Publication Data

1. Women executives—United States. 2. Board of directors—United States. 3. Sex role in the work environment—United States. 4. Success in business. 5. Businesswomen. 6. Corporate Culture. 7. Leadership in Women. 8. Leadership, women, glass ceilings.

To my mother, who never left her children's side, and who made us believe in ourselves and believe *anything* was possible for our lives.

And to my beloved husband, best friend, and ardent supporter, Peter, who made *so many things* possible in my life.

And, foremost, to my Lord and Savior, Jesus Christ, who made *all things possible.*

A portion of the net profits from *Keys to the Corner Office* will be donated to organizations dedicated to ending human sex trafficking, the most common form of modern-day slavery.

Contents

PART II
Unleash the Leader Within

PART III
Ignite Your Management

PART IV
Transform Your Life

Parting Thoughts

ACKNOWLEDGEMENTS

A heartfelt thank you to my many colleagues, friends, and family who shared invaluable time and insights for *Keys to the Corner Office*.

My publishing partners and dear friends, Bryna Kranzler and Karin Eastham, have loyally been there from the early conception of this book and its many iterations. My beloved and patient husband, Peter, lived through nearly four years of research and writing, endless edits, and twenty-plus potential titles—the final title is his. My immediate family—Patricia (my mum), Charlie, Heather, Kelly, Shelby, Jamie, and Alison—encouraged, advised, and believed when I had doubts.

I received invaluable contributions from my incredible colleagues and friends—Lauren Abrams, Emma Brejwo Balina, Amber Bello, Kevin Bello, David Berg, Amy Bergen, Andrew Bergen, Betsy Berkhemer-Credaire, Margaret Bhola, Mindy Bortness, Rebecca Boudreaux, Rick Cantu, Valerie Carricaburu, Jennifer Conklin, Carla Corkern, Jennifer Crittenden, Teresa Daggett, Krista Dalton, Nicole DeBerg, Robbi Denman, Hien DeYoung, Gary Eastham, Kristina Eastham, Kim Weighter Farley, Malli Gero, Jolie Gischer, Cate Goethals, Maria Golovina, Ashlee Gora, Kevin Hammond, Lorraine Herr, Nancie "Gabrielle" Hochberg, Paul Jansen, Kathy Johanson, Deborah Jondall,

Kathie Jordan, Cheri Joseph, Noah Klika, Andrew Lanyi, Paula Levy, Teri Louden, Nancy Lublin, Caroline Mcelligott, Jana Morrelli, Deanna Mowery Nelms, Jamie Huba Oberto, Bonnie Ortega, Saundra Pelletier, Michael Perry, Celine Peters, Rachelle Pizarro, Chris Pliha, Stephanie Pliha, Kelly Powers, Cindy Presar, Philip Press, Lisa Quast, Erik Sabiers, Maureen Sabiers, David Salisbury, Mary Schumacher, Stan Sewitch, Michelle Stewart, Linda Strobeck, Marjorie Swingle, Rachael Tanner, Jim Tanny, Lauren Tanny, Robin Toft, Sigalit "Siggy" Tsadok, Cynthia Valenta, Nicholas Valenta, Kevin Wagner, Nikki Zahl . . . and many others who have influenced my life.

And thanks to my talented, creative, and fun editor and cover designer, Susan Wenger.

Preface
My Story

For the past ten years, I have wanted to share my business experience with others in hopes of accelerating their success. I talked to colleagues about writing a book with topics ranging from the challenges facing first-time managers to self-image. Ultimately, I decided a book on leadership—geared toward women—would be ideal.

Why me, why leadership, and why women? From a very early age, I possessed leadership qualities—focus, drive, perseverance, and vision. The problem was that I did not always execute these skills in the most intelligent manner.

One of my first demonstrations of sheer, but inappropriate, determination came when I was three years old. I was sitting in the backseat of my mother's bicycle when I announced that I was ready to get off. My mother told me to wait as we would be home in a few minutes. In a less-than-intelligent move, I efficiently halted the ride by thrusting my foot into the rapidly rotating wheel. I still bear an ugly scar from that experience.

Shortly thereafter, my mother placed me in a bowling alley nursery instead of allowing me to calmly and maturely watch her bowl. Yes, at four years old, I thought I was mature enough to sit quietly and watch her. I'm horrified to admit this, especially so early in this book, but visualizing my goal of getting out of the nursery, I bit a child. This immediately got me evicted from the nursery and sent to join my mother, thereby achieving my coveted goal of being able to watch her bowl. After these early triumphs, however, I expanded and refined my leadership skills to include patience, communication, and emotional restraint.

Another critical leadership skill I lacked early in life was a positive self-image. I was the youngest child in a family of four—basically the runt. Although I knew I was loved by my family, I grew up in the shadow of a magnificently beautiful older sister, Heather, whom the entire world adored.

When I was in sixth grade, I wore a size 6X dress, a size that fit most first graders. In high school, my brother told me I was "indented," meaning that I had no breasts. Determined to escape this chapter of my life, I rushed through high school, graduating at sixteen years old, and left for college weighing less than one hundred pounds at a height of five feet, six inches.

One person made all the difference. Throughout my early life, my mother consistently told me I was intelligent and beautiful, and could achieve anything—and I mean anything—I put my mind to. And that one day I would run a company and be on the cover of *TIME* magazine—right! Although I did not believe her, she successfully brainwashed me into developing a positive self-image. I truly believe if you tell yourself—or if someone else tells you—something long enough, you come to believe and achieve it.

In college, I excelled and graduated at the top of my pharmacy class, not because I was the smartest, but because of my focus, drive, and perseverance. Originally, when I left for college, I expected to continue on to medical school. However, instead of pursuing premedical studies or biology as my undergraduate major, I selected pharmacy to provide a stronger medical and technical foundation, as well as a profession should I decide not to pursue medical school.

After earning my bachelor of pharmacy degree, I decided that medical school was not the career path I sincerely wanted to pursue; this was difficult to acknowledge as continuing on to medical school was a long-stated goal of mine. Instead, after graduation, I worked in retail and hospital pharmacies. But within three years, I was ready to pursue another career. Although I had been strongly advised to go into the pharmaceutical industry, pharmaceutical sales did not require the professional rigor I wanted for my career. Instead, I believed I could find a medical device company that would gamble on me.

Ignoring my lack of experience and demonstrating my usual persistence, I secured a medical device sales position and advanced into sales management. Due to my success and some fortuitous networking, I was offered an incredible, albeit risky, opportunity to become vice president of sales and marketing for a start-up biotechnology company. I was also promised a shot at the corner office if I performed well. Again, due to sheer tenacity and hard work—and the grace and direction of God—I surpassed expectations and was promoted to CEO and board director of Culture Technology, Inc., a privately held biotechnology company, at thirty-one years old. Over the next three years, I established the company as a market leader and grew revenue by 347 percent compound average growth rate (CAGR).

Due to this success and my prior networking, Allen Paulson, founder of Gulfstream Aerospace, recruited me to lead CardioDynamics, a publicly traded medical device company. In this case, much as it had been earlier in my life, my leadership abilities lagged behind my opportunities. I had no real mentors, especially among women. Ironically, I had sponsors, mostly men, who provided opportunities. (I explain the differences between mentors and sponsors, and their importance, in chapter 4, "Sponsors and Mentors.")

So, in my mid-thirties, I became chief operating officer

and, shortly thereafter, president of CardioDynamics. I learned about leadership along the way mainly from what I did wrong and some from what I did right.

After CardioDynamics was sold in 2009, I took time off to travel with my husband—whom I had never lived with—and to contemplate life and my next professional move. During this time, I started writing *Keys to the Corner Office* based on what I had learned about leadership. I also started a consulting company to keep "in the game" and to keep abreast of medical advancements and innovative medical technologies. And in 2013, I returned to work full-time as CEO, president, and board director for Prevencio, a development-stage cardiac biomarker company.

As I edited *Keys to the Corner Office,* I was kindly, and rightly, encouraged by my publishing partners and colleagues to add more personal stories. This was excellent advice that was difficult for me to implement as I prefer not to talk about myself. However, in the spirit of transparency, vulnerability, and authentic leadership, I have earnestly attempted not only to share wisdom, but also to share the experiences that led to that wisdom.

In *Keys to the Corner Office,* I often refer to "positive thinking" and "taking control of one's life." Although many people believe I have led a "charmed and privileged" life, the truth is, it has been my positive attitude and belief in God that makes it seem "perfect." For example, just before my tenth birthday, my father, although extremely successful and highly intelligent, abandoned our family; he literally left us on the street without a home or money. Shortly thereafter, unfortunately, he committed suicide. But my mother, in her usual positive way, forged ahead. She made each of her children believe we had the "perfect life." Oh, thank God for her! The positive attitude she embodied has prevailed throughout my life and carried me through many challenging personal and professional times.

The result of my hard-earned wisdom is *Keys to the Corner Office*. It is intended to be used for reference to provide guidance over the course of your career. The book provides background information, *Key Action Tips*, and additional recommended reading to accelerate your career.

The book is divided into five sections: Turbocharge Your Career, Unleash the Leader Within, Ignite Your Management, Transform Your Life, and Parting Thoughts. The focus of *Keys to the Corner Office* is to educate, encourage, and train the reader to level the playing field for herself as well as enhance career opportunities for all women.

My recommended approach to *Keys to the Corner Office* is to read the book at a rate of, perhaps, one or two chapters a day over the next month, and then decide which areas you want to focus on first. Alternately, you may elect to browse through the entire book and identify specific chapters that resonate with you or apply to the stage you're at in your career. Regardless of your approach, identify one to two areas you want to develop and, after adding those skills to your repertoire, choose other areas. Inasmuch as you may not read *Keys to the Corner Office* from cover to cover and may selectively read chapters out of order, I have reiterated important concepts throughout the book.

I thank you for considering my mistakes, successes, and wisdom as a learning path for your career, and as the keys to your own corner office—or at least the keys to your success.

Introduction

We've Come a Long Way Baby— and the Best Is Yet to Come!

Energy and persistence conquer all things.
—Benjamin Franklin, US founding father

In her speech endorsing Senator Barack Obama for president after she failed to gain the Democratic nomination, Senator Hillary Clinton declared, "Although we weren't able to shatter that highest, hardest glass ceiling this time, thanks to you, it's got about eighteen million cracks in it."[1]

We've all heard of the "glass ceiling" and intuitively know what it means, but when and how did that phrase originate? Ironically, the term developed as a result of *progress* in the women's movement. Although women were beginning to achieve greater success in every field, including those that had not previously been open to women, people became aware that there were some subtle obstacles to success.

In 1979, Katherine Lawrence and Marianne Schreiber of Hewlett-Packard coined the term "glass ceiling" to describe an invisible but real barrier through which the next level of advancement was unobtainable for women. It became such a recognized phenomenon by 1991 that the US Department of Labor issued an official definition of the glass ceiling and established the Federal Glass Ceiling Commission in an effort to level the playing field for women.

During the last few decades, awareness of glass ceilings has significantly increased. It has been the subject of research, books, business publications, and blogs. But despite Clinton's optimism, women remain underrepresented in positions of power in almost every sector across the US. In management, women account for approximately one-third of MBA classes, but only 6 percent of top earners, 8 percent of top leadership positions, and 16 percent of board directors and corporate officers. In law, women constitute about half of new entrants to the profession, but less than one-fifth of law firm partners, federal judges, law school deans, and Fortune 500 general counsels.[2]

Furthermore, labor statistics report that the number of women reaching the C-suite (CEO, COO, CFO) decreased by 12 percent between 2000 and 2010.[3] With fewer women reaching senior management, the pool of qualified women for board seats shrinks, making it more difficult for companies to diversify their boards.

But women are making progress on several fronts. With the appointment of Marissa Mayer as Yahoo's CEO in July 2012, the number of Fortune 500 female CEOs hit twenty, or 4 percent—a new record. Then, in January 2014, the number of Fortune 500 female CEOs hit twenty-three, or 4.5 percent, when Mary Barra became the CEO of General Motors.

Additionally, according to an October 2013 Bureau of Labor Statistics report on 2012 earnings,[4] women made about 81 percent of the median earnings of men, up from 62 percent in 1979. The positive: a 19 percent gain in a little more than twenty-two years. The negative: there is still a 19 percent disparity.

Thanks to research highlighting a correlation among gender diversity, good corporate governance, and positive long-term corporate performance, there's now a strong push to add women directors to corporate boards. This push comes from institutional investors and many others.[5] The research is so compelling that in August 2013, the California State Senate and Assembly passed a breakthrough resolution taking the next step in "encouraging" and "urging" California companies to have equitable and diverse gender representation.[6] Specifically, Resolution 62 urges every publicly traded company in California to have one to three women directors on their boards, depending upon the total number of directors.

Momentum is growing with other initiatives, including 2020 Women on Boards, Thirty Percent Coalition, and 85 Broads. The 2020 Women on Boards movement is a national campaign to increase the number of women serving on corporate boards and in executive leadership. Its mission is to increase the percentage of women on US corporate boards from 15.6 percent to at least 20 percent by the year 2020. With even loftier goals, Thirty Percent Coalition is a group of senior business executives, institutional investors, corporate governance experts, board members, national women's organizations, and state elected officials who are working to ensure that by 2015, at least 30 percent of the people on US public company boards will be women. Another initiative, 85 Broads, is a global network of trailblazing women using their intellect and ambition to change the game for all women globally. Even Girl Scouts of USA are engaged; they've launched a national campaign called "To Get Her There" to give girls the skills they need to become leaders in twenty-five years.

Almost a century prior to Lawrence and Schreiber describing the glass ceiling, Susan B. Anthony was fighting hard for women's right to vote. In 1920, fourteen years after

Anthony's death, the US Constitution's Nineteenth Amendment was passed, barring voting discrimination based on gender. What's astonishing is how much longer it took to prohibit wage differentials based on sex—forty-three years, to be exact—with the passage of the Equal Pay Act of 1963. Then, in 1964, the US Civil Rights Act outlawed major forms of discrimination in public facilities based on race, ethnicity, religion, and gender. With California's Resolution 62, twenty-first-century US legislation *may be* right around the corner.

Despite the progress we're making, the fact remains that we are not at par. Eighteen million cracks and counting, glass ceilings still exist—for now. There are certain societal challenges beyond our immediate control, and they will take time, education, and possibly more legislation to conquer. But there are also critical areas of our lives that we do control. *Keys to the Corner Office* provides insights and *Key Action Tips* to help you navigate those critical areas.

My hope is that after reading *Keys to the Corner Office,* you will be better equipped to shatter glass ceilings and secure your own corner office. Read on and enjoy!

PART I

Turbocharge Your Career

Advancing your career isn't just about your next salary increase, promotion, change in companies, or degree. Career advancement requires thought, strategy, skill development, management, and the help of others. It also requires believing that you are in control and must drive your own career.

Many women believe that if they work hard enough, the rewards they deserve will follow. This is a flawed belief and sure-fail strategy, especially if you want to expedite your journey to the corner office.

This section provides insights on key elements that will help you turbocharge your career.

1

Your Career—Care the Most

Successful careers don't just happen. They require thought, strategy, and management.

—Denise Morrison, Campbell Soup Company CEO and board director

Your career—it's where you spend approximately 40 percent of your time for most of your adult life. It's most likely your largest financial resource.

Companies can provide career paths, but they will never care more about your career than you. They make decisions that ultimately best serve their own interests—and so should you. Consider your career as your own business, and don't turn it over to anyone else to run. Don't assign its management to your boss, your human resource department, or your spouse. Take control and care the most!

Careers require strategy and management. Denise Morrison, president and CEO of Campbell Soup, is a good example of somebody who did it correctly. "I knew from an early age that I wanted to lead a company," she declared in a *Wall Street Journal* article.[1] "I developed a strategic process for my career plan that set the final destination, developed

At every stage in your career, stay focused on the big picture.

the career track, identified skills to build, took line positions to gain experience, and sought leadership and management training on the job, through special assignments, coaching, and networking." Wow, don't we all wish we'd had this insight and approached our careers with strategic planning and management!

It's never too early—or too late—to start thinking ahead. Upon entering college, I had my sights set on becoming a physician. Fortuitously, I also considered that I might change my mind about medical school, and decided to obtain an undergraduate degree in pharmacy as opposed to a typical premed degree in biology. My rationale: a pharmacy degree qualified me for a good profession if I elected to forego medicine. It also provided a technical background for careers in other fields, including the medical technology industry.

At every stage in your career, stay focused on the big picture—your career destination. Create a career road map. If you need direction, consider reading *Career Development and Planning: A Comprehensive Approach* or engaging a professional career consultant. It will be money well spent. Once you have your road map, regularly assess your goals and your progress, establish new goals, seek feedback and direction from more experienced professionals, and invest in your development.

Key Action Tips

To enhance your ongoing career management and development:

1. *Acknowledge that your career is your own business.* Take control. Be proactive. Strategically plan. Don't depend on anyone else to manage it. If you do, you'll limit your achievements.

2. *Assess yourself.* Objectively assess your skills, natural talents, strengths, areas of development, likes, and dislikes. Consider utilizing an online assessment or a book such as *Now Discover Your Strengths* or *Strengths Finder* 2.0.

3. *Define your brand.* See chapter 2, "Brand Yourself—Unique, Memorable, and Authentic."

4. *Map your career plan and strategic process.* Envision your ideal career. Describe where you want to end up, or at least where you want to be in ten years. Document what career steps are ideal, what you need to do to get to each step, and who can help you. Seek the advice of a professional career counselor if you're unsure, and read one of the books on road maps in the Recommended Reading section.

5. *Set career goals and take risks.* People don't plan to fail; they fail to plan. On a monthly, quarterly, and annual basis, take time to assess your goals, objectively evaluate your progress, and set new goals. Define detailed steps to reach your goals. Seek help

and change your approach if you are not achieving your goals. Ask yourself whether you feel aligned with the goals of your company. Consider the outlook for your position and how your role might develop. Don't back away from the "risk" of a new job.

6. *Document your accomplishments.* Your accomplishments will largely determine your ability to move into higher positions. Make a focused effort to make meaningful, measurable contributions every day. You are being paid to do so and, in fulfilling your side of the bargain, you'll serve yourself and your career in immeasurable ways. Catalog your achievements in a lifelong career journal.

7. *Continue your development.* Keep learning, whether it's new technology or different professional roles. Stay current on market trends and industry developments that affect your business sector. Doing so makes you an impressive job candidate and a successful executive.

8. *Network, network, network.* Always be networking. Networking is essential to every stage of your career development. Your professional contacts can provide feedback and direction. They can enhance your industry knowledge, assist in your career path, and recommend you for jobs. LinkedIn, industry meetings, and professional organizations are invaluable networking tools for facilitating contact with professionals. Read chapter 5, "Networking—Not a Dirty Word."

9. *Identify sponsors and mentors.* Seek sponsors and mentors. Read chapter 4, "Sponsors and Mentors," for an explanation of the differences between the two.

2

Brand Yourself—Unique, Memorable, and Authentic

Are you known for something of value or are you a victim of others branding you?

—Karen Kang, CEO BrandingPays

The value of branding is well understood. Some companies are known for a specific branded statement, such as Nike's "Just do it." Others associate their brand with an area of excellence, such as Nordstrom's exemplary customer service, Google's search engine, or Apple's design and innovation. Nike, Google, and Apple also have iconic logos. No one would dare argue against the value of these well-defined brands. In fact, in 2013, Interbrand, the world's leading brand consultancy firm, valued Google's brand at $93 billion and Apple's at $98 billion![1]

Just as these companies have staked out clearly differentiated market niches, you, too, must distinguish yourself from innumerable other professionals. "These days, branding your company isn't enough. The world wants to hear what you have to say. If you aren't building your own brand, you and your company will suffer," claims Dan Schawbel,

What is your brand? A strong personal brand is key to influence, opportunities, advancement, and the corner office.

author of *Promote Yourself: The New Rules for Career Success.* To excel, "become an expert in your field, claim a website under your own domain name, connect with the media, and build relationships with your audience."[2]

Karen Kang, author of *BrandingPays: The Five-Step System to Reinvent Your Personal Brand,* agrees. "Thanks to social media and extreme job competition, your image has never been more important. A changing world makes a strategic personal brand the single factor that will make or break your next career opportunity. Consider yourself a free agent—no one else is looking out for your best interests but yourself. You need to be crystal clear about who you are and the value you bring to a world where constant change is the only norm."[3]

A critical success strategy in my move from San Diego, where I was well established, to Seattle, where I was unknown, was branding myself as an expert in commercializing innovative medical technologies for early-stage companies. It truly made the difference for me and my company, Rhyne Life Sciences Consulting. I was overwhelmingly well received, and immediately had more consulting opportunities than I could fulfill. And within six months, I also had three corner office opportunities.

To brand myself, I had to be bold, unique, and memorable. It paid off, though sometimes it felt uncomfortable to toot my own horn so loudly. At times, I did not feel humble.

"Many people are raised to believe humility is a virtue and don't feel personal branding aligns with being humble," observes Deborah Jondall, CEO of Sabra Marketing. "This is especially true for women. We need to change this mindset. Personal branding is essential and educates others who can benefit from knowing your unique value."[4]

Mary Schumacher, principal of Career Frames, a branding, resume, and career advancement firm, adds, "Your personal brand should authentically represent you. Don't just parrot what you think others expect of you because you'll end up looking like a hollow copy of everyone else and miserably unhappy if you're in the wrong job or the wrong company. Instead, by understanding what makes you tick, you'll be able to demonstrate your expertise, individuality, and zeal for solving problems. You'll remain faithful to your values, making you irresistible for new opportunities because you're strong, memorable, and effective."[5]

What's *your* brand?

Key Action Tips

1. *Define your unique value proposition and brand.* Who are you? What differentiates you? What makes you unique, memorable, and authentic? What are your interests and strengths? What do you offer? What do you do better than most other people? Be able to articulate your valuable skills.

2. *Share it.* Be prepared to intersperse your conversations with your unique value proposition. Your goal should be to have everyone walk away from a conversation with you knowing what makes you unique. Read chapter 45, "Roosters Crow, Hens Deliver—Successful Women Do Both."

3. *Become an expert.* By being an expert in an area related to your business or profession, you can enhance or expand your brand.

4. *Generate your brand awareness with a strong online presence and face-to-face networking.* Work with a resume writer or branding expert to create a powerful LinkedIn profile. Connect with other professionals in your industry via social and professional networks/groups, including LinkedIn.com and blog comments. Join relevant online groups, including those associated with your industry, colleges, and past companies. Establish yourself as a "thought leader" by forwarding articles or starting conversations on your Internet professional groups. Don't limit yourself to online activities; face-to-face networking is one of the best ways to become known in your industry.

5. *Establish a website and/or blog under your full name.* Customers, media, and executive recruiters conduct Internet searches by people's names, subjects, and specialties. If you establish a website or blog with a URL that is the same as your name, you'll own the first result for your name in Google and other search engines. Add your picture, biography, email address, and links to other sites where you have an online presence, such as LinkedIn and Twitter. Claim your name before someone else does. If you have a blog, regularly post so it is always current and relevant.

3

Executive Presence

Dress shabbily and they remember the dress; dress impeccably and they remember the woman.

—Coco Chanel, founder of Chanel brand,
French fashion designer

Do you have executive presence? If you don't know, you're not alone. In a recent study by the Center for Talent Innovation, women found feedback about executive presence so contradictory and confusing that 81 percent said they didn't know how to act on it.[1]

It is well known that leaders at the highest echelons of business tend to be taller and deeper voiced.[2] Since women usually lack the "height premium" and deep voice, our executive presence will naturally differ from that of a stereotypical successful male executive. We need to develop a corporate persona appropriately matched to our profession, personality, style, and gender.

Executive presence encompasses numerous components, including dress, physique, body language, self-confidence, verbal and nonverbal communication, speaking tone, and emotional intelligence; for women, it also includes makeup and hairstyle. The list goes on. It even extends to

> If you want people to take you seriously as an executive, you have to look and act the part.

online presence, including your LinkedIn profile. In this chapter, I focus on the physical components of executive presence.

Let's start with something easy—your body language. Your body language defines who you are, and it does so in as little as two minutes. In a TED talk, social psychologist Amy Cuddy shares an easy way to change not only others' perceptions of you, but also the way you feel about yourself. It simply takes two minutes of "power posing." Power posing is standing with arms or elbows out, chin lifted, and an expansive posture. Cuddy's research, done in collaboration with Dana Carney, has shown that adopting a body language associated with dominance for just 120 seconds is enough to create a 20 percent increase in testosterone and a 25 percent decrease in cortisol, a stress hormone. In other words, adopting these postures makes a person feel more powerful.[3] That's amazing!

Don't stop there. Cuddy advises that "many leaders focus so much on demonstrating power and competence that they fail to communicate warmth and trustworthiness... and warmth may actually be a truer, deeper source of power to begin with." Her research indicated that women are much more likely than men to be seen as high on one dimension and low on the other; such images include the sweet, incompetent, fragile, feminine woman and the strong, cruel, masculine woman who has no heart.[4] This is an area in which I have struggled. Given my competence and drive, some employees did not believe that I could also be genuinely warm and caring. Sad, but true. Eventually, I found it was highly effective to build trust and demonstrate warmth prior to exerting authority.

What about dress, hair, and makeup?

Your choice of work attire is partially driven by your workplace culture, but regardless of the culture, women should err on the side of dressing more professionally. While men can get away with wearing golf shirts in a business casual workplace, the same look doesn't work as well for women. Gloria Star, an image and etiquette consultant, advises female executives to dress in one color, which adds height, wear plain fabric rather than patterned styles, and avoid open-toe sandals, bare legs, and dangling or sparkling jewelry. "Trust is higher when an elegant sophisticated business look is consistently presented," she explains.[5]

There was a time in my professional life when I felt open-toe shoes were an absolute no-no. After working in San Diego and now Seattle—two cities that embrace more-than-casual business dress—I have loosened my standards for everyday work attire. In my experience, however, it's still better to be slightly overdressed, especially if you have meetings with more conservative investors or customers. In summary, know your audience and err on the formal side.

"Many women believe it is more important to develop their intellect, allowing their style to play second fiddle. And with the advent of business casual, many women have allowed themselves to slump into a fashion malaise," observes Deborah Jondall, CEO of Sabra Marketing. "Image is everything and negative first impressions are difficult to overcome. Wrapping your intellect in a head-to-toe style that communicates professionalism and proficiency instills confidence and respect. Own the room. Own your leadership and be a role model to others by ensuring the outside package is as together as the inside."[6]

In the professional world where first impressions are critical, your hairstyle can work for or against you. Regardless of color, length, or style, select the combination that is flattering, is polished but not overdone, is appropriate for the workplace, and makes you feel confident. Unless you are in a creative industry, avoid extremes in color, cuts, and stiff hairspray.

Like it or not, research has shown that wearing makeup enhances people's perceptions of a woman's competence, trustworthiness, and likeability.[7] Frankly, I'm thankful for this. I feel more confident and attractive when I'm wearing makeup, and believe that it provides a finishing look for women. It all adds up—look your best, be your best, and do your best!

Key Action Tips

1. Practice "power posing." Watch Amy Cuddy's TED video at http://www.huffingtonpost.com/amy-cuddy/body-language_b_2451277.html?utm_hp_ref=email_share. Conduct two minutes of power posing prior to meetings and demonstrate open, confident body language during meetings.

2. Assess your professional clothing and image. Compare your attire with that of successful women in your industry and company. If there are gaps, consider adjustments or consulting with a wardrobe consultant. Many department stores offer consultations at no charge.

3. Maintain healthy, professional hair. Visit your hairstylist for a cut and, if applicable, coloring every four to six weeks.

4. Visit a makeup artist annually—at Sephora, a local department store, or any other source with trained professionals—to get a makeover and learn about new products and makeup applications.

4

Sponsors and Mentors

People will forget what you said, people will forget what you did, but people will never forget how you made them feel.

—Maya Angelou, American author, poet, Pulitzer Prize nominee

We've heard it over and over: to get ahead, you need a mentor. It's good advice. Research has demonstrated that mentors improve job satisfaction, skill development, and the chance for promotions.

But it's not enough.

There are numerous mentoring programs, networking opportunities, and initiatives specifically for women. In fact, a recent study[1] found women have three times as many mentors as men. But despite this seeming advantage, women are still not reaching the highest echelons of large corporations in significant numbers.

A lack of *sponsorship* for women may be the culprit. The aforementioned study revealed that while women have more *mentors*, men have more *sponsors.*

What's the difference? Typically, mentors help more with *tactical* areas whereas sponsors are more *strategic,*

Mentors encourage you. Sponsors challenge you.

focusing on longer-term career advancement. Mentors encourage and advise you, but sponsors challenge you to reach higher and take on tougher assignments. Mentors often work behind the scenes and are willing to work with low performers, while sponsors are out front promoting high performers—and risking their reputations by doing so.

Sponsors provide stretch assignments, advocate for promotions, and facilitate important relationships. They expand your professional network through introductions to key people both inside and outside your company. They may help overcome women's oft-cited discomfort with asking for or pursuing highly visible, risky assignments.

Women tend to underestimate the power of the sponsor effect, believing that hard work and mentors will get them ahead. This is alarming considering that sponsorship conveys a 30 percent benefit in stretch assignments, promotions, and pay raises—a boost that mentoring alone can never hope to match.[2]

"Thirty-four percent of the marzipan layer, that layer just below senior leadership, is made up of women," says Sylvia Ann Hewlett, chairman of Center for Work-Life Policy (CWLP). However, only about 21 percent of senior leadership is female, and this number hasn't increased in years. "It's about relationship capital," Hewlett explains.[3]

If you need more convincing, McKinsey & Company, in partnership with *Wall Street Journal*'s Executive Task Force for Women in the Economy, interviewed successful executive women and found that 90 percent reported sponsorship as significant to their success.[4]

"Sponsors have made *the* difference in my career advancement," notes Cynthia Valenta, Life Care Solutions manager for GE Healthcare. "They have provided stretch goals, special assignments, coaching, promotions, and a vision for my career. As important, my sponsors have helped me gain visibility at the executive levels of a very large corporation." Valenta adds, "I highly recommend having more than one sponsor at a time. By doing so, you gain different perspectives, access to broader networks, and are covered should one of your sponsors leave your company."

As I indicated in the preface, it was sponsors—most of them male—who provided critical career opportunities for me. They pushed me to take on risky, but key, roles. So don't give up your mentors, but definitely pursue sponsors; they're critical if you want to expedite your progress to the corner office.

Key Action Tips

Here are some steps you can take to find mentors and sponsors.

1. Assess your needs. Determine whether you need support in your:
   a. career path;
   b. functional skill development;
   c. communication, leadership, and interpersonal skills; or
   d. work-life balance.

2. Define your goal for one or two of these areas.

3. Identify successful people in your company, in professional organizations, or on LinkedIn who you can approach. If appropriate, talk to your human resource department for suggestions.

4. Mentors are usually asked to fulfill the mentor role, whereas sponsors usually do the asking. This means you must approach them differently.
   a. Ask a potential mentor to coffee or lunch. If they don't accept, then they probably don't have time to mentor you. If they do, tell the person how much you respect them, inquire about the keys to their success, and ask if they would be willing to meet with you for one hour per month for six months to help you with "X" goal. Start your first meeting with goal setting and go to your meetings with an agenda. Implement suggestions from your mentor, and at each monthly meeting, discuss your progress against your goals. After six months, summarize what you have achieved and ask to continue meeting monthly or periodically stay in touch.
   b. Sponsors can be found inside or outside your company. After you have identified a potential sponsor, attempt to get on a strategic or visible project with them so you can demonstrate your skills and potential. If this is not possible, ask them to coffee, tell them you respect them, and ask about their secrets for success. As you form a relationship, if they see potential in you, they will naturally take you under their guidance. You can share your career aspirations and ask for advice on developing and advancing within the company or industry.

5. Sponsors will likely be men as they are in the majority of upper management and executive positions. Meet in public, if possible, and maintain professionalism. Be prepared for others to question your relationship. You must decide whether you

will forego the help of a male sponsor to avoid potential gossip—which I do not recommend. Always engage a sponsor—male or female—in the most professional manner possible.

5

Networking—Not a Dirty Word

It's not who you know, but who you can get to know.
—Lauren Tanny, CEO, author

Networking is not a dirty word. It's something you *absolutely* must embrace if you want to *significantly* advance your career and secure the corner office.

Let's be candid. Do you know anyone who loves networking? Most people rank it right up there with public speaking or dental extraction. Yes, there are the few rare anomalies out there—people who actually enjoy it; some are even good at it. For the vast majority of us, however, a room full of people drives us right to the bar to drink up some courage before trying—one more time—to make the experience bearable.

Do we really need to network? The answer is a resounding *yes*! Effective networking cultivates long-lasting, influential relationships. Networking makes it easier to secure your next job, promotion, or board position. It can also lead to higher compensation. A recent study quoted in *Harvard Business Review* compared the number of former colleagues that executive directors (board members who were executives within the company) had currently sitting on other boards. On average, those with twice as many former colleagues sitting on boards were paid 6 percent more. More significantly, female executive board directors earned 17 percent less than their male counterparts due to their lack of such a network. Men leveraged their large networks into more senior positions or seats on a higher-paying board.[1]

> "Building relationships is the thrilling if delicate quest to at once understand another person and allow that person to understand you."
>
> —Reid Hoffman, cofounder, LinkedIn

Kathryn Minshew, CEO of the Muse, says, "When new entrepreneurs ask me for advice, I sometimes tell them to NYFO—Network Your Face Off. Nearly everything I've accomplished in the past two years, from speaking on CNN to watching my company cross 1.7 million users in less than a year, can be directly traced back to connections I've made and help I've received from a network that is vast, diverse, and active."[2]

I can vouch for the wisdom of Minshew's advice. Every significant professional job I've had was a result of my diverse network. It's truly about whom you know and can get to know, and only then what you've delivered. Unfortunately, I'm acquainted with plenty of male colleagues who have delivered less but know more people, and thus have risen above more qualified women.

"The best networking suggestion I can offer?" Minshew says. "Always say yes to invitations, even if it's not clear what you'll get out of the meeting. I'm not arguing for long, pointless, unstructured conversations with everyone you meet. But many of my most fruitful relationships have resulted from a meeting or call in which I was not entirely sure what would or would not come of the conversation."[3]

Reid Hoffman, cofounder and chairman of LinkedIn and author of *The Start-up of You,* believes that networking gets a bad rap because most people don't enjoy it. "It's the presumption that building relationships in a professional context is like flossing," he writes. "You're told it's important, but it's no fun."

To motivate yourself for network building, consider the fact that your happiest memories probably involve spending time with someone else. As Hoffman says, "We're not suggesting that you have to be an extrovert or life of the party. We just think it's possible to appreciate the mystery of another person's life experience. Building relationships is the thrilling if delicate quest to at once understand another person and allow that person to understand you."[4] Eloquently put!

A great way to network is to join professional networking groups or industry organizations. One of the many I joined was Athena San Diego, an organization for executive and rising female managers in the life sciences industry. It focuses on mentoring, sponsoring, educating, and networking with other female professionals. Whereas many of the industry organizations I participated in had a ratio of nine men to one woman, Athena San Diego's members are primarily women.

Lorraine Herr, Marketing Showroom Director, Sub-Zero Group Midwest, advocates finding your "tribe." "After relaunching my career in 2011, I felt the distinct longing to connect with women who were successful, had taken atypical career paths, had the fortitude and perseverance to advance professionally, and knew how to laugh. Having access to an authentic tribe builds my network and also helps me successfully navigate the culture at my current company."[5]

So let's move beyond the adage "It's not what you know, it's who you know." Let's embrace *From Ramen to Riches* author Lauren Tanny's sage advice: "It's not *who* you know, but who you can *get* to know."[6] Go out there, have fun, and just do it!

Key Action Tips

1. *Change your attitude about networking.* Remind yourself that networking is a critical tool for your career success. Embrace the art of it.

2. *Join industry groups and professional associations.* Attend at least four but preferably twelve industry-specific meetings annually. At each meeting, show up early and plan to stay late to ensure maximum networking time. Set a goal of meeting at least three to five new contacts, and find out how you can assist them (and follow through). Connect with all your new contacts on LinkedIn and follow up immediately to schedule additional time to meet over coffee or lunch. Set a goal of having each new contact introduce you to two additional, worthwhile contacts.

3. *At each meeting, bring something that will benefit the other person.* Effective networking is a two-way street. By offering to help others, you'll establish yourself as a resource and people will, in turn, want to assist you.

4. *Perfect your brand, elevator pitch, and eight-second hook.* Read chapter 2, "Brand Yourself—Unique, Memorable, and Authentic," chapter 49, "Roosters Crow, Hens Deliver—Successful Women Do Both," and chapter 6, "Talk—to Anyone, Anytime."

5. *Bring yourself fully to every interaction.* Disengage your phone, engage the other person, and focus on your goal. Lean forward, ask questions. Others will notice your interest and respond to your engagement with their own.

6. *Truly listen to and care about others.* Hone your listening skills and focus on others. When you get other people talking about themselves, they believe *you're* incredibly interesting. If you listen well, others will take care of you.

7. *Follow through.* People will respect you and invest more in their relationship with you if you actually do what you say you will—such as make an introduction or send information.

8. *Reach out to maintain and develop your contacts.* Email relevant articles or items of interest to people in your network. Engage them socially. Oftentimes, business connections are facilitated and deepened through shared hobbies or social interests. Maintain a list of your contacts and their interests. Every week, set a goal of meeting with at least one person in your network and emailing one contact daily.

9. *Seek input.* Share exciting ideas and developments with colleagues. As you let them know about your activities or other opportunities, they will be

inclined to be forthcoming with ideas and resources. Engage them in interesting conversations.

10. *Express gratitude with a note of thanks.* Whenever anyone helps you, express your appreciation in email or, better yet, with a handwritten thank-you note. Don't save your gratitude until you get a promotion or new job. Thank those who help you each step of the way.

6

Talk—to Anyone, Anytime

One of the greatest skills—and gifts—is focusing on other people. Make each person feel as if he or she is the only person in the world.

—Anonymous

How comfortable we feel about talking to others often depends on who we are talking to and how we are feeling about the situation. For the sake of personal and professional success, however, it's important to be able to talk—to anyone, anytime.

Stanford University School of Business tracked MBAs ten years after they graduated and found that grade point average had no bearing on their success. What made the difference was their ability to converse with others.[1]

Some people have a natural ability and comfort level when it comes to talking. And then there are other people, like me, who must work at it. If you have an extroverted personality, you probably do very well in any social or business setting. If you're at the other extreme—an introvert—it's a constant struggle. My guess is that the majority of you fall somewhere in between. My hope is that, after reading this chapter, you'll gain confidence and feel more at ease, or at least learn how to make people believe you're a natural conversationalist.

The easiest way to accomplish this is by asking questions, being a good listener, and relaxing. "Keeping a conversation rolling is simple when you learn to listen and ask appropriate probing questions that naturally grow from the dialogue. You only need a couple of questions in advance. If there is a genuine connection then you can proactively engage in conversation," advises Allison Graham, author of *From Business Cards to Business Relationships: Personal Branding & Profitable Networking Made Easy.*[2] "The real key to great conversations is to relax. Let the conversation flow naturally. That's easiest to do when you're fully engaged and genuinely interested in the conversation topic and the person with whom you are talking."

With small talk, people may forget your words, but they will remember how you make them feel.[3] By actively listening, maintaining eye contact, and keeping your focus on the other person, you can make them feel as though they're the only person in the room, or quite possibly the world—and that they're important to you. This is what is truly important in connecting with people.

When should you end a conversation? Susan RoAne, author of *How to Work a Room,* advises, "Your objective in all encounters should be to make a good impression and leave people wanting more. To do that, be bright. Be brief. Be gone."[4]

Most importantly, embrace the opportunity to meet someone and have fun in the process.

Key Action Tips

1. Develop five to ten open-ended questions that can easily be modified depending on the person to whom

you're speaking, the function you're attending, or what's going on in the world. Examples include:

   a. What products or services does your company specialize in?
   b. What do you like most about your company?
   c. What challenges are most pressing for your company or the industry?
   d. How do you see the industry changing over the next five years?
   e. What disruptive technologies do you envision?
   f. How did you end up in this field?
   g. What are your interests or hobbies?
   h. Today's speaker sounds fascinating. What other events have you attended through this organization?
   i. Current event X is capturing the attention of the world. Where do you think it will lead?

2. Listen thoughtfully; don't interrupt.

3. Give nonverbal cues that show you're engaged and feeling good about the interaction: smile at appropriate times, maintain eye contact, and nod in response to what the other person is saying.

4. Give verbal cues to indicate you are listening and supportive: "Uh huh," "Right," "Yes."

5. Be interested in what the other person is saying; clarify their responses with follow-on questions.

6. Be empathetic, but try not to shift the focus back to you with comments such as "I know how you feel." Empathetic statements include:
   a. "How frustrating."

   b. "Oh, my."
   c. "That must have been upsetting."

7. Don't talk too much about yourself but be open and honest if asked questions. Have your elevator pitch ready.

8. Be enthusiastic and interested in what you're doing in your life.

9. Share new perspectives or differing points of view.

10. Regularly read industry publications to stay current.

11. Stay informed about current events and subjects beyond your specialty. Read the news, listen to public radio, or watch a newscast on a daily basis.

12. Tell yourself that you are interesting, fun, and successful. Embrace your next opportunity to engage others in a dynamic conversation.

13. Observe and take note of how others interact and converse, especially those you admire. Watch television, online, and in-person interviews.

14. Develop hobbies and outside interests and share them with others.

15. Have a good sense of humor.

7

To Golf or Not to Golf—the Power of Informal Networks

The most important thing about playing golf is access—access to other people. If you have golf in your portfolio, it gives access that you can't buy and that education cannot guarantee.

—Rose Harper, *Grass Ceiling president and* CEO

Golf may seem as revolting to you as networking. I entirely understand. However, the sad fact remains that the majority of managers, directors, and executives are men, and most men love golf and other sports. If we ignore these opportunities for connections, we lock ourselves out of conversations and connections with those who can make a difference in our career's progression.

Rose Harper is president and CEO of the Grass Ceiling, Inc., a business empowerment firm that uses golf to level the playing field for executive women. She ardently advises, "Golf is one of the most effective tools for networking and deal making in today's business world. It promotes and encourages communication and positive bonding between professionals and their peers—and that can have positive impact in many ways."[1]

> The golf course provides many opportunities for connecting.

"Golf facilitates one-on-one time for four to five hours leading to relationship development and critical business decisions," adds Jamie Cantu, CEO of Premier Corporate Productions. "It's hard to find another setting where you have this much concentrated time with decision makers."[2]

That said, don't play golf with male colleagues unless you have reasonably developed your game or your male counterpart is a beginner. Agree to a game only if you can score close to 100 or within 20 percent of the person you're playing with. You must also commit to knowing and following the rules of the game and its etiquette, and keeping pace on the course.

There's hope if playing golf is entirely off the table. You can learn to "talk" golf and other sports. And thankfully, most men and women have broader interests, including travel, art, theater, history, skiing, wine, fine dining, cooking, and investing. It's important to join groups and informal networks that provide access to a wide variety of business professionals, especially men. Your career advancement will frequently depend on whom you know and how you connect with others. By developing and sharing outside interests, you facilitate informal networks and oftentimes enhance your chances for success.

Key Action Tips

1. Seriously consider playing golf. If you don't play, are you willing to try it? Do you have the time and

money for lessons? There's a wide range of options, from group lessons to private lessons. Try it for three to six months. At a minimum, you'll have a better understanding of the swing and game.

2. Consider attending a multiday clinic. Intense and focused lessons can expedite your learning curve.

3. Recruit a colleague—preferably male!—to take golf lessons with you.

4. Commit to watching or, better yet, attending a few golf tournaments a year. This makes the game more interesting. The commentators will give you a different perspective on the sport.

5. Peruse quick-read books on golf theory, rules, and etiquette. There are also books on "learning how to talk sports," such as *Game Time: Learn to Talk Sports in 5 Minutes a Day for Business.*

8

FEAR—THE GREAT PARALYZER

We gain strength, and courage, and confidence by each experience in which we really stop to look fear in the face... we must do that which we think we cannot.

—Eleanor Roosevelt, longest-serving
United States first lady

Fear. It's one of life's greatest paralyzers. It robs you of your life. As Robert H. Schuller put it, what would you attempt—and achieve—if you knew you could not fail?[1] Think about how many things you have *not* attempted because of fear.

Each day we are confronted with a multitude of choices. Do your options make you feel confident, empowered, and strong, or do they leave you feeling fearful, paralyzed, and helpless? If you are in the latter camp, read on and take action. Otherwise you'll die never knowing what a great person you might have become.[2]

"Every time we make a choice that is based in fear, we are sealing in the belief that we are unworthy, that we are not good enough or strong enough to be in control of our own lives, our thoughts, our beliefs, our choices—and,

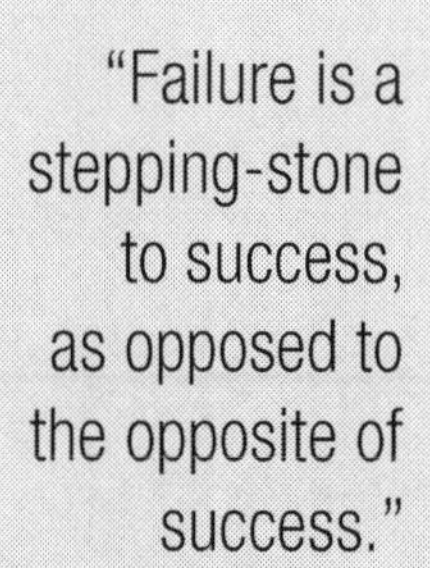

> "Failure is a stepping-stone to success, as opposed to the opposite of success."
>
> —Arianna Huffington

most, important, our future," says Debbie Ford in *Courage: Overcoming Fear and Igniting Self-Confidence.*[3] If you start confronting your fears today, you will start to control your future—personally and professionally.

The first step toward triumphing over fear is developing *awareness* of the significant anxiety and missed opportunities that fear has caused in your life. Then it's critical to identify and analyze the *source* of the fear. Is it fear of failure, fear of success, fear of the unknown, fear of change, fear of adversity, fear of rejection, or fear of your inner critic? At one time or another, you've probably experienced all of these fears and allowed them to paralyze you.

Once you truly understand the source of your fear, it's helpful to put things into *perspective.* A favorite question I ask myself is, "What's the worst that can happen … being fired?"

A few of my favorite pieces of wisdom:

- We don't regret the things we do in life … we regret the things we don't do.
- We learn much more from our failures than from our successes.
- We could attempt wondrous things if we knew we could not fail.

"My mother used to call failure a stepping-stone to success, as opposed to the opposite of success," says Arianna Huffington, cofounder and editor in chief of *The Huffington Post.* "When you frame failure that way, it changes dramatically what you're willing to do, how you're willing to invent, and the risks you'll take . . . a key component of whatever successes I've had has been what I've learned from my failures."[4]

A dear friend and longtime colleague, Ashlee Gora, went through a challenging time of professional self-doubt—which we all do—and successfully used the above principles. "When I realized the destructive manifestations of my self-doubt, I finally asked myself, 'what's the worst thing that can happen?' Once I answered that question, mentally I had an instant change for the better," Ashlee declared. "Fear of failing is a big trap. The focus should be on whether there is a good corporate match, whether I can change the circumstances or develop my skills, or whether I should find a better fit at another company."[5]

Once you change your perspective about fear—and failure—you'll likely stop being paralyzed and take action! With action, amazingly, you'll discover that your fears abate. You gain strength, courage, and confidence. And confidence is critical. Confidence (and lack of fear) is the little voice in the back of your head that says, "you belong."[6]

Key Action Tips

1. *Awareness.* The first step to addressing any issue in life is awareness. Acknowledge the significant limitations and losses that you have experienced because of fear.

2. *Analysis.* Identify what you're most afraid of and why. Is it fear of failure, fear of success, fear of the unknown, fear of change, fear of adversity, fear of rejection, or fear of your inner critic?

3. *Journaling.* Once you've identified your fears, it's helpful to write them down. Stop the negative, nonproductive replaying in your mind.

4. *Perspective.* After writing down your fears, put them into perspective by listing the pros and cons of overcoming the fear and situation. Make sure you identify a ratio of two to one of positives to negatives. Ask and answer: "What's the worst that can happen?"

5. *Positive thinking.* If fear arises, immediately stop yourself from thinking about the negative. Envision overcoming your fear, and envision what success will look like and feel like. Document a few favorite, positive quotes. Read chapter 33, "In Piles of Crap . . . Find the Pony."

6. *Action.* If you're taking action, it's more difficult to focus on the fear. Once you take action, your fears will abate and you'll gain amazing strength, courage, and confidence. The more action you take, the more confidence you'll gain and the more results you'll see. Read chapter 29, "Just Do It—with Confidence, Passion, and Sensitivity."

7. *Development.* Our fear may have to do with a lack of experience or skill in a particular area. While this doesn't seem unreasonable, most leaders have never previously done that which they undertake. You're not alone. As John F. Kennedy said, "Leadership and learning are indispensable to each other." Just remember, you are intelligent, resourceful, and tenacious. With those three qualities, you will be undefeatable.

9

If You Don't Risk Anything, You Risk Everything

A ship in port is safe, but that is not what ships are for. Sail out to sea and do new things.

—Rear Admiral Grace Hopper,
American computer scientist pioneer

To what degree are you comfortable taking risks? Do you get *a thrill, embracing it*? Or are you *uneasy, running in the opposite direction*? The answers to these questions have a lot to do with your leadership potential, as leadership is largely about risk-taking.

The *Wall Street Journal* queried eighteen Fortune 500 female CEOs on what it takes to make it in the male-dominated C-suite. Former Wellpoint CEO Angela Braly answered, "The most important factor in determining whether you will succeed isn't your gender, it's you... Be open to opportunity and take risks. In fact, take the worst, the messiest, the most challenging assignment you can find, and then take control." Keycorp CEO Beth Mooney added, "I have stepped up to many 'ugly' assignments that others didn't want."[1]

I completely concur with Braly and Mooney. The

"The most important factor in determining whether you will succeed isn't your gender, it's you . . . Be open to opportunity and take risks."

—Angela Braly, former Wellpoint CEO

majority of my career opportunities occurred because companies had failures and ugly messes prior to hiring me. If they hadn't, there wouldn't have been an opportunity for me. And I was confident—even if I knew very little about the science or technology—that I could do a better job than the status quo of "failure."

According to Cate Goethals, professor in women's leadership and creator of the award-winning Women at the Top MBA class at the University of Washington, Foster School of Business, "The female CEOs who speak to my students are constantly stretching and testing themselves, trying new things, and broadening their knowledge, skills, and network. They'd much rather try something that doesn't work than stand still. As one CEO put it—'If you're not failing, you're not growing.' The trick is to fail quickly and move on to a better plan or opportunity."[2]

There's considerable debate on whether women are more risk-averse than men.[3,4,5] Regardless, if you're not comfortable with risk, seek to understand the underlying reasons and address them. There are numerous factors that influence whether you'll engage in intelligent risk taking, including:

Background. Most entrepreneurs and leaders are more resilient due to significant challenges in their personal life or career. Resilience and tenacity are necessary for overcoming career setbacks. We often hear that the greatest people have experienced the most failure. They're the ones who demonstrate resolve and commitment by continually picking themselves up, making necessary changes, and forging forward.

Embracing challenge and adaptability. Challenge deters many people from taking risks and making changes. Embracing challenges and adapting to situations is essential to effecting change and leading people. Challenges help people develop perseverance, build confidence, continue learning, and hone skills. As German philosopher Friedrich Nietzsche said, "What does not kill me, makes me stronger."[6]

Shattering comfort zones. If you are fearful and unwilling to step outside your comfort zone, you won't be able to take risks necessary for effective leadership. As Eleanor Roosevelt said, "The danger lies in refusing to face the fear, in not daring to come to grips with it. If you fail anywhere along the line, it will take away your confidence. You must make yourself succeed every time. You must do the thing you cannot do."[7]

Viewing risks and changes as opportunities. In order to embrace risk-taking, one must view risks as opportunities to learn. Exemplary leaders learn from their good decisions as well as their mistakes. Personally, I have learned far more from my so-called mistakes or failures than I have from my successes. As Thomas Edison said to a colleague, "I have not failed. I've just found 10,000 ways that won't work."[8]

Having confidence. Our willingness to take risks is blunted by our fears. This, in turn, stunts our growth. Embrace Babe Ruth's advice: "Never let the fear of striking out get in your way."[9] Learning to manage fear is something that comes with experience. To build the confidence you need to make difficult decisions, practice by making less difficult decisions.

Taking action. To make risky but effective decisions, one must research a situation and conduct an appropriate amount of analysis before taking action. The key word here is "appropriate." All too often, people look at the negative consequences of a wrong decision and fail to make one at all. It's paralysis by analysis. With regard to risk-taking and change, I fully embrace the proverb "Any decision is better than no decision."[10] An early decision can initiate progress, and it can be modified later to optimize the outcome.

Possessing emotional intelligence. Chapter 32, "Intelligence—IQ versus EQ," is devoted to the importance of emotional intelligence, also referred to as emotional quotient. Without strong self-awareness, self-regulation, motivation, empathy, and social skills, the ability to take risks in an intelligent way is significantly lower.

Driving innovation: Innovation is necessary for people, companies, and societies to progress, and risks are inherent in innovation. A large part of any leader's responsibility is setting the vision for an organization. Hopefully, that vision includes an innovative culture that helps employees take intelligent risks.

Cate Goethals aptly sums up career risks this way: "If a new project or position feels safe, it's the wrong opportunity."

Key Action Tips

To enhance your risk-taking ability:

1. Read about risks, change management, and emotional intelligence. Incorporate some of the ideas into your thinking and actions.

2. Have the confidence to say (and believe), "What is the worst thing that can happen? I'll fail, or I'll get fired." This mindset is quite liberating and empowering. Failing and being fired usually aren't the worst

things that can happen to you. We learn much more from these two experiences than from success and staying employed. In my experience, most competent people—and often incompetent people—who have been fired move on to better opportunities.

3. Do as Eleanor Roosevelt encourages: do that which you believe you cannot do. Journal the fear, your response, and what it felt like once you took action. Review your journal every week.

4. Identify a person who is a change agent in your organization. Meet with them to discuss their views on change and seek them out as a mentor.

5. Volunteer for a risky assignment.

10

Seek Revenue-Producing Jobs and Profit-and-Loss Responsibilities

Sales and positive cash flow—the lifeblood of every person, every business.

—Anonymous

This chapter was originally titled "Seek Line Positions." Then I got feedback from women who were at earlier stages in their careers and weren't familiar with the term "line position." *Line jobs* make direct contributions to a company's profits. They involve the design, manufacture, marketing, or sale of a product or service. *Staff positions* support those functions and include human resources, finance, billing, purchasing, information technology, and investor relations.

In general, line roles provide a clearer path to senior management. Line people are viewed as essential to a company, tend to be paid more, and have more power than staff, who are seen as an expense. One significant difference between women and men in the workplace is that women typically spend much of their careers in staff positions, also known as "sticky floor positions," such as human resources and finance. This may be due to women seeking more traditional jobs or believing staff jobs are less risky—but the result is that they tend to be less networked and less often considered for promotional opportunities.

If you have a positive impact on your company's revenue and profitability, you can more quickly move up the ranks where you'll eventually have a shot at profit-and-loss (P&L) positions. P&L responsibilities range from overseeing a departmental budget and generating profitability for the company through that department to overseeing the budget for the entire division or company. It involves monitoring net income and having a direct influence on how resources are allocated. P&L is one of the most important responsibilities for rising managers, directors, and executives; it's a steppingstone to the corner office.

One of my critical early career moves was a transition out of the pharmacy profession into medical device sales and management. Initially, the thought of telling people I was in sales was embarrassing as I mistakenly did not have respect for the profession. Furthermore, I was not naturally an outgoing, gregarious person. But as much as a sales job did not excite me, I wanted to leave pharmacy and had a great mentor[1] who strongly encouraged me to move into sales—or possibly shoved me into it. This changed my life, both professionally and personally. Sales forced me to become more extroverted, engaging, and most importantly, respectful of this critical corporate function. It also cleared a path for my ascension into P&L responsibility and executive management.

Other senior women have benefited from similar paths. Michelle Stacy, president of the Keurig unit of Green Mountain Coffee Roasters, was originally hired as a brand manager at Gillette and progressed to overseeing acquisitions. Then she wanted to work more directly with customers, so she took a step back and became a sales representative for the company. "My experience working closely with retail-

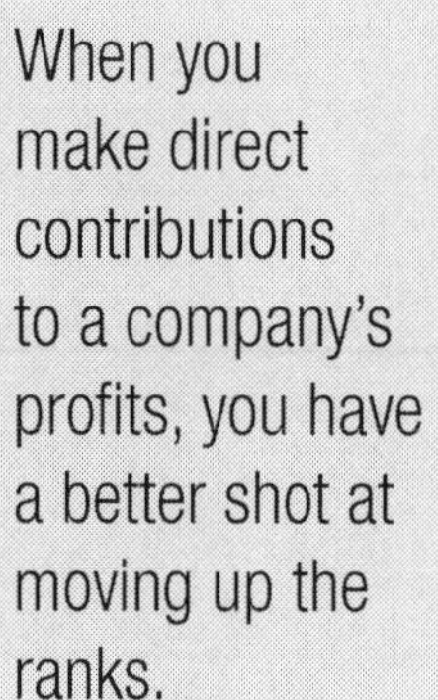
When you make direct contributions to a company's profits, you have a better shot at moving up the ranks.

ers helped me win a promotion the next year, as Gillette USA's vice president of marketing," she recounts.[2] Similarly, Anne M. Mulcahy, former Xerox chairman and CEO, started as a sales representative and progressed to the corner office. As president, she became the first woman to run a $20 billion company.

As you plan and progress in your career, aggressively seek out line positions, including a stint in sales, with eventual P&L responsibilities. These are integral components to every successful company and are requisite experience for successful executives. Conquer these areas and you gain recognition, job security, compensation, and advancement.

Key Action Tips

1. Network with two or three of your company's top sales representatives and sales management.
    a. Let them know you respect the importance of the sales function.
    b. Without experience, it's difficult to move into sales. You have a better chance of gaining sales experience if you do so after being established in a company. Work with your boss, human resource department, and sales management to get authorization to spend a minimum of one day per quarter in the field with sales personnel.
    c. After gaining exposure, let it be known that you would like to work in a sales role.

2. Read and master basic sales techniques such as cold-calling, listening, negotiating, and closing.

3. Identify a timeline for gaining this critical experience.

4. Gain comfort with P&L statements and other financial statements. Read chapter 11, "Know Thy Numbers," and one of the books in the Recommended Reading section. Familiarize yourself with your company's financials, if available; if not, work with your manager to understand your department's budget and how you and your department contribute to the company's top and bottom lines. If you control your department's budget, gain an understanding of how it rolls up into the corporate budget.

5. Take continuing education classes and meet with different department personnel to gain a better understanding of the different line functions and how each contributes to a successful company.

11

Know Thy Numbers

Every success, every strategy, every vision is told through the numbers.

—Nicola (Nikki) Zahl, board member, So Cal Entrepreneurial Ecosystem Development

The one feature that every department and organization has in common is numbers. Does financial data scare you? If so, this chapter is critical. Your financial literacy contributes to the success of your people, your department, your company, and you.

Managers need to understand financial data to make intelligent decisions. Employees perform better when they understand how financial success is measured and how their department, as well as others, affects a company's performance. The more intelligent and comfortable you are with financial data, the more adept you'll be at allocating resources and budgeting expenses. You also need to be able to speak the language of finance to be taken seriously and to communicate effectively across your company.

Research has shown that women, even professional women with good jobs and successful careers, tend to be less financially literate than men.[1] Lack of financial literacy

> If you want to understand the business, you have to understand the numbers.

hinders our performance and upward mobility. It's easy to believe that because you're in marketing, sales, engineering, or some other non-finance department you don't need to develop this expertise. If this is your attitude, I can attest from personal experience that you're limiting your potential. I lost a shot at being CEO at one company because I wasn't familiar with stock warrants. I won't go into details but, trust me, sophisticated investors and board directors speak in terms of finance, numbers, and percentages. If you are not financially savvy and tuned in to the numbers, you will be not be respected.

In summary, if you're not in finance, you need to embrace the numbers even more. Why? As with all skills, you must not only learn them, but you must also practice and apply them if you want to retain the knowledge. Most of us could significantly improve our financial literacy. Let's start today.

Key Action Tips

1. Begin by gaining a basic understanding of financial statements: profit and loss (also referred to as the income statement), balance sheet, and cash flow statement.

2. Learn about separating the actual numbers from the assumptions and estimates.

3. Learn about ratios, return on investment (ROI), and working capital. I highly recommend the easy-to-comprehend book *Financial Intelligence, Revised Edition: A Manager's Guide to Knowing What the Numbers Really Mean.*

4. If you work at a publicly traded company or have access to your company's financial statements, review them quarterly, run ratios, and ask questions. If you don't have access to your company's financial reports, select a couple of interesting publicly traded companies and ask to be added to their press release distributions; you will also get their quarterly financial reports. You can also easily obtain various filings and other official financial statements online through the Securities and Exchange Commission (SEC), with whom these reports are filed.

5. Get actively involved in your company's budgeting process. Review how your department's numbers roll up into the corporate numbers.

12

Ongoing Education—Invest in You

Education is power.

—Oprah Winfrey, American producer and philanthropist

Recession, unemployment, debt, and uncertainty. The past few years of economic calamity and soaring college costs have raised doubts about the value of education. However, the stats still demonstrate that a person with a college degree is better off in terms of employment, salary, and lifetime earnings, especially in a challenging job market. During the 2008–2011 economic crisis, the average unemployment rate for people with a bachelor's degree or higher was less than 5 percent, compared to more than 10 percent for those with only a high school diploma. More compelling, employers pay college graduates 84 percent more than they pay high school graduates; compensation is even higher for those with graduate degrees.[1]

It's surprising that only 25 percent of adults in the US have bachelor's degrees.[2] You would think that means a bachelor degree is sufficient in today's market, but today's undergraduate degree is the equivalent of a high school

> "A good leader will recognize what she does not know and be willing to learn all the time."
>
> —Anne M. Mulcahy, former Xerox chairman and CEO

diploma years ago, while a graduate degree is similar to a bachelor's degree years ago. A master's in business administration (MBA) is nearly essential if you want to achieve an executive position—and it's more important for women aspiring to rise through the corporate ranks. Even if you don't have your eye on the corner office, you acquire more skills, gain access to more opportunities, and make more money with a graduate degree than you do with a bachelor's degree.

And it's never too late to go back to school. Not only do many graduate programs value prior work experience, most require it. They know the importance of real-life experience prior to entering an advanced educational program. I earned my executive MBA in 1999, while I was president of a publicly traded medical device company—more than fifteen years after earning my bachelor's degree. And in our wired world, it's easier than ever to get your advanced degree while continuing to work.

If you do go back to school, be sure to take advantage of your "student" title. "Being a student is a golden ticket that opens doors left and right," shares Jana Morrelli, entrepreneur and University of Washington MBA graduate. "I was able to get informational interview meetings with CEOs, business owners, investors, and major players in my community, simply by letting them know I was a student and would like to learn from them. Those connections often led to internships and have been long lasting and invaluable to my business experience."[3]

When considering schools, select the best school you

can afford. According to research conducted at Arizona State University, the "benefits to an individual from a university education vary with the quality of the institution attended. Those who graduate from an elite university earn substantially more than those who graduate from a lower-quality institution."[4] Some of this relates to the quality of education, but it also has to do with the people you meet at school; there are potential lifelong networking contacts. Additionally, a school's brand recognition can be connected to future opportunities.

Be a lifelong student.
—Pam Alabaster, L'Oréal senior vice president

Whether you have an MBA or not, commit your life to continuous learning. "Continuous learning leads to continuous improvement," says Pam Alabaster, senior vice president of L'Oréal. "Commit yourself to advancing your knowledge, skills, and expertise. The business environment is quickly changing, and your understanding of leading practices, thinking, and emerging tools will help you manage for better results. Be a lifelong student."[5]

Key Action Tips

1. Consult with peers who have obtained an advanced degree, especially an MBA. Inquire about the pros, the cons, the expense, the types of programs, and whether they would do it all over again. I am biased, but I have never heard anyone say they would not.

2. Start to explore your options. Every school has different program offerings. Identify which type would work best for your life. Make a list and consider the pros and cons.

3. Inquire with your company about corporate educational benefits and flexibility provided to employees who are pursuing advanced education.

4. Talk with your boss to gauge whether they would be supportive of your advanced education quest. Discuss the benefits to the company. If you don't have internal support, consider changing companies or leaving to attend a full-time program. If you go to a good school, you'll have recruitment opportunities upon completion.

5. If you're married or in a serious relationship, discuss your goals, the time involved in completing an advanced degree, the financial commitment, benefits, and concerns.

6. Make a decision and plan.

7. If your decision is to seek an advanced degree, it will be a two-to-three-year (or more) sacrifice, but once you obtain the degree, no one will ever be able to take it away.

8. Regardless of whether you have an advanced degree, make annual plans for continuous learning. Regularly read industry and business periodicals and attend industry meetings, seminars, and webinars.

13

LOYALTY—A TWO-WAY STREET

Ultimately, companies must do what's in their best interest. You, too, must do the same.

—Charles Kendrick, entrepreneur

Let's face it—women, in general, are more loyal than men.[1,2] And there are plenty of reasons to move beyond our loyalty. Companies are under more and more pressure to be lean and flexible, which results in reorganizations and layoffs. This means that even if we want to work for only a few companies throughout our careers, the odds of our doing so have greatly decreased.

Proactively changing positions, divisions, or companies isn't just defensive play. The payoff for doing so every three to five years is compelling: higher pay, promotions, a broader skill set, expansive knowledge of corporate best practices, a burgeoning professional network, intellectual stimulation, and, more often than not, a greater feeling of engagement.

Why every three to five years, specifically?

If you leave a company within a year or two, you risk being labeled as "unstable," especially if you've done this repeatedly or in succession. "Don't change positions just for

It serves you well to experience other corporate cultures.

the sake of change," says Betsy Berkhemer-Credaire, president and cofounder of Berkhemer Clayton Retained Executive Search and author of *The Board Game: How Smart Women Become Corporate Directors.* "We only look for people who have been working at a company for three to five years or more. We look for performers—we cannot consider people who don't stay long enough to make a difference wherever they've worked." On the other hand, if you stay too long in one position, you risk being viewed as unmotivated, passive, or inept. Far worse, you risk boredom, burnout, and obsolescence.

There are exceptions. Early in my career, I was offered a position with significant career advancement. I agonized over leaving a well-respected company where I had been for less than one year. I felt guilty about the investment the company had made in me. After several discussions, a trusted mentor (my brother) wisely convinced me that companies ultimately do what's in their best interest—and I needed to do the same. I made the move. It was the best advice I could have gotten, and the best career decision I could have made.

At the other extreme, I also served as president of a publicly traded company for twelve years. Although the experience was incredible, I stayed too long for my own good, and possibly for the good of the company. I stayed as long as I did in large part because of loyalty to long-term shareholders and employees. If I had taken one of the many exciting opportunities I had been offered during that time, however, I would not only have broadened my experience and boosted my career, but I would have also been able to offer former employees opportunities to expand their careers. As Lauren Tanny, author of *From Ramen to Riches,* points out, "You can still be loyal to the company and its people even after you move on."[3]

Loyalty isn't a terrible thing when it's a two-way street. If your company boasts an exciting, progressive, growth-oriented environment, then stay longer, but seek high-profile assignments that lead to promotions and opportunities in other functional areas. This facilitates your career growth. But even under the best of circumstances, given enough time, it will serve you well to experience other corporate cultures, processes, technologies, and coworkers.

Key Action Tips

1. *Live your career map.* If you have not defined and mapped your career goals for the next ten years, do so. This keeps you focused on the big picture of your career and is especially helpful if you're feeling discouraged. Read chapter 1, "Your Career—Care the Most."

2. *Consider your employer.* Know your employer's needs as well as your own. Provide a quality product (you and your work) for fair pay. Look at your position as a three-to-five-year assignment. When you achieve a major milestone, assess what else you can do for your company, explore opportunities to move to other functional areas to broaden your experience, and evaluate whether it's beneficial to your career to remain at your company. Engage your boss, your boss's boss, and the human resource department in career discussions.

3. *Know your industry trends.* Discuss where your industry is headed with senior professionals and colleagues. Is it expanding, contracting, or stagnant? If your industry is expanding, seek the areas of fastest growth. If it's contracting, consider entering into parallel industries or another industry with higher growth. Subscribe to Internet sites offering daily news regarding your industry. Use LinkedIn Pulse, a LinkedIn news offering, to keep abreast of your industry and interests.

4. *Regularly update your resume and LinkedIn profile.* Hire a professional resume writer to create your resume, cover letter, and LinkedIn profile. You can do regular updates yourself, but invest in a professional update every two years. Also, establish a relationship with a professional photographer and post a flattering, professional picture.

5. *Connect, endorse, recommend, and be recommended on LinkedIn.* Make connections with the professionals in your day-to-day network and continue to do so with every new introduction. Expand your connections with professionals you would like to know by personalizing invitations with a valid reason to connect. Post your skills and endorse the skills of people in your network. Also, seek recommendations for your profile and post recommendations for your colleagues.

6. *Regularly network with colleagues, senior professionals, and recruiters.* Join industry and professional organizations and regularly attend meetings. Update relevant regional recruiters and national executive search firms, including Korn/Ferry, Heidrick

& Struggles, Spencer Stuart, Russell Reynolds, Berkhemer Clayton, Sanford Rose, The Domann Organization, and Kazan International.

7. *Annually source your pay range.* Consult with recruiters and Internet salary or job sites, including www.salary.com, www.vault.com, and www.payscale.com. This enhances your knowledge of the current market and how other companies value experience and skills similar to your own. Use this information to negotiate with your current or future company.

14

Never Pass on New Jobs Because of "Inexperience"

I've been lucky. Opportunities don't often come along. So, when they do, you have to grab them.

—Audrey Hepburn, British actress, humanitarian

Women are more likely to pass up promotions and decline new opportunities than men. It's one of the things holding us back. Cynthia Good, Little Pink Book's CEO, poignantly notes that men, who tout their accomplishments more than women, are promoted and hired based on potential. Women, who can be more reticent, "are promoted and hired based on if they can do the job."[1]

The good news is that your response to opportunity is largely under your control. Change your thinking, or at least your words and your actions, and don't allow so-called inexperience to stop you from raising your hand at the next opportunity.

"I still think we have a dynamic, even among successful women, to be less forthcoming with their accomplishments. Be confident and willing to talk about them," advises Lisa Sawicki, national diversity leader of PwC's (formerly

PriceWaterhouseCooper's) assurance practice.[2] "What I wish I had known when I started my career is that there is no one right path to take . . . you have to take advantage of opportunities as they arise."

"You have to be very confident, even though you are so self-critical inside."

—Virginia Rometty, IBM CEO

I strongly believe there are self-esteem and confidence issues at play. Speaking at a *Fortune* Most Powerful Women Summit, IBM CEO Virginia Rometty shared an early career experience in which she was offered a "big job" that she didn't think she was prepared to take. Rometty told the recruiter "I'm not ready for this job. I need more time, I need more experience and then I could do it really well . . . I need to go home and think about it." When Rometty's husband heard this, his response was, "Do you think a man would have ever answered the question that way?" That was a wake-up call to act more self-assured and have the courage to take professional leaps. Rometty concluded, "What it taught me was you have to be very confident, even though you are so self-critical inside about what it is you may or may not know."[3]

I have been "inexperienced" in every job I ever started. However, I was confident that with perseverance, time, and resources, I would figure it out, or at least I would do better than the person who preceded me. And thankfully, that's what happened. If I hadn't tried, I would still be practicing pharmacy—a great career, but not what I was destined to do.

Key Action Tips

1. Hire a professional coach and resume writer to help package and position yourself. I can't count the number of women—and men—I've suggested this to and who have thanked me profusely for the results.

2. Know your brand and elevator pitch, and always be prepared to share it! Read chapter 2, "Brand Yourself—Unique, Memorable, and Authentic."

3. Don't minimize your accomplishments; to the contrary, talk them up. Read chapter 49, "Roosters Crow, Hens Deliver—Successful Women Do Both."

4. Be confident in spite of the little voice in the back of your head saying you shouldn't. Read chapter 29, "Just Do It—with Confidence, Passion, and Sensitivity."

5. To progress in your career, do a great job in your current position for two or more years, then begin to prospect for your next job. Read chapter 13, "Loyalty—a Two-Way Street."

6. Follow your career map. Return all recruiter calls and never, ever say you don't have enough experience. If it were that far off from what you've done, you probably wouldn't be talking about the job in the first place.

15

Recruiters—Yes, Return All Calls

Nothing is so often irretrievably missed as a daily opportunity.

—Marie von Ebner-Eschenbach, Austria's premier female author

Executive recruiters, also referred to as headhunters, become more and more crucial as you ascend in your career. Therefore, nurturing relationships with executive recruiters is a key component to building your network for future career advancement. Additionally, by being a helpful resource to search firms, you benefit by learning what's going on in your industry and what the current salaries are at your level and above. It also enables you to refer executive colleagues for positions.

I'm sorry to admit that I probably did not return 99 percent of recruiter calls—I was "too busy." Looking back, I wish I had returned all of them. What would it have taken ... ten minutes each? At the least, I would have developed a tremendous network of recruiter relationships, and it's highly likely that I would have advanced faster than I did.

There are three kinds of recruiters: retained, contin-

Nurturing relationships with executive recruiters is a key component to future career advancement.

gency, and in-house. Retained executive search firms typically specialize in particular professional functions or industries. Engaged by corporations for senior-level management positions, they have an exclusive arrangement to handle a specific position for a client organization. Retained firms are paid their fees (customarily one-third of the first-year base salary, plus bonus) during the first three months of the search, which they are committed to completing. Retained firms present only three to five well-qualified and fully vetted candidates to their client company, and they interview those candidates in person prior to that. As a career strategy, you want to develop relationships with retained recruiting firms that specialize in your professional function or industry. You may trust retained firms to keep your information confidential.

Contingency recruiters most often handle middle-management, sales, and technical positions. They receive a fee (approximately 20 percent of base salary) from the employer only if their candidate is hired. Contingency recruiters want to know you so they can keep you in mind for openings they hear about or represent. They then put forward your resume for searches related to your background. If you're currently employed, ask the recruiter about confidentiality and how your resume will be used.

In-house corporate recruiters are employees of the company where they work, and they tend to handle numerous open searches simultaneously. Their job is to find candidates for multiple internal clients, so they generally focus on their current priorities. They often don't have time to develop relationships with potential future candidates.

By returning recruiters' calls, you gain much more than you give up in time. As an added benefit, you learn to craft your verbal self-presentation and hear feedback about the value of your skills and experience. If you receive a call from a recruiter, treat it as a lucky break. Gladly take the call and build a two-way trusted relationship. Ask for their feedback about your presentation and your resume. And if you know of any corporate openings that the recruiter might want to pursue for search engagements, let them know—they'll appreciate it.

Betsy Berkhemer-Credaire, president of Berkhemer Clayton Retained Executive Search, recommends researching executive search firms and attending events where consultants are speaking so you can meet them in person. "Keep alert to executive searches they are handling. Send an email introduction that gives three bullet points demonstrating your track record that's pertinent to a specific position, with your resume attached. Include results of your work with measurable achievements, the range of budgets you have handled, and the number of employees you have managed. Such numbers and strategic success stories are the keys to capturing a busy recruiter's attention."[1]

Additionally, she urges, "Don't use empty words like *transformational, indispensable,* or *unprecedented.* Instead, use facts and figures to paint the picture of what you have accomplished—even if you are still working your way up the ladder. You have success stories at every level that you can use to your advantage."[2,3]

It's a small world and gets smaller within industries, so be cautious about confidentiality. When you return recruiters' calls, ask if they're a retained or contingency recruiter and be aware that your confidentiality is at greater risk with the latter. It's a given that if you initiate your own search to find other opportunities, your employer might find out. However, that shouldn't necessarily stop you from exploring your options. Your employer might proactively reengage you.

If you are a high-performing contributor at your company, I recommend that you return every recruiter's call. After all, they're reaching out to you because they've heard about you. You can nurture relationships by helping them, and you can reassure your boss that you're not looking to leave. They called you.

Key Action Tips

1. Return all calls from recruiters and create a spreadsheet with your current recruiter contacts. Proactively reach out to recruiters who have contacted you in the past. You know the saying: it's easier to get a job (or reach out) when you have a job. It's all right to let them know that you want to establish a relationship and have your contact information in their database. But know that when you initiate the call, the recruiter will ask you why you want to leave your current job. There should be a strategic reason—you want to be on their radar for certain positions so that you can move up to the next level.

2. Expand your recruiter contacts by identifying and introducing yourself to appropriate regional and national executive search firms, including Korn/Ferry, Heidrick & Struggles, Spencer Stuart, Russell Reynolds, Berkhemer Clayton, Sanford Rose, The Domann Organization, and Kazan International.

3. Ask recruiters about the process they use to present qualified candidates to employers (e.g., a blind resume), how your information will be shared,

and whether your resume will be stored in their database. With retained firms, your resume won't be shared without your knowledge (and a personal interview with the firm). With contingency firms, your resume may be shared with potential employers without your advance knowledge. Be sure you're comfortable with that before giving them your information.

4. Contingency recruiters won't disclose the name of the employer they're working for until your qualifications and experience are identified as a match by the employer. They cannot reveal the name of the company because candidates might go directly to the company—and the contingency recruiter would not be paid. That's a no-no—you can ask for industry, location, and other details, but don't go direct to the employer even if you guess which company.

5. Many of the retained executive search firms will not consider unemployed candidates. If you're unemployed, ask about their policies. And if you have gaps in your resume—or you left your career trajectory to take time out for having babies—be candid. Explain that you are now committed to finding a place where your track record will be value-added. You may be looking for a job that allows you to spend time with your family if you have young children, so be honest with yourself and recruiters about your availability.

6. Use caution if a contingency recruiter has told you about a position and you're later contacted by another recruiter or learn of the same opportunity

elsewhere. It's best for you to stay with the original recruiter. If you don't, you risk a disagreement between the recruiters and the company, which may jeopardize your chance of being hired.

7. Build trusted, long-term relationships with recruiters. These relationships become even more important as one ascends the corporate ladder. Even if a few positions go to other candidates, there will be more opportunities. Assuming you remain professional, the recruiters will still want to place you.

8. Email or call the recruiters on your contact list annually to update them (and remind them what an incredible professional you are). Update the date on your resume's document title every time you send it, even if you have not made major changes to the text. Providing a more recent date shows that you respect the search consultant and are providing the most current information.

9. If you're not already on LinkedIn (www.linkedin.com), register as a user and create a profile that precisely mirrors your resume. Use key words about your industry and functional expertise. Be accurate about dates, titles, and achievements. If there are discrepancies between the LinkedIn profile and your resume, that's a red flag to executive search recruiters. For the photo you provide, use a professional headshot. Do *not* use personal photos or casual snapshots as you would on Facebook. If you don't have a professional photo and your profile is too cute and personal, most recruiters won't call.

10. Be very cautious about anything you post on Facebook and other social media sites. All executive search consultants will look at your LinkedIn profile and your other social media platforms prior to calling you. Google your own name to see what comes up about you on the Internet. If anything needs to be removed to protect your image, find ways to remedy the situation.

16

The Job Search—Maximize Success Through Due Diligence

Research is formalized curiosity. It is poking and prying with a purpose.

—Zora Neale Hurston,
American anthropologist

Job searches can be exciting, but it takes time to do them correctly. Prior to, during, and after the interview process, continue to learn about the company and position. Your due diligence maximizes success for any new position.

The New Leader's 100-Day Action Plan[1] recommends assessing risks from three perspectives: organizational, role, and personal.

Organizational risk. There are two fundamental factors at play: a winning strategy and the company's ability to implement the strategy. First of all, make sure that the company has a sustainable competitive advantage. Factors include:

- Customers: direct, end-users, influencers
- Collaborators: suppliers, business partners, government

- Capabilities: human, operational, financial, technical, intellectual property (IP), brands
- Competitors: direct, indirect, potential
- Conditions: social, political, economic

Compile this data into a framework, such as a SWOT matrix, which is commonly used to analyze a company's strengths, weaknesses, opportunities, and threats. This helps you identify sources of revenue growth, drivers of revenue growth, and barriers to revenue growth. You can then compare the company's current strategy with where you want the company to go. Question whether the company has the wherewithal to get there.

Role risk. Are expectations and resources aligned, and do major stakeholders agree on those expectations and resources? To evaluate these considerations, you need to:

- Identify stakeholders who had/have concerns.
- Understand the concerns and ask for recommendations on alleviating them.
- Discuss gaps between expectations and resources.
- Learn why the position is open. Who previously held the position? Was he or she successful? What were that person's strengths and weaknesses?
- Learn about your direct boss. What is his or her leadership style? How have other direct reports felt about this person's leadership?

Also, evaluate reporting lines, core team, decision-making power, and whether your role is strategic, operational, or both. Are these areas conducive to accomplishing what you need to accomplish in the organization? Are they aligned with your career goals?

Personal risk. Is it the right position and the right company for *you*? Ask yourself the following:

- What are the three most important elements you

want in your next company or career move? Compensation, benefits, company stability, corporate culture, opportunities for growth?

- Do your strengths align with the company and the role?
- Do you fit in with the corporate culture? In other words, do you share the company's beliefs, attitudes, and behaviors?
- Is this a place you'll want to work a year or two from now?
- Who are the executive leaders? Is their approach to succession planning and career development of staff in alignment with your goals? As important, if not more so, are the executive leaders, board, and investors ethical and respectable?

There is no perfect company, job, or fit. But it's best to identify the risks and address up front as many as you can. Then—if you decide to go forward—communicate early and often about the risks and your responses with your boss or board of directors.

Key Action Tips

1. As you consider a new opportunity, identify the top three elements important in your next career move. Use these as a guide when considering your options.

2. Immediately start your due diligence on the company and position. Assess the company and position from an organizational, role, and personal perspective.

3. Review the executive leaders and, if applicable, other levels of leadership that affect your position. Learn about their backgrounds, their tenure with the company, and how they feel about the company and its culture. Also, learn how others—employees and outsiders—feel about the company leadership and corporate culture.

4. Ask whether the company has a clearly articulated set of corporate values. If so, request the list and assess whether these values are in alignment with the behavior of the company and what is important to you.

5. Verify that the company has the resources to finance operations, ramp revenue, and maintain profitability and positive cash flow. If the company is not profitable, confirm when profitability and positive cash flow is projected and whether the company has the financial resources to get there. Review the last two or three years of financial statements if they are available.

6. Inquire about corporate and departmental-level turnover. Confirm the method by which the company calculates turnover.

7. Search the Internet for a due diligence checklist that applies to your position and industry.

8. If the position is open, find out as much as you can about why it's open. What happened to the last person who held the position? What skills made the person successful, and what skills did he or she lack?

9. Conduct online searches on the company and competitors. Read message boards and blogs, even though you should take information from these sources with a grain of salt.

17

Mission: Interview—Get the Offer

It's your job to sell yourself—do it well.

—Anonymous

So you've identified a company where you might like to work, researched it, evaluated whether its mission motivates you, and considered how your experience and skill set meets its needs. You've customized your cover letter and resume, you've submitted them, and you've followed up. Now what?

To get to an offer, your mission is to diligently prepare for the telephone screening and in-person interview. Make it your top priority.

There are two primary types of interviews: behavioral and traditional. Behavioral interviews assume that past performance is the best predictor of future performance. To determine whether you have the right skills for a position, the interviewers ask questions that require you to provide examples of what you did in specific situations. For instance, they might ask you to describe a difficult situation and how you handled it. Conversely, a traditional interview asks more general questions, such as, "What did you like

> They don't want to know about you. They want to know how you can help them.

most about your job?" or "What did you like most about your company?"

Since it's difficult to anticipate an interviewer's style, I recommend preparing for a behavioral interview. Even if you're asked general questions, you'll serve yourself well by answering with specific examples of your past performance. The STAR method is an effective way of doing this. STAR is an acronym for situation, task, action, and result. First, describe a specific situation and the task required. Then describe the action you took, even if a team was involved. Finally, describe the results, quantifying them if possible, and tell the interviewer what you learned.

Carole Martin, interview coach and author, encourages clients to "Show—don't tell. The secret to doing well in a behavioral interview is showing the interviewer what you have done—not just telling him or her."[1] Painting a picture of your experience with action and emotion makes your answers much more interesting than if you just tell the interviewer about the problem. Use the framework of a beginning (there was a time…), middle (the actions I took…) and end (the results were…).

In addition to preparing your answers, have a list of questions ready. According to Louise Garver, executive coach and founder of Career Directions, LLC, "The best questions are really all about them and not about you. They have one thing at their core: How can I contribute value to the team and the company."[2]

Finally, use psychology to ace the interview. Joy Bridges, recruiter for Legacy MedSearch, recommends using a social style model (similar to the one described in chapter 39, "The Platinum Rule—Know Personality Styles") to identify the interviewer's style and what he or she is looking for in a candidate.

Bridges offers the following descriptions of the different social types and what they want:[3]

a. *Expressive*. Assertive, responsive, energetic, fast-paced, and visionary. May have a flamboyant personality. They're fashion forward in their dress and may have a cluttered office. The desk chair may be beside the interviewer rather than across the desk to allow for more connection during the interview. Expressives want to like and be liked, so building a personal rapport is essential. A career portfolio will help the interviewer visualize your achievements.

b. *Driver*. Assertive, low responsiveness, driven, results-oriented, and bottom-line focused. They're quick decision makers and like to control. The office may be neat and covered in awards and other evidence of the interviewer's achievements. They'll likely be dressed conservatively, and the guest's chair will be across from the desk to build a barrier of professionalism. Elaborate on what you can do for the company and focus your responses in terms of return on investment.

c. *Amiable*. Low assertiveness, high responsiveness, team builder. Amiables want everyone to be happy, want to be liked, and want peace and cohesion in the workplace. The guest's chair will most likely be beside the interviewer. Pictures of friends and family will be displayed prominently in the office. Focus your answers on your ability to work well with others and your ability to build trusting relationships.

d. *Analytical.* Low assertiveness, low responsiveness. Often referred to as "the thinker," they're detail-oriented, methodical decision makers who are focused on facts, logic, and reasoning. Expect a neat, organized office. This personality type is less emotional than Expressives or Amiables, so the interviewer will seem less energetic or opinionated and will likely be dressed conservatively. The guest chair may be across from the desk, as it would be with a Driver.

In general, I am a Driver and prefer candidates who concisely answer questions. Although I attempt to take into account the position for which the candidate is interviewing, I still have a strong preference for those candidates who quickly and confidently answer interview questions.

Key Action Tips

1. As you consider a new opportunity, immediately start your due diligence on the company and position. Read chapter 16, "The Job Search—Maximize Success through Due Diligence."

2. Create a white paper highlighting your strengths, motivation, and fit with the organization. It's all about how you can help the company, why you are the best person for the job, and lastly, why you want to work at the company. Use the white paper contents in all your interactions and for follow-up. Brand yourself as the best candidate.

3. Prepare for a behavioral interview by identifying six or more examples of situations in which you

demonstrated behaviors and skills of interest to the prospective employer. Using the STAR method, prepare three positive examples in which you met a goal and three challenging examples in which you made the best of a situation or turned it around.

4. Briefly and enthusiastically answer each question in a positive manner. Prepare a list of answers to commonly asked questions, including:
   a. *Describe a specific goal or objective you were assigned, the outcome, and what factors led to your success.*
   b. *Tell me about a time when you came up with an innovative solution to a challenge, how you proceeded, and the outcome.*
   c. *Tell me about a time you failed. What did you learn? What would you do over?*
   d. *Tell me about yourself.*
   e. *What are you looking for in your next position?*
   f. *Why did you leave previous companies? Why are there gaps in your employment? What are the reasons for short employment tenures?*
   g. *What do you like and dislike about your current job?*
   h. *Why do you want to work at this company?*
   i. *Why are you the best candidate?*
   j. *Describe the work environment or culture in which you have been most productive.*
   k. *What do you believe is the most effective management style? What is the role of a good manager?*
   l. *Do you prefer to work alone or as part of a team?*
   m. *What is the biggest misperception people have of you?*

5. Prepare a list of questions in advance of the interview. Focus them on how *you* can contribute value to the team and the company.
   a. *How would you describe the ideal candidate or the top qualities in an ideal candidate?* Use this as an opportunity to describe past successful experiences.
   b. *How do you envision this position supporting you?* This implies that you will make the person's life easier.
   c. *How would you define "success" for this position?* This helps you understand how the company will evaluate your performance and may provide insight into the company's culture.
   d. *What are the top three to five areas to immediately address?* This demonstrates a results-oriented focus.
   e. *Do you have any concerns about my ability to excel in the position?* This allows you an opportunity to address any perceived shortcomings.
   f. *How does this position fit into the company's long-term plans?* This gives you an opportunity to describe how you can contribute to meeting the company's long-term strategies.
   g. *What is the company culture?* This demonstrates your interest in understanding the company's philosophy and people. Use the opportunity to show that you thrive in this type of corporate culture—if it's true.
   h. *What can I do as follow-up to move forward as the top candidate?* This demonstrates interest and initiative.

6. Plan to be available for a phone or video interview at least fifteen minutes early to allow extra time to

correct technological issues. For an in-person interview, also plan to arrive early, allowing time for getting lost, locating parking, and feeling relaxed, calm, and ready. Regardless of when you arrive, don't enter the building until ten minutes prior to the interview. From the moment you enter the building, you are being evaluated. Be sure to treat the receptionist as respectfully as you do the interviewer.

7. Greet the interviewer with a warm smile regardless of whether you're on the phone or in the same room. A smile makes a difference even if people can't see you. If in person, maintain good eye contact from your initial greeting through the end of the interview. If there is more than one interviewer, make eye contact with each one as you're answering questions.

8. Remember that even the initial small talk is a way for the interviewer to get you to let down your guard. Regardless of flight delays, time changes, etc., be positive! Review chapter 39, "The Platinum Rule—Know Personality Styles" and employ the Platinum Rule or a similar social style model to identify what the interviewer is looking for in a candidate.

9. Maintain your confidence and calm as you navigate the interview. Some interviewers will attempt to stress you out to see how you respond to pressure. It's critical to be positive, upbeat, energetic, and genuine throughout the entire interview. Turn every potential weakness or lack of skill into a positive.

10. Practice excellent listening skills and never interrupt the interviewer. Take notes so you can add to your list of questions. When invited to ask questions, ask how much time the interviewer has; absolutely do not exceed that time and limit yourself to five questions. Then inquire whether you can count on the interviewer's support of your candidacy and follow up immediately with a thank-you email message.

18

Dare to Ask—Negotiate for Pay Raises, Promotions, and New Jobs

Never allow a person to tell you no who doesn't have the power to say yes.

—Eleanor Roosevelt,
longest-serving US first lady

Would you like to add a million dollars to your lifetime earnings? No one in their right mind would say no. Why then are women, in essence, saying no?

According to a study by economist Linda Babcock and associates, eight times as many men as women (57 percent versus 7 percent) graduating with master's degrees from Carnegie Mellon negotiated their salaries. In doing so, men increased their starting salaries by an average of 7.6 percent.[1] This may sound inconsequential, but starting salary differentials get compounded over the lifetime of a career, resulting in losses of hundreds of thousands of dollars. Without a doubt, they contribute to the gender gap in pay.

The simple fact is that women don't like to negotiate. It's been reported that more than twice as many women than men feel a great deal of apprehension about negoti-

> Women possess significant negotiating advantages—so why don't we use them?

ating. In general, men are four times as likely to negotiate.[2] Sheryl Sandberg, Facebook's chief operating officer, says that women who are great negotiators for other people—doing a business deal, for instance—"are often not good negotiators for their own advancement."[3]

Many women forgo negotiations due to fear, conflict avoidance, and a desire to be liked. Unfortunately, their reservations are not unfounded. Research indicates that women and men are judged differently for negotiating. A Carnegie Mellon and Harvard study gave participants descriptions of male and female job applicants with equivalent qualifications. When examining the candidates who negotiated for a higher salary, the participants found fault with the women twice as often as they did with the men who did exactly the same thing.[4]

To ease the pain and improve your odds, be "promotion-focused": take a minute to focus on what you have to gain, and eliminate all thoughts of what you have to lose. Research has shown that promotion-focused people are more successful in negotiations than "prevention-focused" people who concentrate on what they could lose if they don't succeed. Promotion-focus can also facilitate a win-win scenario in negotiations. If both parties are promotion-focused in a situation where there are multiple issues under consideration, each can yield on lower-priority issues and reach compromises that allow both parties to get what they want the most—a concept referred to as "expanding the pie."[5]

"Yes, I was uneasy about negotiating for myself, but I knew I had to," admits Valerie Carricaburu, director of strategic alliances at Pacific Northwest Diabetes Research

Institute. "If you are apprehensive about negotiating your new job offer or pay raise, 'extract' yourself from the situation and imagine observing someone else negotiating for you. I found it helped me on two levels—controlling my emotions and realizing that it is absolutely reasonable to ask. Also, before and after getting an offer, seek advice from people you respect. You don't have the job until you sign the offer, and the impression you make while negotiating is another test of your skills."[6]

Although cultural and social factors contribute to women's aversion to asking and negotiating, Cait Clark, author of *Dare to Ask!*, argues that women actually possess significant natural negotiating advantages. Clark suggests that these advantages result from social skills in which women generally excel, including communicating, active listening, empathy, willingness to share, and intuition.[7]

From an employer perspective, if you receive an offer, you are the number one candidate. They want you! In fact, if you don't negotiate, the company wonders if they could have secured you for less money. Additionally, by negotiating, you're demonstrating a critical leadership skill. At worst, the company says no. At best, you get a higher salary, better benefits, or more stock options. It's worth asking.

And these principles don't just apply to the initial offer. It's also important to keep asking for your next promotion. "I would not have gotten four promotions within my eight years at Solar Turbines if I had not asked for them," advises Kelly Powers, director of strategic planning at CLINDEVOR 360. "During my annual performance review, each and every year, I would always ask my boss what I needed to do to be considered for a promotion. Several times I got an unexpected and positive reaction from my boss, particularly when I had recently been promoted. I was always steadfast with my intentions on clearly understanding what my goals and objectives were to successfully reach the next level. And it paid off!"[8]

Now that you're motivated to ask and negotiate, follow my top ten salary negotiation tips below. They have helped me and other women make hundreds of thousands of dollars more over their careers.

Key Action Tips

1. Regularly ask and clearly understand what you need to do to be promoted to the next level. Believe in yourself, seek advice, and role-play before you ask for a raise, promotion, or new job. Role-playing can prepare you for a variety of responses and increase your confidence. Practice promotion-focus by taking a minute or two to focus on what you have to gain.

2. Research salary ranges prior to negotiating for a new job or position. Inquire with one to two recruiters not involved in the search. Online sources include www.salary.com, www.vault.com, www.payscale.com, and the salary calculator on www.monster.com. Review these figures before you negotiate your pay requirements and use them for objective rationale. Since money does play a key factor in career satisfaction, it's important not to shortchange yourself.

3. Set your own salary expectations. Define a compensation range and set higher goals. Before negotiations commence, calculate the minimum amount you're willing to accept. If the offer doesn't meet your minimum requirement and cannot be negotiated higher, consider passing on the offer. Also, don't

adopt the mindset that whatever they offer is good enough. If you accept the first offer, the "seller" feels you may have accepted less.

4. Delay salary discussions as long as possible as prospective employers frequently base their offers on current salary. Since women generally start at lower salaries than men and don't negotiate as much, such offers will most likely be undervalued. Additionally, the earlier you are in the interview process, the less your prospective employer knows about you and the value you'll bring to the company. If you're asked your salary, try to deflect the question. Per Jack Chapman, author of *Negotiating Your Salary: How to Make $1000 a Minute,* use the following phrases:[9]
   a. "I'm sure we can come to a good salary agreement if I'm the right person for the job, so let's first agree on whether I am."
   b. "I have some idea of the market, but for a moment let's start with your range. What market data do you have for this position?"

   If that doesn't work, state the range applicable to the position and say you're confident the employer will make a fair and equitable offer. If you cannot get around the question of your current salary, don't lie. Companies frequently ask for paystubs or W-2s.

5. Be positive and understand that practically everything is negotiable. If you have an offer, they are interested in you. After researching the position and assessing your worth, enter into negotiations with a sense of optimism and confidence that will help ensure success.

6. Turn the negotiation into a collaborative, win-win, problem-solving exercise by using "feel, felt, found" throughout the conversation. For example, "I understand how you feel about making salaries equitable within the department. Our human resource department also felt that way, but, over time, we found it was to the company's benefit to stretch and hire more qualified candidates at higher salaries." Another approach is, "You may not be aware of this, but the salary range for this position is $X to $Y." Framing the negotiations as a win-win situation, as compared to a competition, will be better received.

7. Be willing to yield on lower-priority issues in order to achieve your most important priorities. For every concession you make, ask for something in return. For example, if you're accepting a lower salary than requested, request more equity, a higher title, and/or a shorter time until the next salary review.

8. Take time to reflect on each offer before rejecting it, asking for more, or accepting. This will make you appear more reflective, objective, and appreciative of your prospective employer's efforts.

9. Use your natural skills. Negotiate like a woman, not a man. It's better to make your demands known in a thoughtful, respectful, win-win manner than a masculine in-your-face way.

10. If you're offered a promotion or additional responsibilities, thank your boss for the opportunity, say you're confident that you'll do a great job, and then inquire about salary increase. Don't ask, "Is there is

a salary increase?" Instead, ask, "What's the salary increase range?" You can ask your boss for a day to consider the opportunity and use that time to research the appropriate compensation range.

19

First Ninety Days—Critical Success Strategies

What is success? I think it is a mixture of having a flair for the thing that you are doing; knowing that it is not enough, that you have got to have hard work and a certain sense of purpose.

—Margaret Thatcher,
British prime minister, 1979–1990

Transitioning into a new leadership position is one of the biggest challenges you'll face. Whether you succeed is largely determined by what you do, or don't do, during the first ninety days.

Nearly half of all new leaders fail within the first eighteen months.[1] Crucial mistakes include belief that their hiring mandates change, overconfidence in skills and experience, lack of organizational respect, attempting too much too fast, failure to clarify objectives, and failure to establish networks within a new company.

"Forget about 'hitting the ground running' and trying to solve everything in the first month," advises Julie Kampf, CEO of leadership coaching firm Career Central. "Instead, spend your first thirty days listening, and studying the company and the challenges it faces. What are the goals you want to reach, and the obstacles to those goals? Read everything you can, online and elsewhere, about the company and the industry, and seek opinions from the people under you and above you. Ask a lot of questions. Become an expert on the business and build rapport with as many people as you can."[2]

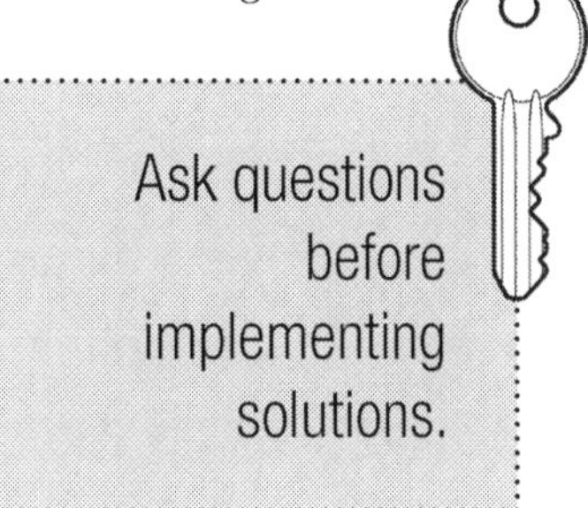

Michael Watkins, author of *Leadership Transitions* and *The First 90 Days*, agrees with this strategy. The first thirty days are for assessing your team or company—taking into account the culture, strengths, processes, and standards—and for establishing your credibility. Once you've laid that foundation, you can spend the next thirty days aligning stakeholders, and the thirty days after that for integrating your leadership style, strategy and vision development, and performance metrics.[3]

Strategies for success can differ depending on whether you have been internally promoted or hired from the outside. They also depend on your level in an organization. Low-status leaders are rated as more effective when they take charge with a directive style and draw on positional power, whereas high-status leaders are viewed as more effective when they use a participatory style and personal power to influence others.[4] In other words, newly hired lower-level managers establish authority, leadership, and respect by taking charge earlier, whereas for executives, minimal change is recommended in the first thirty days.

"Stay as positive and upbeat as you can," emphasizes Kampf. "Acknowledge the problems, but focus the people on the future, and what specifically you can do to make things better."[5]

Key Action Tips[6]

Before you start

1. Meet/speak with critical stakeholders.
   a. Ask questions about their priorities and what would constitute success in your first 90, 180, and 360 days.
   b. Ask questions related to customers (end-users, influencers), collaborators (suppliers, business partners), organizational capabilities (human, operational, financial, technical, IP, and brand assets), competitors (direct, indirect, potential), and conditions (government, regulatory, macro- and microeconomic).
   c. Ask about preferred communication in terms of mode (email, voicemail, in person, memos), manner (formal versus informal presentation, scheduling notice), and frequency.

2. Collect/organize important corporate information.

3. Match your strategy with the company's, division's, or department's situation. You'll usually be dealing with one or more of four situations:
   a. *Start-up.* You'll need to make decisions quickly, often without perfect information. Take risks, and direct your company's actions toward common goals.
   b. *Turnaround.* Employees are rarely enthusiastic and may be demoralized. Make decisions quickly, including layoffs and other cost-cutting measures, and reenergize your team. Educate others on why measures are being taken.

c. *Realignment.* Start slowly and learn as much as you can before taking action. Educate people as to why change is necessary and how it will benefit employees. Involve people in change management.
d. *Sustaining success.* Learn everything you can about the culture, politics, and key players. Focus strategy on defense. Develop a solid group of supporters and a good business case for any change.

4. Plan/outline your first ninety days.

Day One

a. Your first impression is the longest lasting, and the impression you leave people with is the second longest lasting. The middle portion of your interaction will be largely lost.
b. Understand the culture; dress and plan accordingly.
c. Meet with your direct reports.
d. Conduct a department-wide meeting or, if applicable, a company-wide meeting.
   v. Your goal is to make people feel comfortable and feel your energy and enthusiasm about the company or department, the employees, and the opportunity.
   vi. Recognize the to-date progress; talk about your belief in the mission and your desire to work as a team to move the company, division, or department to its next level.
   vii. Have as many one-on-one meetings with key employees as you can to hear about their projects, outstanding issues, concerns, etc. Take notes, listen, and thank them for their

input. Be sure to schedule proper follow-up on any urgent outstanding issues.

First Thirty Days

a. Begin executing the strategy you planned based on the situation (see above).
b. In general, learn as quickly as you can and accelerate the transition. Become an expert on the business.
c. Identify and spend time with key players who can help support your efforts.
d. Ask questions, listen, study the company, and identify challenges. Seek opinions from the people under you and above you.
e. Build rapport with as many people as you can.
f. Define the goals you want to reach, and the obstacles to reaching those goals. Identify a few significant challenges you can address with quick fixes to establish credibility.
g. Be positive and maintain the attitude that the challenges are solvable.

Days Thirty-One to Sixty

a. Conduct strategic planning sessions with your team to identify challenges and potential solutions. Create or modify the vision *with* your team to encourage involvement and buy-in.
b. Set short-term goals with metrics and strategies to achieve in the next 60, 90, 180, and 360 days.

Days Sixty-One to Ninety

a. Develop a performance scorecard.
b. Maintain balance with careful scheduling, limited changes, and maintaining contact with your mentors.

20

Marriage, Motherhood, Career Advancement—a Perfect Storm?

I've yet to be on a campus where most women weren't worrying about some aspect of combining marriage, children, and a career. I've yet to find one where many men were worrying about the same thing.

—Gloria Steinem, American feminist and political activist

Can women simultaneously pursue marriage, motherhood, and the ladder of success? Should they make sacrifices rather than attempt to have it all? There is no clear-cut answer. Many women have experienced tremendous career success while balancing the rewarding yet demanding jobs of spouse and mother. Others become caught in a second tier, the "marzipan layer." Others drop out.

Let's first talk about two-career marriages. Much of what has been written about glass ceilings attribute the lack of female CEOs to men holding women back *at work*. This may not tell the entire story. *Financial Times* management columnist Lucy Kellaway argues, "The biggest reason alpha women don't become CEOs is because they have made the

We can have it all . . . but we can't get it without support..

common error of marrying an alpha man . . . [who] insisted on putting their own careers first."[1]

Kellaway reports that most women on the list of "the most powerful women in world business" have children, but don't have alpha male husbands—or at least not so alpha that they won't sacrifice their careers for their wives' careers. Examples include Indra Nooyi, Pepsi CEO; Irene Rosenfeld, Kraft CEO; and Ursula Burns, Xerox CEO. Moreover, surveys of executive women reveal that the majority of executive married women are the breadwinners in the family. Either the two-alpha marriages did not work, or they did not occur to begin with. There are exceptions, but a long-term two-alpha marriage is not the norm.

If you're an alpha woman who wants a husband who is in the supportive role, I share sage advice I received from a male mentor: men are wired to be respected, women to be adored. A woman needs to ensure that her non-breadwinning husband feels respected and appreciated. Likewise, she should feel adored—as well as respected—by her husband.

This is even truer for dual-alpha marriages. When you come home, take off your corporate, tough-as-nails shell and show love and respect for your husband. You may be rolling your eyes, but trust me, your ultra-alpha husband needs respect from you, or he may find it elsewhere.

What about motherhood? While society no longer has a problem with women pursuing careers, working outside the home doesn't exempt women from the societal expectation that caring for the home and raising children is (mostly) their responsibility.

A National Parenting Association survey reports that successful working women are much more likely to assume primary home and childcare responsibilities than their husbands. Fifty percent of successful married women were primarily responsible for meal preparation, as compared with 9 percent of their husbands. Fifty-one percent of women took time off to care for a sick child, compared to 9 percent of husbands. Career women also contributed eleven hours more per week toward household work than men.[2]

So is it hopeless? Not according to Ilene Gordon, CEO of Corn Products and an advocate of having it all: "The biggest myth that I'd like to set to rest is that women can't have a family and a successful career. The skills that make a good business leader—organization, drive, trust, delegation, and compassion—also go a long way to balance the responsibilities of work and family life."[3]

"I remember when I used to prepare for my workday with four children," says Celine Peters, vice president of CRISI Medical Systems. "I would get up early while it was still dark outside, and the children were sleeping. The quietness of the house provided a relaxing environment to review my day's schedule and contemplate work issues."[4]

As in business, scheduling is also key for your personal life. Christine Osekoski, publisher of *Fast Company*, offers her top life/work balance tip: "I schedule everything—I have to. I schedule phone conversations with friends, yoga, personal training, and every personal appointment. I even schedule in preparation and travel time in between."[5]

What about the guilt-inducing societal message that good moms raise their children themselves, whereas bad moms work and leave childrearing to others? Don't worry about it. In a study of more than one thousand American children over a fifteen-year period, children who experienced no outside childcare didn't fare any better than children who received non-maternal care.[6] In fact, children who spent time in *high-quality* childcare settings demonstrated higher cognitive skills, better language skills, and better school readiness scores than those with stay-at-home moms.

I have tremendous respect for women who achieve the ultimate trifecta: a happy marriage, well-adjusted children, and a successful career. The challenge lies in balancing all of it while remaining sane, healthy, and happy.

Key Action Tips

To maximize your chances of a good life/work balance, try the following.

At work:

1. *Organize, establish priorities, and execute.* Make a list of priorities each day and prioritize longer-term projects over the week, month, or quarter. Focus on priorities and understand that working efficiently is more important than the number of hours spent at work.

2. *Delegate, stop taking others' responsibilities, and say no.* Reserve your time for the tasks and projects that only you can accomplish. Almost everything else should be delegated if there is someone else to delegate to; if not, work with your boss to set priorities that accomplish the most vital objectives.

3. *Focus on the big picture.* Work the large issues of a project. Then, if possible, pass on to another capable person to complete.

4. *Eliminate distractions.* Don't allow "urgent, unimportant distractions" such as email or phone calls

to interrupt your schedule. Schedule two to three blocks of time daily to respond to email messages. Return calls while commuting or at an established time.

5. *Schedule everything.* This includes everything at work and at home. It may seem excessive, but if something doesn't get scheduled, the likelihood of it being accomplished is significantly lower.

6. *Plan time off.* Plan for and take family vacations. Ensure vacations and project/quarter-end deadlines don't overlap.

7. *Schedule specific nights that you'll leave work "on time."* Establish certain nights for family dinners and leave work at the appointed time on those nights. Worst case scenario, you can go in early the next morning to address unresolved tasks.

8. *Leave work at work, if possible.* Develop a mental switch to create a boundary between work and home. Use your commute time to transition between the two. Enter each arena with a positive attitude. If you need to work at home, reserve it for later in the evening after you have spent time with your family.

At home:

1. *Build a support network.* Share parenting duties with your spouse, parents, in-laws, neighbors, friends, or others. Arrange with your network a few hours weekly where they will take your children and vice versa. Your network can also serve as support in emergencies.

2. *Find reliable childcare.* Leave your children with someone capable and confident. Communicate with the caregiver and facilitate positive interactions between your children and caregiver.

3. *Let go of guilt.* Guilt is bad for morale. It wastes valuable time and energy. It keeps you focused on the past rather than being present. Whatever is making you feel guilty, identify it and make a plan to approach it differently.

4. *Set boundaries.* Boundaries are necessary for balancing work and family and acknowledging your limits. Boundaries allow you to take charge of your time, space, and feelings. When asked to do something, take a deep breath and think about it. Most of the time it will be acceptable to tell the person it's an interesting idea and you'll get back to them. This allows you time to think through your response and ensure that it's in alignment with your goals.

5. *Create time for yourself.* Too much work at home (and the office) can lead to stress, anxiety, and even health problems. Allow thirty to sixty minutes daily to exercise, pray, and/or read. Eat healthy and get sufficient sleep.

6. *Get organized at home by creating family routines.* Organize and schedule your family activities as you do at work. Have regularly scheduled times for starting the day, meals, and ending the day. Prepare things like clothing and lunches the night before.

7. *Be flexible and keep striving for balance.* Understand that the best-laid plans are only plans and will never

go as intended. Leave time for the unplanned and continue your pursuit to achieve a healthy balance.

8. *Include fun family activities in your schedule.* To optimize your time, plan activities all of the family can do together. Get involved with hobbies. Give your family your full attention. Develop rituals or family habits that become a positive part of your family culture.

21

Sexual Harassment

Sexual harassment is complex, subtle, and highly subjective.

—Kathie Lee Gifford, US talk show host

Sexual harassment... a very sensitive and difficult topic. How is it best handled? Some feel it's a damned if you do, damned if you don't situation. Left unaddressed, sexual harassment only gets worse.

What exactly is sexual harassment? The Equal Employment Opportunity Commission (EEOC) defines sexual harassment as:

> Unwelcomed sexual advancements, requests for sexual favors, and other verbal or physical conduct of a sexual nature when submission to such conduct is a condition for employment, or such conduct interferes with work performance or creates an intimidating, hostile, or offensive working environment.

"Unwelcomed" is the critical word. A victim may fail to protest certain conduct even though it's offensive, and this may still constitute sexual harassment if it is unwelcome. Sexual harassment runs the gamut from unwanted phone calls, letters, or emails to invading someone's personal space, whistling, personal questions about the person's sex life, following a person, staring, looking a person up and down, telling sexual jokes, making sexual innuendos, showing pornography, leaving questionable pictures out in the open, touching a person's hair, gestures like winking or throwing kisses, discussing topics of a sexual nature in front of another individual, and intimidation. The list goes on.

Employers have a responsibility to protect their employees.

Employers have a responsibility to protect their employees from sexual harassment, both from other employees and from customers and vendors. Managers may have personal liability for engaging in sexual harassment, though they may not be individually liable for sexual harassment between coworkers. (The employer may be liable for such coworker sexual harassment if the manager knew or should have known about it and failed to take action to stop it).

"In communications, the speaker is responsible for the message that is delivered. It is the same for sexual harassment situations," says Hien DeYoung, vice president of human resources at Acucela, Inc. "The target of the sexual harassment is not responsible for preventing or stopping the harassment. If someone says 'no' to sexual conduct, once is generally enough for a reasonable person to know to stop such conduct immediately. If it does not stop, legal liability to the employer may be created."[1]

So what should you do if you feel you're in an intimidating, hostile, or offensive work environment?

Key Action Tips

1. Directly and clearly inform the harasser that the behavior is offensive and you want it to stop. Keep to your agenda and don't respond to a harasser's excuses or diversionary tactics. When addressing the individual, use direct eye contact and a strong, serious stance; do not smile.

2. Keep a journal of all the incidents and your attempts to stop the behavior. Document the dates, times, places, and names of other people who were present.

3. If you don't feel comfortable speaking directly with the harasser, then discuss the situation with your manager and/or the human resource department. Find out whether your company has a sexual harassment policy or procedure. Adhere to the procedure. If your manager is the harasser, report your situation to the human resource department or next-level manager. Document the report in your journal and follow up all in-person meetings with written correspondence, such as an email message, so you have documentation that you brought the matter to management's attention. Follow up to ensure your complaint is investigated.

4. If the harassment is causing stress, depression, or other symptoms, seek professional assistance or see your physician.

5. Seek the advice of an attorney if the actions persist. While it's far better to get the situation resolved internally and avoid further disruption, obtaining external help may be the only way to bring internal attention to the situation.

6. If you are a manager and you witness or are informed of a potential sexual harassment situation, closely follow your company's sexual harassment policy or procedure. Ignoring or not properly addressing the situation can result in corporate liability and you being disciplined or terminated.

22

"Fair" Is Where You Go on Rides and Eat Cotton Candy

Above all, be the heroine in your life, not the victim.
—Nora Ephron, American screenwriter, producer, and director

Life's not fair. Sometimes you get burned by inequity; other times, you benefit. Either way, it's a fact of life. Accept it. Once you eliminate the fairness factor from your mindset, you'll be less likely to expect fairness and less affected when it rears its ugly head—and it will, time and time again.

Once you stop worrying about fairness, you minimize the risk of feeling like a victim. This is essential, as defining yourself as a victim significantly limits your ability to move forward and dramatically affects the way others view you. Mary Engelbreit, world-renowned artist and illustrator, wisely states, "If you don't like something, change it; if you can't change it, change the way you think about it."[1] In other words, take control of what you can and realize there will always be things we cannot control.

This doesn't mean denying that unfairness exists. As women—for now—we need to acknowledge that sexism

> Don't obsess over past injustices. Think about what you can change right now.

and discrimination *do* exist and are *not* going away anytime soon. A common mistake women make is believing that the playing field is level. By acknowledging the barriers, we can better prepare and plan our careers.

I have heard it said many times that women need to outperform men to be considered as good or be promoted. So be it. But we cannot allow double standards to hold us back. We have to keep forging ahead, controlling what we can, learning what we do that contributes to the existence of glass ceilings, and mounting strategies to shatter every last piece of glass!

It's been helpful for me to keep life's challenges in perspective, be they professional or personal. I don't often share intimate details of my personal history with most people, but when I do, I always hear, "I am so sorry." Well, thankfully, I'm not. My challenges have made me stronger, resilient, and empathetic. They have made me who I am. Without those challenges, I would not be as determined, positive, or loving. Everyone has his or her own trials and tribulations. We need to make the best of them. And we need to keep reminding ourselves that "fair" is where you go on rides and eat cotton candy![2]

Key Action Tips

1. Stop expecting life to hand you a fair deck. If something unfair happens, remind yourself that you may not have benefited this time around, but *there is a reason it happened, time will reveal that reason, and most things work out for the best.* It just takes time to

understand. Identify how the situation could have been minimized, better dealt with, or prevented. Be introspective and, if necessary, obtain objective feedback. Take as much responsibility as you can, but don't beat yourself up. The world already does a good enough job of doing that for us (just a little humor). Look at it as a learning moment: grow and improve from the experience.

2. Keep your life in perspective. Every day, look into the mirror and say, "Life may not be *fair*, but I will level the playing field as much as I can, and have fun in the process. I accept this, embrace it, and am thankful for the personal and professional opportunities and blessings I have." Make a list of your blessings and, while forging ahead, constantly be mindful of them. If you tell yourself something long enough, you'll come to believe it... and even feel better about it. Look around and realize that whatever you're dealing with, it's not nearly as bad as the circumstances faced by billions of other people in the world.

3. Identify charities or people where you can donate time, money, or experience to others in need. Giving to others takes the focus from ourselves and is fulfilling.

4. Remember, life is full of different opportunities. If one door shuts, don't stay stuck. Run for the next door! Somehow, somewhere, something will open.

5. Every day we wake up with a choice—it's going to be a great day or not. Choose great no matter what.

PART II

Unleash the Leader Within

We all have a leader inside of us, yet most of us are so busy doing our job that we fail to set aside time for developing our leadership skills. I'm here to tell you that leadership can be learned, and there are many great role models—from both history and the present day—to inspire us. Whether you look to Mother Teresa, Susan B. Anthony, Abraham Lincoln, Gandhi, or modern-day figures, you find that leaders are always learning, gaining insights from others, and raising their own bar. You can do this too.

As women, we have innate strengths that can make us great leaders. Some of us achieve this without really thinking about it—it comes naturally. The rest of us just need guidance and tools.

Part II of *Keys to the Corner Office* provides insights on the key elements you need to master to unleash your leader within.

23

Refine Your Leadership—Before It Defines You

Leaders aren't born. They are made.
—*Vince Lombardi, American football coach*

Have you given much thought to what kind of leader you are? What would your colleagues say? What would your friends and family say? How do you lead so that others will follow? How much time do you spend studying other leaders and developing your own leadership? Sadly, for most of us, the answer to that last question is "not enough." But developing leadership is incredibly important as demands for leadership occur in every area of our lives.

Heed the adage "Your reputation precedes you." It truly does. Take time to develop and refine your leadership—before it defines you. Once you gain a reputation, good or bad, it's very difficult to shed.

Marissa Mayer, CEO of Yahoo and former Google executive, is an unfortunate casualty of this. When she was appointed CEO of Yahoo, horror stories of her leadership, or lack thereof, were highlighted in the news. People weren't as focused on her strengths—off-the-chart intelligence, an

> "Success means having the courage, the determination, and the will to become the person you believe you were meant to be."
>
> —George Sheehan

exemplary work ethic, and a successful career. Instead, they paid more attention to her early leadership years when she had a tyrannical managerial style and made people line up outside of her office so she could see them in five-minute increments.[1]

Fair or not, Marissa's early leadership style overshadowed her Yahoo appointment and incredible accomplishment—the youngest Fortune 500 CEO and one of only a few women running a Fortune 500 company. This was the case even though, according to a former subordinate, Marissa had "matured" in her leadership style.[2]

I strongly doubt male leaders would have been judged as harshly for the same behavior. They might even be praised, as Steve Jobs had been. "Leadership experts say women must navigate a 'double bind,'" a *Wall Street Journal* article explains. "If they assert themselves forcefully, people may perceive them as not acting feminine enough, triggering a backlash. But if they act in a stereotypically feminine way, they aren't seen as strong leaders."[3]

In my own career, I've faced similar challenges. I had a reputation for being decisive, driven, and results-oriented—traits that were respected for male executives but were sometime interpreted as too hard-charging for a woman. And when I empathized with the people I led, they didn't always believe I was sincere. They actually questioned—behind my back—how I could care for employees the way I did. Caring didn't seem congruent with my hard-charging side.

It seemed that my colleagues and subordinates either

loved me or feared me. Though I never threatened or bullied people, my drive, intensity, and strong work ethic were intimidating to many. They believed I held them to the same standards I held myself. They developed anxiety about me because they didn't know me. While I could have taken the position that this was their problem, I ultimately realized *I needed to change* in order to soften these perceptions and increase my effectiveness as a leader. It would have been ideal if I had been more self-aware and refined my leadership earlier in my career, before it defined me.

"Invest in self-assessments of your communication style, competencies, core motivators, and emotional intelligence," recommends Mindy Bortness, president of Communication Works, Inc. "These will provide strong validation and understanding of your strengths as well as areas to improve. These self-assessments nicely complement 360 analyses which focus on others' perception of you."[4]

Key Action Tips

To develop and refine your leadership:

1. Read, reflect, define, and refine. Make yourself a student of leadership.
   a. Read leadership books.
   b. Subscribe to leadership blogs, such as *Harvard Business Review Blog Network* (blogs.hbr.org), and join women's leadership groups on LinkedIn and other professional social media sites.
   c. Start a lifelong leadership journal and define what great leadership means to you. Identify leaders you respect and document the skills and qualities they possess.
   d. From your leadership journal, create your *own*

personal definition of leadership. Commit the definition to memory so you can live it, articulate it, and check your actions against it.

   e. Develop your own leadership brand. An example of a common leadership brand is the policeman's credo: "To protect and serve." My seven point brand is "To trust, serve, respect, empower, encourage, develop, and achieve."

2. Conduct a gap analysis.
   a. From the skills and qualities of respected leaders, identify areas you lack or need to develop.
   b. Conduct 360 analyses (a process to obtain confidential feedback from managers, peers, and direct reports) with the help of your boss, your human resource department, or an Internet-based source like the Center for Creative Leadership (www.ccl.org), STAR Leadership 360 (www.star360feedback.com), CustomInsight (www.custominsight.com), or LPI (www.lpionline.com). Alternatively, create your own online survey through Zoomerang (www.zoomerang.com) or SurveyMonkey (www.surveymonkey.com).
   c. Conduct a communication self-assessment with the help of Communication Works (www.communicationworksinc.com) or TTI Success Insights (www.ttisuccessinsights.com).

3. Develop a leadership map and development plan.
   a. From your gap analysis, create a plan and time frame for acquiring the skills you need.
   b. On an annual basis, evaluate your progress and shortfalls and reinforce your plan.

4. Take an hour or two per week or month to think and garner feedback.
   a. How is your leadership perceived?
   b. Where are the gaps?
   c. What's important to your people?
   d. What's important to you?
   e. What are you passionate about?
   f. How can you apply what other successful leaders are doing in their businesses?

5. Organize a personal board of directors.
   a. From your development plan, identify potential board members and/or committees for each skill area. Identify people you know or people you can meet to help you develop the skills you need.
   b. For each potential board member, make an initial contact, request help, and create an action plan.
   c. Engage your board members and keep them updated on your progress.
   d. Acknowledge their support in creative ways that are memorable and meaningful.

6. Seek assistance from leadership professionals.
   a. Hire a local leadership or executive coach. You can search the Internet for local sources.
   b. Attend an intensive weeklong leadership course, such as a Center for Creative Leadership (www.ccl.org) program.

7. Identify and engage female role models.
   a. Identify one or two respected female leaders in your company. Request their assessment of your

style and their ongoing guidance, feedback, and support.

b. Join community or professional women's leadership organizations, such as National Association for Female Executives (NAFE), National Association of Professional Women (NAPW), National Association for Women Business Owners (NAWBO), Financial Women's Association (FWA), Women in Technology International (WITI), Women in Bio (WIB), and Athena San Diego. For more senior, board-level women, consider Women Corporate Directors (WCD). Many of these organizations offer mentoring, networking, and educational opportunities.

c. Assume leadership roles outside of the office to further develop and test leadership styles.

24

Servant Leadership—It's About Others

If we do not lay out ourselves in the service of mankind whom should we serve?

—Abigail Adams, second US first lady

What makes a great leader? What is exemplary leadership?

Innumerable sources have examined the attitudes, activities, and actions of leaders. Examples of well-known leaders include Jesus, Moses, Gandhi, Nelson Mandela, Mother Teresa, Hitler, and Jim Jones. What differentiates them? What separates the esteemed from the despicable, the good from the evil?

Motivation makes the difference. Do they want to serve themselves or to serve others?

Servant leaders work to ensure that other people's needs are being served ahead of their own. According to Robert Greenleaf, the management development expert who coined the term "servant leadership," they enable those served to become healthier, wiser, freer, more autonomous, and more likely to become servant leaders themselves.[1]

Good leadership is about the welfare of others.

It's human nature to be self-serving. In your leadership development journey, you need to move from serving yourself to serving others. Regardless of your position in a company or your life, you have daily opportunities to lead, whether formally or informally. "You can rise to be a servant leader among a small group, a community-at-large, on a national scale, or on an international scale," says Mindy Bortness, president of Communication Works, Inc. "It's all good."[2]

View every interaction as an opportunity for service, development, and growth. Each time we lead in a serving manner, we develop others, as well as ourselves, and take a step closer to becoming a pure servant leader.

Your motivation as a leader will define your destiny. Never forget that great and effective leadership starts from within and is about genuinely serving others.

Key Action Tips

1. Think about whether your current leadership is helping those you serve grow as professionals and people. Are they edified and empowered? Are they more confident, wise, and autonomous? Are they likely to become servant leaders?

2. Identify situations where you can improve your servant leadership.

3. Organize leadership discussions focused on servant leadership. Get others thinking, talking, and implementing servant leadership principles.

25

Primal Leadership

A leader takes people where they want to go. A great leader takes people where they don't necessarily want to go, but ought to be.

—Rosalynn Carter, US first lady, 1977–1981

Servant leadership is about serving others and putting their needs ahead of our own. What about primal leadership? Primal leadership is about changing your leadership style to fit the needs of the individuals you're leading, the demands of the situation, and the challenges of the company.

"Companies need both traditional hierarchy and empowered employees," argues Clara Shih, Starbucks's youngest-ever board director and CEO of the social media firm Hearsay.[1] Although command-and-control leadership may sound anachronistic, there are processes and quality controls that require clear rules and hierarchical decision making. "Where hierarchy clearly fails the modern organization is in fostering and encouraging the creative ideas needed to stay agile in today's networked world."[2] The challenge is to encourage creativity and agility while retaining the advantages of hierarchy.

Daniel Goleman, psychologist and renowned author

of *Emotional Intelligence* and *Primal Leadership,* has found that the most effective leaders employ six distinct styles of leadership and transition amongst these styles, adopting the one that best meets the needs of the situation. Knowing and adapting your leadership style to the needs of the employee, situation, or company is key.

Based on research data from almost four thousand executives, Goleman describes six styles of primal leadership.[3]

Visionary leadership. This style focuses on long-term goals and is most appropriate when an organization needs a new vision and direction. A visionary leader listens to the values held by the individuals and lays out a direction or end goal, but doesn't say how to get there. This empowers employees to innovate and take calculated risks. Susan B. Anthony, Winston Churchill, Martin Luther King, Jr., Ronald Reagan, Oprah Winfrey, and Blake Mycoskie (founder of TOMS shoes) are examples of visionary leaders.

Coaching leadership. This one-on-one style focuses on developing individual employees, improving performance, and connecting individual goals to organizational goals. It's about delegation of decision-making authority to employees within their area of responsibility, including the power to make, and learn from, mistakes. Coaching leadership accelerates innovation and learning at all levels of the organization. It is most productive for employees who take initiative and desire advanced professional development. Meg Whitman, former chief executive of eBay and president and CEO of Hewlett-Packard, is an excellent example of a coaching leader.

Affiliative leadership. This style emphasizes teamwork and a people-focused working atmosphere. The leader utilizes listening skills to understand the emotional needs of employees. It's constructive for optimizing team harmony, boosting morale, and improving communication and trust in an organization. The downside is that group praise may

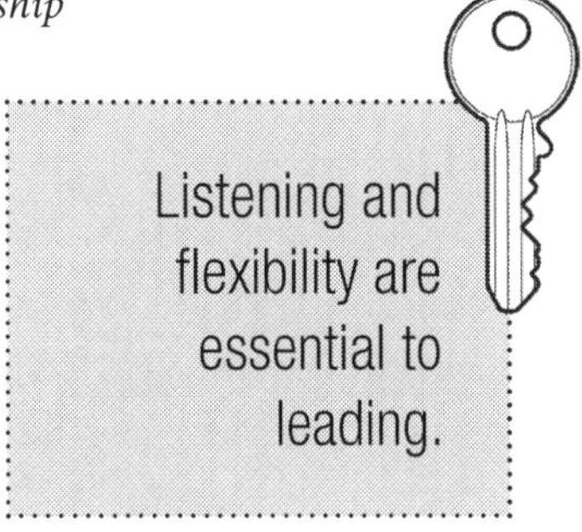
Listening and flexibility are essential to leading.

allow poor individual performance to go unaddressed, leading employees to believe that mediocrity is tolerated. It should be used with other leadership styles, especially the visionary style. Andrea Jung, former CEO of Avon, and Susan Lyne, chairman of the Gilt Groupe, are examples of teamwork-focused leaders.

Democratic leadership. This style is also known as consensus building and draws on people's input, commitment, knowledge, and skills. It encourages commitment to the group, more active listening, and goal creation. It works best when the organizational direction is unclear and the leader needs to secure feedback from the group. However, this leadership style can be ruinous in times of crisis, when critical events demand immediate decisions. Indra Nooyi, CEO of PepsiCo, Beth Mooney, CEO of KeyCorp, and John Mackey, co-CEO of Whole Foods Market, are exemplary examples of democratic and consensus-building leaders.

Pacesetting leadership. This style involves setting high standards for performance and continually monitoring progress against those goals. The leader is obsessive about doing things better and faster, and expects the same of everyone else. Although a superior motivator for certain types of employees and certain situations, the unrelenting pressure over long periods of time can result in burnout and loss of both creativity and productivity. In the long term, this leadership style poisons the climate, reduces morale, and makes people feel as if they're failing. It should be limited. General Electric, under the leadership of Jack Welch, and Intuitive Surgical, Inc., under Gary Guthart, are classic examples of companies driven by pacesetting leaders.

Commanding leadership. This is classic military-style leadership. It rarely involves praise, frequently employs criticism, and erodes motivation and commitment; consequently it leads to low job satisfaction, low morale, and high turnover. Apple and Microsoft endured commanding leadership, especially during the early tenures of Steve Jobs and Bill Gates, respectively. Goleman believes it's probably only effective in a crisis, when urgency is required; otherwise, it's the least effective of all leadership styles. Clara Shih, however, argues that command-and-control, hierarchical leadership is an "effective tool for streamlining decision making, disseminating information, and making sure stuff gets done."[4]

In *Primal Leadership*, Goleman describes the first four styles as resonance builders. He refers to the last two styles as dissonant because they don't value listening. Empathic listening and resonating to others' thinking enables a leader to more effectively influence emotions and provide a sense of direction, both for individuals and the company as a whole.

Key Action Tips

To enhance primal leadership:[5]

1. Commit to improving your listening skills. This requires listening to oneself and to others with empathy and self-awareness, conducting 360 analyses, and coaching. To improve empathetic listening, practice the three steps of active listening:
    a. Hear the message communicated by the sender; encourage the other person to express him- or herself; be quiet and don't dominate the conversation; shut the meeting room door and elimi-

nate all other distractions, including those in your mind.

b. Ask open-ended questions (what, how, when) to better comprehend the meaning; don't challenge the content; paraphrase the important elements and confirm that you understand.

c. Respond appropriately to the message, taking into account the feelings attached to the spoken words.

2. Identify your ideal self by identifying and listening to your core values and beliefs. Define:
   a. What's important to you?
   b. What are you passionate about?

3. Identify the discrepancy between your real self and how you appear to others. This can be achieved through coaching, behavioral style and emotional intelligence assessments, and feedback from your 360 analyses from peers, subordinates, superiors, and customers. The difference between your perception of yourself and others' perceptions of you is often strikingly different. Comparing your ideal self to your real self is essential to identifying strengths and gaps.

4. Create a plan to build on strengths and reduce gaps.

5. Experiment and practice new skills to further develop strengths and reduce gaps.

6. Concurrently develop trusting, encouraging relationships that provide support during the process.

7. Study the six primal leadership styles and employ the appropriate style depending on the unique requirements of an individual, situation, or specific company challenge.

26

Respect-Centric Leadership

When people honor each other, there is a trust established that leads to synergy, interdependence, and deep respect. Both parties make decisions and choices based on what is right, what is best, what is valued most highly.

—*Blaine Lee, coauthor of* The Power Principle: Influence with Honor

Can a woman lead in the same way as a man and be as effective? It largely depends on the leadership style. Men who lead in an autocratic, commanding, power-oriented, or positional manner are more likely to get away with it. Women who choose that style are often considered disrespectful—or worse, bitchy—and tend to meet with resistance from the people under them.

What compels you to follow a leader? What traits repel you? Chances are that respect is at the core of your decision. The simple fact is that people want to be led not only by someone they respect, but by someone who respects them.

John C. Maxwell, leadership expert and author of more than thirty books, including *Developing the Leader Within You* and *The 21 Irrefutable Laws of Leadership*, believes that

People want
to be led by
someone they
respect.

"People don't follow others by accident. They follow individuals whose leadership they respect . . . people who are better leaders than themselves."

Leadership based in respect is key for effectively leading others, rising through the ranks, garnering the corner office, and shattering the "bitch" myth. So what does it take to develop respect-centric leadership?[1] Seven essential principles include:

- Authentically demonstrating respect for others
- Placing others' interests ahead of your own through servant leadership
- Employing primal leadership
- Creating vision and inspiration
- Becoming a change expert
- Promoting ethics, trust, and empowerment
- Establishing priorities and results-oriented principles

Key Action Tips

To develop respect-centric leadership:

1. Authentically demonstrate respect.
    a. Communicate in a thoughtful, respectful manner.
    b. Listen to others' ideas, goals, and aspirations.
    c. Help them achieve their professional and personal goals and aspirations.
    d. Encourage and edify others. Believe in and find their strengths; overlook the negative traits and/or help people to overcome them.
    e. Forgive past transgressions.

   f. Don't allow others to be disrespectful to you, and don't stay in disrespectful companies or situations.

2. Practice servant leadership.
   a. Win the hearts of people by serving and caring.
   b. Put others' interests ahead of your own.
   c. Ensure that others are becoming healthier, wiser, and more autonomous under your leadership.
   d. See chapter 24, "Servant Leadership—It's About Others," for more details.

3. Employ primal leadership.
   a. Apply appropriate leadership styles depending on the individuals, situations, and companies involved.
   b. See chapter 25, "Primal Leadership," for more details.

4. Demonstrate vision and inspiration.
   a. Be forward-thinking.
   b. Be optimistic and tenacious.
   c. Be passionately self-assured and possess the belief that your life exists for a purpose.
   d. Demonstrate awe-inspiring belief and passion in the organization's vision.

5. Develop change agent expertise.
   a. Learn to embrace change.
   b. Develop your skills for implementing change and helping others deal with change.
   c. See chapter 34, "To Lead, Inspire and Drive Change," for more details.

6. Promote ethics, trust, and empowerment.
   a. Create an atmosphere of ethics, trust, and empowerment by incorporating them in your vision, values, strategy, goals, and organizational culture.
   b. Empower others to create strategies that support the organization's vision.
   c. Make your actions consistent with the organization's values.

7. Emphasize priorities and results-oriented principles.
   a. Set goals and specific actions to support achievement of the goals.
   b. Ensure that goals are SMARTER (specific, measurable, attainable, relevant, time-bound, evaluated, and rewarded).
   c. Limit your focus to no more than three top-priority goals.
   d. If goal setting for others, involve them in the process.
   e. Regularly review progress against goals.

27

Communication—More Important Than Ever

[Leaders] realize that their power lies less in any title they hold than in their ability to move others.

—Judith Humphrey, author of *Speaking as a Leader*

Communication is critical to a leader's success. Leaders who communicate effectively are better able to motivate employees and build successful companies.

Three major steps in leadership communication involve *defining* your message, *delivering* it with passion, and *advancing* it through ongoing relevance to corporate success. In each of these steps, describing a vision or "painting a picture" is key. Martin Luther King's "I Have a Dream" speech is one of the best examples of painting a picture.

Once you've defined your message, how you deliver it is at least as important as what you say. "You can have brilliant ideas, but if you can't get them across in a way that engages, excites, and motivates others to believe and act, those ideas will remain unrealized," warns Judith Humphrey, author of *Speaking as a Leader*. "And as a leader you will have missed an opportunity to create followers."[1]

"Leaders of the future will have to be visionary and be able to bring people in—real communicators. These are the things that women bring to leadership and executive positions."

—Anita Borg, founder of the Institute for Women and Technology

Tone of voice is more critical for women than men. Both women and men prefer female leaders who have lower-pitched voices to those with higher voices, even in stereotypically female positions.[2] According to Kristen Powers, Fox News analyst, "Women, when they are talking loudly … often sound like they're screeching." Her advice: "Get voice coaches."[3] Hiring a vocal coach may sound excessive, but some of the world's most successful female leaders, including Hillary Clinton and Margaret Thatcher, did just that.

After defining and delivering your message, be mindful that all of your efforts will be in vain if you don't sustain and advance the message you have communicated. "One of the ways I've been able to sustain a message is literally painting a picture," says Kathy Johanson, CEO of ReJuVey. "On one occasion, we decided to dedicate an entire wall in the leadership conference room to a message of vision by drawing a 'yellow brick road' with all of the actions that were needed along the way in order for the message to become a reality. It was quite powerful."[4]

I have experienced firsthand the importance of frequent and sustained communication. At CardioDynamics, we were on the public company revenue and earnings treadmill. Toward the end of every fiscal quarter, I shared with employees how many sales and shipments we needed to meet analyst expectations. With passion and encouragement, I delivered the call-to-action updates in person to corporate personnel and via voicemail to others, focusing my messages on the importance of teamwork. The messages grew in frequency as we neared the end of the quarter. As a result, everyone understood the goal, and everyone understood how he or she personally contributed to the company's success.

Effective communication in three critical areas is key to winning employee trust and confidence: Employees need an understanding of the company's overall business strategy; their contribution to achieving key business objectives; and how the company and employees' divisions are doing relative to strategic business objectives.[5]

John Baldoni, leadership consultant and author of *Great Communication Secrets of Great Leaders,* sums it up nicely: "Just as there is no single way to lead, there is no single way to communicate—in fact, there are countless ways. What matters most is the willingness to do it, with a consistent message, a constancy of purpose, and a frequency of performance."[6]

Key Action Tips

To enhance your leadership communication:

1. Educate and engage your employees in establishing the vision, mission, and goals. This is part of developing your message.

2. Engage management and employees to define specific quarterly objectives that contribute to the achievement of the overall business strategy and goals. The goals can be driving organizational vision,

product or service promotion, transformational change, or a call to action.

3. Have employees publicly and/or visibly post quarterly objectives, also detailing how the objectives tie into key business strategies. This focuses them on their objectives while also helping them understand how each employee's objectives contribute to the company's success.

4. Obtain buy-in through talk, walk, and emotion. Get everyone communicating the goals, strategizing how to best achieve them, and living the goals through actions and emotions. As a leader, you must set the example and demonstrate through actions that you would not ask your employees to do anything you are not willing to do. This is an important part of delivering your message.

5. Be authentic and passionate in your communication. Deliver your messages with conviction and belief.

6. Get feedback on your delivery and tone. If necessary, get coaching.

7. Be visible and available. Meet with direct reports regularly to provide coaching and feedback, both on what's going right and on how to correct course. Make sure employees at all levels are regularly meeting with their superiors, reviewing progress against goals, and receiving positive feedback and coaching.

8. Regularly communicate and confirm employees' understanding of the company's overall business strategy and how the company is doing, as well as how their own division is doing relative to strategic business objectives.

9. Facilitate frequent and regular communication throughout management ranks to teams, departments, or divisions. Discuss how the unit is doing relative to the company's strategic business objectives. Praise interim progress, discuss challenges, collaborate on solutions, and encourage perseverance.

10. Issue short-term action calls. Part of leadership is communicating where you are relative to the goal and what needs to be done to surpass the goal. This is part of sustaining your message.

11. Use the message in the poem below as a cornerstone of everyday business communications:

Key Words to Human Relations

Six most important words: I admit I made a mistake
Five most important words: I am proud of you
Four most important words: What is your opinion?
Three most important words: If you please
Two most important words: Thank you
One most important word: We
Least important word: I

—Anonymous

28

And Then There's Public Speaking

For a leader, the mike is always on.

—Judith Humphrey, author

If public speaking strikes fear in your heart, you're not alone. Public speaking is frequently ranked among people's top two or three fears—sometimes higher than the fear of death. Comedian Jerry Seinfeld has joked that "at a funeral, the average person would rather be in the casket than giving the eulogy."[1]

While more than 70 percent of people experience nervousness when publicly speaking,[2] research suggests that men tend to feel more comfortable speaking in larger groups than women.[3] My goal for you is to become more confident and excited about public speaking. Try to view it as an opportunity. Communicating to large groups with confidence is a fundamental leadership skill, and you'll need it if you want to reach the corner office.

In addition to advancing your own career, your willingness to speak in public will contribute to a more egalitarian environment. "As long as women remain a vocal minority in corporate boardrooms, on TV talk shows, and in the halls of Congress, we pay the price of being voiceless," says

Christine K. Jahnke, advisor to Hillary Clinton's presidential campaign. "The world needs well-spoken women to state opinions in every venue ... It is not that a woman's perspective is better. What matters is that it is different."[4]

So now that I've got your attention and convinced you of the absolute need for good public speaking skills, let's master the art and overcome your fears.

Effective pubic speaking involves six facets: attitude, planning, organization, practice, delivery, and reflection. If you educate yourself on all of these facets and gain enough experience, you'll seem almost as prepared for an impromptu speech as you are for a planned presentation.

Attitude

Regardless of whether the talk is impromptu or planned, anyone can convey the right attitude. To make an impact on your audience, you must demonstrate confidence, conviction, and enthusiasm. You can immediately start developing a confident delivery style by reading books, watching videos on YouTube and elsewhere, listening to podcasts, analyzing speakers at events you attend, or getting coaching from a mentor or other professional. Always envision a successful talk or presentation when planning and delivering. There is power in positive thinking and visualizing success.

Planning

If you have the time to plan and prepare, use that time. Think about the who, what, where, and why. Who is your audience? What is the purpose of the presentation, what is the best means of delivering the content, and what is the benefit to the audience? Where is the venue? Why are you the one delivering the message?

With those considerations in mind, prepare the content. Do research and gather materials, making sure to document your sources. To make your talk interesting and

"The human brain starts working the moment you are born and never stops until you stand up to speak in public."

—George Jessel, (known as "Toastmaster General of the US")

interactive, I encourage you to include quotes, statistics, analogies, pictures, cartoons, memorable stories, questions, straw polls, or invitations to audience members to take the stage. Use limited self-effacing humor or personalize some part of your talk to make your audience feel you're approachable or similar to them. Lastly, if possible, get input on your content from someone who will be in the audience.

Organization

Using the "rule of three"—splitting your speech into three parts—is a good way to structure your talk. For an impromptu speech, the simplest application is to divide your message into an introduction, middle, and close. Your introduction may include a thank-you to your audience for their time, or a thank-you to an organization for an award. The middle is where you deliver the message, preferably no more than three points. Betty Sue Flowers, writer and contributor to *Harvard Business Review,* recommends that you organize the "raw material into a sensible outline" and "distill your ideas into three main propositions."[5] Then close with an inspiring, motivational, or call-to-action ending.

Another example of the rule of three is telling the audience what you're going to tell them, telling them, and then telling them what you told them. Then, all you need to do is prepare three elements for the body of your talk. I used this format during my only visit to Toastmasters when we were required to give an impromptu speech. Mine went something like this:

> I like California for three major reasons. The reasons include the warm weather, friendly people, and healthy lifestyle. Let's first talk about the warm weather. In San Diego the average daytime weather is approximately 70 °F, with very little rain, and little to no snow. The second reason I like California is the friendly people. It seems like people are usually smiling, seeking new friends, and including you in their adventures. The third reason I like California is the healthy lifestyle. People are outside and enjoy walking, running, and cycling. Who wouldn't find joy in the three greatest parts of California: the weather, the people, and the healthy lifestyle? Come join us!

Truly, impromptu speeches can be this simple. Use the rule of three and build on those points. Add a little humor or encouragement at the end, as I did with "Come join us!"

Practice

Many people will spend 90 percent of their time planning a speech or presentation and 10 percent practicing it. I encourage you to shift that ratio to 30 percent on planning and 70 percent on practice. As you progress in your experience, you may need less practice, but I find too many professionals do not practice enough.

Your opening is the most important part. This creates a first impression and sets the stage for the remainder. The closing is the second most important part, followed by the body of the talk. Don't just rehearse the words—rehearse your delivery as well.

Delivery

Relax, envision success, and smile. Take a moment to scan the room and connect with individual audience members for one to three seconds.

Start with an enthusiastic, confident tone, and never—ever—apologize for nervousness, technological challenges, or anything else. Deliver your well-rehearsed opening and continue to scan the room and connect with individual audience members for longer periods, around three to five seconds. You are now ready for the body of the talk or presentation. Pause, keep smiling, and continue to scan the room and connect with audience members as you begin the middle of your speech. Enjoy the moment. If appropriate, ask questions and engage your audience.

Finally, you're ready for your strong, inspirational, well-rehearsed ending. Pause as you move into your close. Smile and use a transition, such as, "In closing…," or "In summary…" Congratulations, you have just delivered an amazing speech or presentation!

Reflection

Keep a public speaking journal or add a section to your leadership journal. After each speech or presentation, record three areas that you felt went well and three areas in which you would like to improve. Also record any feedback you receive from the audience and, when possible, seek feedback from trusted colleagues. Feedback will help you prepare for the next speech. No matter what, encourage yourself and remember that public speaking is a lifelong development opportunity.

Key Action Tips

1. Read about public speaking. Watch speakers on the Internet, at events, or on television. Listen to podcasts. Get coaching from a mentor.

2. Identify leaders, especially women, whose public speaking skills you respect. Study their delivery so you can emulate it.

3. Identify a person in your organization or someone you know who is a memorable speaker. Ask to meet with them to discuss how they developed their public speaking skills.

4. Join a local Toastmasters group or find a public speaking class.

5. Seek and accept opportunities to give toasts, speeches, and presentations. Start small and build confidence with experience.

29

Just Do It—with Confidence, Passion, and Sensitivity

Don't live down to expectations. Go out there and do something remarkable.

—Wendy Wasserstein, American playwright and author

Confidence is an absolute requisite for leadership and career advancement. A study of more than five hundred students, academics, and workers reported that people with extremely high confidence are often promoted over people with greater ability, in part due to others overlooking mistakes of the high-confidence professionals.[1]

That's the good news about confidence. The bad news is that confident people can also seem mysterious, threatening, and unapproachable—not qualities an effective leader desires. Earlier in my career, I paid a price for not knowing how to use my confidence to motivate and inspire others. It inspired fear in more timid people.

So how do women leaders convey confidence and passion while not intimidating people? The answer lies in five qualities. The first four are typical of strong leaders, male and female alike:

1. *Passionately self-assured.* Optimistic about life, have high self-esteem, and passionately believe their life exists for special purposes.

> "No one can make you feel inferior without your consent."
>
> —Eleanor Roosevelt

2. *Ambitiously perseverant.* Focused on meaningful goals, demonstrate strong work ethic, and persevere to destroy challenges standing in the way of goals.

3. *Competitively risk-taking.* Thrive on competition, exhibit a strong desire to win but not fearful of loss, and seek intelligent risks.

4. *Socially adept.* Skillfully extroverted, comfortably relate to a wide variety of people, and demonstrate a broad range of interests.

There is a fifth leadership quality required for motivating and inspiring others:

5. *Outwardly sensitive.* Acutely aware of others and environment, genuinely listen, encourage others, and desire success for all.

This fifth quality is critical, especially for female leaders. Why? In part, it involves the double standard that has contributed to glass ceilings. Men and women are often judged differently for the same behavior or lack thereof. Women are expected to be sensitive toward others; if we're not, we're judged more harshly than men. We have all witnessed a confident, direct, and not-so-sensitive man who is praised for his leadership skills while a woman demonstrating the same qualities is often considered a poor leader and labeled a "bitch."

Double standards aside, think of the truly effective leaders in your life. They balance confidence and passion with outward sensitivity for others. If you're not a confident person, don't give up. Each of us deals with a certain amount of insecurity.

Key Action Tips

To build and effectively implement passionate confidence:

1. Conduct a self-assessment of the five qualities of confident people. Embrace your areas of strength and focus on improving the other areas. Discuss your assessment with someone you trust. Get their feedback and make a plan for further development.

2. Think, speak, and act in a positive, confident, yet humble manner. Envision and describe your endeavors as successful; smile and speak with excitement; affirm several times daily that you are a likable, interesting, and intelligent person; have good posture, a strong handshake, and excellent eye contact. You'll be amazed by how people perceive you when you do these things.

3. Engage others by asking questions and actively listening; seek to understand their careers, personal lives, and interests.

4. Eat healthy, exercise daily, and get enough rest. You'll feel better!

5. Be mentally, spiritually, and physically active and balanced. This gets the blood flowing in your brain and the rest of your body. Spend time each day, even if it's only fifteen minutes, focusing on your mind, spirit, and body.

6. Improve your self-esteem by focusing on your strengths, doing things to improve your confidence and skills, or helping others. Read a book on self-confidence, take a class to develop a new hobby or skill, or volunteer for charities. Even better, do all three!

7. When a negative thought enters your mind or speech, stop! Replace it with a positive thought.

8. Expand your network and your relationships by joining a new organization and getting actively involved.

9. Think of all the things you have wanted to do or needed to do. Write them down and prioritize. Every day, tackle one thing, or one part of a larger project, that scares or overwhelms you. You'll feel stronger and more empowered once you conquer it.

10. Don't allow others to discourage you or make you feel inferior. There will always be naysayers. And remember Eleanor Roosevelt's advice: "No one can make you feel inferior without your consent."[2]

30

Perseverance Is King—Make That Queen!

When I thought I couldn't go on, I forced myself to keep going. My success is based on persistence, not luck.

—Estee Lauder, cofounder
Estee Lauder Companies

Nothing in the world takes the place of perseverance. It is the key to lasting success. The world's most successful people identify perseverance and determination as crucial factors in their success. They are essentially one and the same. Calvin Coolidge, the thirtieth president of the United States, is famously quoted as saying:[1]

> Nothing in this world can take the place of persistence. Talent will not; nothing is more common than unsuccessful people with talent. Genius will not; unrewarded genius is almost a proverb. Education will not; the world is full of educated derelicts. Persistence and determination alone are omnipotent. The slogan "press on" has solved and always

will solve the problems of the human race.

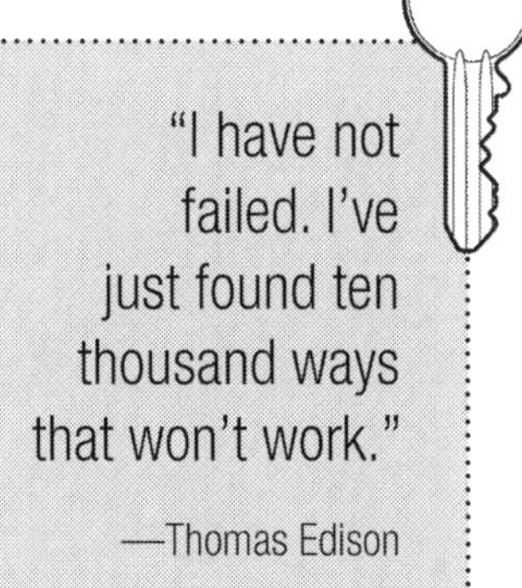
"I have not failed. I've just found ten thousand ways that won't work."
—Thomas Edison

Leaders solve problems by defining a vision, strategy, or solution, collaborating with their team to understand issues, and creating actionable plans. Then perseverance becomes the critical driver and determinant.

Albert Einstein purportedly declared that insanity is doing the same thing over and over and expecting different results.[2] Persistence doesn't mean repeating actions that don't work. Initial plans rarely achieve success. Evaluate your progress. If your plans are not producing the desired results, it's your responsibility (and opportunity) to revise them. Effective leaders rally others to believe in the vision, to persevere through challenge and change, and to eventually achieve success.

One of my business mantras is *failure is not an option.*[3] I have long subscribed to the philosophy that one does not fail until one gives up. So why do people give up? Why have you given up? Many cite lack of true commitment or belief in a mission or goal.

In one of my companies, we sponsored a high-visibility clinical study. A successful outcome was critical for our company's existence. There were numerous challenges throughout the study, and the preliminary results were not promising. Some executives conceded defeat. Instead of accepting the initial impressions, I said, "Failure is not an option, and we must find a way." I directed the resources of our most brilliant employees[4] to work with the principal investigator to meticulously sort through the data—some called it crap—and "find the pony." It took the better part of a year, but we worked together to understand the issues and figure out how to solve them. To everyone's relief, pride, and, frankly, amazement, we ethically validated a positive clinical application.

Can you imagine what life would be like if we did not have people who persevered? Give thanks to Thomas Edison for the light bulb, phonograph, and motion picture camera. Edison is famously quoted as saying, "I have not failed. I've just found ten thousand ways that won't work." Give thanks to Steve Jobs for MacBooks, iPhones, iPads, and iPods. Give thanks to Hedy Lamarr for coinventing a torpedo guidance system with frequency hopping and spread spectrum radio, which is the technology used in today's cell phones, Wi-Fi, and GPS—yes, the glamorous 1940s Hollywood actress Hedy Lamarr did all that. Women, in particular, have been ardent inventors of a variety of important products, ranging from submarine telescopes to the steel-like fibers used in radial tires and bulletproof vests to Liquid Paper.[5]

As women, we can be especially thankful for Susan B. Anthony's perseverance in her lifelong fight for women's suffrage. Although she did not achieve this goal in her lifetime, Susan's work laid the foundation. Fourteen years after her death, following persistent campaigning, women were granted the right to vote on August 26, 1920, by the Nineteenth Amendment to the US Constitution. Following Susan's death, the New York State Senate passed a resolution remembering her "unceasing labor, undaunted courage, and unselfish devotion to many philanthropic purposes and to the cause of equal political rights for women." Susan's perseverance also led the way for future legislation advocating the rights of women (and others), including the Equal Pay Act of 1963, the Civil Rights Act of 1964, and, in 2013, California's Resolution 62, encouraging US public companies to have a more equitable number of women board directors. With additional perseverance, Resolution 62 will progress to legislation.

As leaders, it is our responsibility to persevere and encourage others to do the same. Nothing is more empowering for you and your team than achieving a goal, especially one that many thought was improbable. Your legacy is defined, in part, by helping others accomplish goals bigger than themselves.

Key Action Tips

1. Whatever the challenge, chart an action plan. Collaborate with your team and mentors to make one. Don't procrastinate. You'll feel productive, encouraged, and less overwhelmed when you make a plan and then act on it.

2. Analyze and change plans that aren't working. There's no sense in persevering for the sake of plans that don't work. Analyze and understand the issues. Identify critical steps or adverse external factors that may have been overlooked. Revise your plan based on your findings.

3. Don't give up. Remind yourself of the original reason you set the goal; you felt it was important and worthwhile. Remember that you owe it to yourself and your team to push through the challenges and seek new ways of approaching the problem. It's all right to question your true motivation, but don't take the easy way out and give up if this is something you truly still want to achieve.

4. Focus on the positive. Take a break and focus on positive areas of your life, including spending time with loved ones who are optimistic and encouraging. Watch inspirational movies such as *Braveheart, Chariots of Fire, Dead Poet's Society, Erin Brockovich, Pay It Forward, The Pursuit of Happyness, Ray, Seabiscuit, Secretariat,* and *Simon Birch.* Envision your success.

5. Identify and stop self-defeating actions. Identify habits or negative thoughts that are inhibiting the achievement of your goal. Make plans to overcome each impeding habit. Eliminate negative thinking. Repeat to yourself that you were born to succeed, you have a special purpose, and you can achieve anything for which you're willing to persevere.

6. Set smaller, attainable goals. Divide your project into segments or milestones. It will seem less overwhelming.

7. Do activities you're good at. You'll rebuild your confidence by taking a break and switching your focus to something in which you excel.

8. Remind yourself of reality. Anything worth achieving is not easy.

9. Post reminders of people who have persevered.
   a. Helen Keller lost her sight and hearing at a very young age, yet her indomitable spirit, perseverance, and faith made her a truly inspiring icon.
   b. Wilma Randolph, an Olympics Gold medalist in track, was not able to walk properly as a child.
   c. Thomas Edison, the most successful inventor

in human history and holder of more than one thousand patents, had a learning disability.

10. Post motivational quotes.
    a. "What would you attempt to do if you knew you could not fail?" —Robert Schuller
    b. "Victory belongs to the most persevering." —Napoleon Bonaparte
    c. "The difference between a successful person and others is not a lack of strength, not a lack of knowledge, but rather a lack of determination." —Vince Lombardi

31

Relativity Applies to Physics—Not Ethics

Our deeds determine us, as much as we determine our deeds.

—Mary Anne Evans (aka George Eliot), English novelist

Companies are increasingly developing a corporate code of ethics for employees to follow, espousing transparency with stakeholders and the public at large. There is a high degree of interdependence between corporate ethics and personal integrity. It's difficult for a person of high integrity to work for an unethical company. It's also impossible to have an ethical company without employees of high integrity.

Each day, we are confronted in our personal and professional lives with decisions that test our integrity. One of the most important lessons I've learned is that you must protect your integrity at all costs—it's all you've got! And it's far easier to establish and retain your integrity than it is to regain it once lost.

A recent study suggests a disarmingly simple way to achieve better ethics on the job—slow down. Eighty-sev-

To make ethical decisions, give yourself more time for decision making.

en percent of research subjects opted not to lie for self-gain if they were given three minutes to contemplate their choice, compared with just 56 percent of participants who were told to make an immediate decision. The researchers suggest that in companies with a "fast pulse" and a tendency to reward quick decision making, employees may make ethical missteps because they lack adequate time for contemplation.[1]

As much as I believe that relativity applies to physics, not ethics,[2] ethical decisions are not always black and white. Take an oft-cited hypothetical example of a company whose products are made offshore in a country where child labor is accepted practice. The majority of the company's revenue and profits are derived from this source. Should the company immediately cease using this source, jeopardizing its own existence, or should it explore means of addressing the issue over time, only gradually adjusting its business plan? I think you'll agree it is not always an easy answer.

Apple faced a similar dilemma over alleged abuse of Chinese workers at Foxconn Technology Group, one of Apple's biggest manufacturing partners. Foxconn was accused of having an oppressive work culture that contributed to a slew of suicides, purportedly prompting the company to install nets on its buildings to prevent employees from jumping. Apple CEO Tim Cook toured the facilities and worked with Foxconn and the Fair Labor Association to make changes. Did he make an ultimatum to Foxconn to change their ways or lose Apple's business? We don't know. In the meantime, most consumers—including me—did not boycott Apple products. Conditions have reportedly improved, but what does this say about our commitment to integrity and humane working conditions?

Regardless of Apple, or more egregious examples like Enron and WorldCom, it's crucial for each of us to demonstrate integrity in both our personal and professional lives. Your company's success depends on the integrity of its people. Your personal success depends on your own integrity.

Key Action Tips

1. Think about your integrity and how is it perceived by those around you. Consider the following:
   a. Do I have compassion and understanding toward others?
   b. Do I balance my needs with the needs of others?
   c. Am I respectful of differing views?
   d. Do I seek the advice of others?
   e. Am I open to feedback?
   f. Do I accept personal and/or professional responsibility?
   g. Do I automatically act with integrity when no one is looking, or is it difficult?
   h. Do I honor my word and adhere to agreements?

2. When making a decision, ask yourself the following questions:
   a. Am I acting in a fair, objective, honest, and considerate manner?
   b. Do I believe this is the right course of action?
   c. Would I want someone else to make this decision if I were the one affected?
   d. Is there someone I can consult who might enhance my perspective?

   e. Is this the right time, intention, person, place, and style?
   f. Can I modify my decision to decrease or prevent harm to others?
   g. How does this decision affect the entire organization?

3. If you feel someone doubts your integrity, have a thoughtful, candid discussion to address and attempt to resolve any misperceptions.

4. Discuss integrity and ethics with your spouse, family, friends, and personnel to understand their thoughts and to share yours.

5. Begin reading about ethics to further develop your understanding. Consider one of the books in the "Recommended Reading" section.

32

Intelligence—IQ Versus EQ

The sign of an intelligent people is their ability to control their emotions by the application of reason.

—Marya Mannes, American author

What comes to mind when you hear the names Bill Clinton, Arnold Schwarzenegger, and General Petraeus? Sex scandals? That's tragic, as these men have impressive career accomplishments. How could these intelligent, successful men do something so emotional, so insensitive, and—yes—so stupid? I venture to say that they allowed their emotions to hijack their rational, logical minds.

The downfall of these men highlights one of life's greater challenges: balancing emotions with intellect. Passion, when properly controlled, enables us to achieve great things. Uncontrolled, emotions damage reputations and create mayhem.

Though women are less known for the rampant emotions that lead to sex scandals, we are thought of as emotional creatures. We are also held to higher standards than men when it comes to emotional intelligence.[1]

During the past twenty years, our definition of intel-

> When it comes to emotional intelligence, women are held to higher standards.

ligence has expanded from that of a limited intelligence quotient (IQ), focused on mathematical and linguistic skills, to a broader, real-world measure incorporating emotional, personal, and social components. Social scientists discovered that emotional intelligence (EI)—encompassing interpersonal and intrapersonal skills—was more important to happiness and success than IQ.

Emotional Intelligence: Why It Can Matter More Than IQ, authored by internationally known psychologist Daniel Goleman, resonated with many business leaders when it was published in 1995. The term quickly became a buzzword in corporate America. Goleman defined EI as the capacity for recognizing our own feelings and those of others, for motivating ourselves, and for managing our emotions in ourselves and in our relationships.[2] Many business leaders agree that success is strongly influenced by personal qualities such as perseverance, self-control, and getting along with others.

EI includes the following abilities:

- *Self-awareness:* accurate self-assessment, emotional awareness
- *Self-regulation:* self-control, trustworthiness, adaptability
- *Self-motivation:* initiative, drive, commitment
- *Empathy:* understanding and helping others, service orientation
- *Relationship management:* communication, creating collaborative teams, conflict management

EI is necessary for success in both your personal and professional life. It's critical for leadership development and career advancement. Goleman's research reported that almost 90 percent of executives' leadership success is due to high EI. Unsuccessful executives had low EI, demonstrating rigidity and inability to adapt to changes in corporate culture. They also had poor relationships and were viewed as insensitive and overly critical. High IQs and strong technical expertise could not compensate for low emotional competence.

Does your EI need improvement? It isn't learned in the standard intellectual ways, such as from reading a book. EI development engages emotional parts of the brain and is based on sensory, nonverbal learning and real-life practice. The great news is that EI can grow with effort and time.

Key Action Tips

To enhance your EI, focus on the following:

1. Quickly reduce stress. Stress reduces your ability to accurately read a situation, hear what others are saying, communicate clearly, and make rational decisions. To improve:
    a. Realize when you're stressed—how does it feel compared to your calm state?
    b. Recognize how you respond to stress—do you become angry, agitated, or anxious?
    c. Identify stress-reducing techniques—deep breathing, exercise, listening to music, or taking a break.

2. Understand your emotions. If you're aware of how your emotions affect your thoughts and actions, you'll understand your needs and be able to effec-

tively communicate them. Following are signs of your ability to understand your emotions:

a. Do your feelings change as your experiences and situations change?
b. Do you experience discrete feelings such as anger, sadness, or joy, each evident in facial expressions?
c. Do you experience feelings that are noticeable to yourself and others?

3. Use nonverbal communication. This is emotionally driven and provides evidence that you're listening, you understand, and you care. It produces a sense of interest and trust. To improve, use:
   a. Good eye contact
   b. Positive facial expressions
   c. Affirmative head nodding
   d. Positive tone of voice
   e. Good posture and body language (facing the person, open stance versus folded arms)

4. Resolve conflict positively. This strengthens trust and creativity between people. To improve:
   a. Focus on the present and not past conflicts. Forgive and forego the desire to punish another for past conflicts.
   b. Carefully select your battles and consider what's worth arguing about and what's not.
   c. Disengage and end conflicts that can't be resolved. Agree to disagree.

5. Use humor. Occasional self-deprecating humor and keeping situations in perspective is key. To improve:
   a. Don't be afraid to be imperfect, highlight your gaffes, and have a good laugh.

b. Ask yourself, will this really matter in one year?
c. Help others to realize that it's best to preserve relationships and recognize the lighter side of life.

33

In Piles of Crap ... Find the Pony

Life is not about waiting for the storm to pass, it's about dancing in the rain.

—Anonymous

Positive thinking is *essential* to an empowered life. Think about it. Your attitude fuels the energy and passion you inject into your life. Research shows that optimism pays off when it comes to jobs, promotions, and professional success, as well as longevity, physical and mental health, and coping with adversity.[1,2] "Optimists are more successful because they are willing to overcome obstacles and problem solve, which are critical skills to advancement in any work environment," explains Susan Segerstrom, research psychologist and author of *Breaking Murphy's Law*.[3]

Optimism is also a *critical* leadership quality. It affects how those around you feel and act, as well as their desire to follow you. No one wants to be led by a Debbie Downer. A positive attitude promotes employee engagement, productivity, and success. Yes, productivity can happen in an oppressive, negative environment, but it's short-lived.

A significant factor in my success is my optimism—an invaluable gift from my mother. One of the most memora-

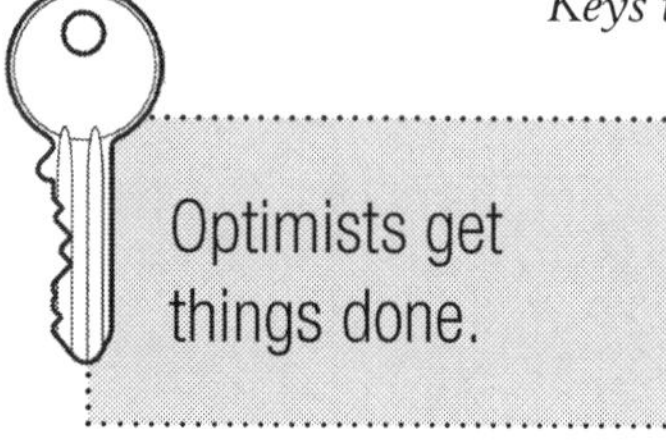
Optimists get things done.

ble examples involved a world-renowned cardiologist who I met when I was president at CardioDynamics. His brilliant but pessimistic mind intimidated most of his colleagues, and we were warned not to engage him. My approach was to make him part of the solution. We needed to educate him about our technology and include him in the design of our clinical study on heart failure. We developed a strong, positive, respectful professional relationship. After working together for more than a year, he said to me, "Are you always *this* positive?" It was a major compliment. My optimism was a driving force in our company's successful relationship with him.

The best part: optimism costs nothing and can be learned.[4,5] It's a life-changing, daily gift you can give yourself, your coworkers, and your family. If you have it, keep practicing it! The best professionals in the world train every day. If you don't have an optimistic attitude, please—for yourself and others—focus on developing it.

In the same vein, *never* speak disparagingly about your colleagues, company, or others. Focus on the positive. Find the pony!

Finally, do your best to limit your exposure to negative people. They're a drain and tend to drag you down with them. You know the adage "Misery loves company"? It's true. If you're in a work situation with a negative colleague, boss, or—worst of all—CEO, do your best to extricate yourself.

Key Action Tips

1. Examine your internal dialogue and mindset. Is it more positive or negative? Whenever a negative thought or "voice" enters your head, stop and focus

on a positive thought or envision a positive outcome. If you can't, then change what you're thinking about and focus on something positive. Remember the Norman Vincent Peale quote: "Change your thoughts, and you change your world."[6]

2. Find the silver lining. You can usually identify something positive even in the direst of situations. Identify the opportunities in each challenge.

3. When things go badly, analyze the extenuating circumstances and identify the uncontrollable and controllable aspects; determine what you can do in the future to produce a different outcome.

4. Resolve that each day, one day at a time, you will be joyful, grateful, and positive—unless something truly life-threatening is happening. Just do it! You'll truly feel enlightened at the end of the day. When someone asks, "How are you doing," reply, "Great, thank you! How are you?" It will be a ray of sunshine for the receiver. How many people respond that way? Too many complain about life, and the truth is, people would rather hear something positive.

5. Identify your purpose and remind yourself daily. If we feel our lives and work have purpose and meaning, we feel more positive.

6. Believe in yourself, stay focused on your goals, and envision success. Remind yourself daily why your goals are worthwhile.

7. Recharge yourself with motivational conferences and seminars. Try to attend at least one annually.

8. Smile—yes, as simple as it sounds, people feel more positive when they smile or see someone else smiling.

9. Surround yourself with positive people. As much as you can, minimize your contact with negative people. If you're in a conversation with another person and a negative subject comes up, try this: "I understand how you might feel that way—let's focus on how best to resolve the issue," or "Let's focus on the person's strengths," or "Let's focus on something more positive." You can always allow the person to continue for a brief time and then quickly and politely change the topic.

10. In your leadership journal, create a section for inspirational, positive quotes. Memorize and recite them. Some quotes that have made a positive impact in my life include:

    "If you don't like something, change it; if you can't change it, change the way you think about it." —Mary Engelbreit, world-renowned artist and illustrator

    "Life is change; growth is optional. Choose wisely." —Karen Kaiser Clark, motivational speaker

    "The thoughts one thinks and the words one speaks create one's experiences" —Unknown

34

To Lead, Inspire and Drive Change

Change is the new status quo.

—Susan Lyne, chairman, Gilt Groupe

Due to rapid technological advances, the world is changing faster than ever. The companies—and people—that succeed will be agile and ever-adapting. To be a successful leader, start embracing and driving change today. Remind yourself that change is the new status quo. Make your daily mantra, "What can we change to drive progress?"

What does it take to become a chief change agent? Jack and Suzy Welch, authors of *The Welch Way,* believe that it requires vision, bravery, power, and support.[1]

Vision

To create positive change, you need to understand where your industry is heading and what customers need (as opposed to what they think they need). Then you need to translate this understanding into initiatives to produce top-line growth while improving bottom lines. A vision of what "can be" will help you challenge long-held corporate and industry strategic assumptions.

To develop greater foresight, push yourself and your teams to learn, develop, and innovate. Understand your industry, your industry's challenges, your customers' challenges, and innovative technologies that can leapfrog yours. We live in a world that never stops changing; therefore, we can never stop learning.

"No matter how good your business is today, some young entrepreneur is working hard to disrupt it," warns Susan Lyne, Gilt Groupe chairman. "Next year, I'll spend more time soaking up inspiration anywhere I can find it."[2]

Visionary thinking enables you to find opportunities your competitors haven't identified. This should result in big, hairy audacious goals (BHAGs), a venerable term coined by Jim Collins and Jerry Porras in their highly acclaimed business book, *Built to Last: Successful Habits of Visionary Companies.*[3] BHAGs are goals that are bold and audacious but not impossible—although many may believe they are impossible.

Bravery

It's not enough to ponder where your industry is headed. A change agent must also demonstrate courage to bet their own future, and often their company's future, on fulfilling the vision.

At CardioDynamics, I bet our future on expanding the marketplace for our *noninvasive,* innovative medical device. The device's data was originally used only for intensive care patients in the hospital, and physicians were trained to use an *invasive* heart catheter to obtain the data. We received significant opposition to our *noninvasive* approach. Based on my pharmacy background, I believed the data would also be useful in managing cardiac patients' medications in the physician's office where the *invasive* catheter was not an option. Making this happen was no small feat. We had to secure Medicare and private reimbursement coverage, obtain reimbursement pricing sufficient for private practice physicians to afford the $40,000 cost for our technology, conduct clinical trials, and literally create the marketplace—one physician-customer at a time. We piloted, course-corrected, and transitioned. The move became the cornerstone for the company's success. If it had failed, the company would have eventually failed. But if we had not envisioned the need and implemented the change, the company would not have helped millions of patients or survived the near-term.

> Make your daily mantra, "What can we change to drive progress?"

Power and Support

Vision and courage alone are not enough. You need power and support to successfully effect change. Someone in an official position of leadership should already possess the power to make change decisions, but the ability to inspire and implement lies in the velvet glove, a soft-handed approach to presenting change and difficult tasks. As you've likely guessed, velvet gloves are especially important for women leaders.

"Every company needs people who can successfully facilitate change. If resources allow, it's also very important for companies to have a permanent, professional position for a Change Manager," advises Kathy Johanson, CEO of ReJuvey. "This person's sole purpose is to seek out and, with the full support of leadership, implement crucial changes throughout the company."[4]

Let's face it: people tend to be paralyzed by fear and resistant to change. They must understand what's in it for them, receive careful guidance and training, and be motivated more by carrots than sticks. Harvard Business School professor and author Rosabeth Moss Kanter observes, "Change is a threat when done *to* me, but an opportunity when done *by* me. Resistance is always greatest when change is inflicted on people without their involvement, making the change effort feel oppressive or constraining." Her advice: "If it is possible to tie change to things people already want, and give them a chance to act on their own goals and aspirations, then it is met with more enthusiasm and commitment. In fact, then they seek innovation on their own."[5]

As Rosalynn Carter sagely put it, "A leader takes people where they want to go. A great leader takes people where they don't necessarily want to go, but ought to be."[6]

Key Action Tips

To enhance your ability to become a chief change agent:

1. Read, read, read about your industry and change management. Understand change and become an expert. If you are relatively new to inspiring change, start by reading *Managing the Dynamics of Change: The Fastest Path to Creating an Engaged and Productive Workforce* by Jerald M. Jellison, PhD. This book provides a good framework for the psychological stages a person goes through during times of change, as well as a means of facilitating transition and maximizing productivity.

2. Assist employees in developing courage and tolerance for ambiguity. You can be a role model in helping them to function effectively in uncertain environments.

3. Encourage employees and colleagues to research and present industry trends and next-generation technologies to your teams. Provide resources or time off for employees to attend conferences, seminars, and webinars that help them evolve into strategic thinkers, one-of-a-kind idea generators, and change agents.

4. Engage your employees in change by obtaining their opinions and implementing their ideas. Demonstrate respect for others' ideas and have the humility to admit you don't have all the answers. Some of the most powerful contributions come from employees, customers, and suppliers.

5. Conduct team-building activities around a specific change.

6. Bring together key employees and establish effective working groups. Clearly define and delegate responsibilities. Set timelines. Then let your people become fully engaged in implementing the change. Your role will transition to reinforcement, encouragement, and follow-up.

35

Get Strategic—Think Big but Simplify Concepts

The only thing worse than being blind is having sight but no vision.

—Helen Keller, American author, first deaf and blind person to earn a bachelor of arts

Strategic thinking is about the big picture and the long term. It's about the big hairy audacious goals (BHAGs) that change the way a company does business, the way it's perceived in the industry, and possibly the industry itself.[1] It means defining where you are, where you want to be, and how you will get there.

The three stages of building a strategy are analyzing, planning, and implementing. A strategic framework involves analyzing data to understand your position; pinpointing your competitive advantage; identifying market and technological trends; defining products and markets; deciding where to focus limited resources; identifying, prioritizing and implementing change; and, finally, monitoring performance and reviewing strategy. Strategy directs employees to work toward common goals and ensures that daily decisions are aligned with long-term plans.

> To come up with the best solution, you have to understand the problem.

Successful leaders not only think strategically—or "big"—but also communicate the concepts that make up their big visions as simple, easily understood ideas. "Every *thing* starts with an idea, but the truly great ideas are built on concept," says Winston Perez, creator of Concept Modeling℠, a process for getting to the essence of things.[2] Perez uses the sleeve around a Starbucks cup as an example of Concept Modeling. Originally, paper cups had handles similar to those on ceramic coffee mugs. The coffee cup sleeve inventor understood that optimal coffee mug holding required more than a handle on the side of a cylinder; the handle alone did not incorporate the concept of cool fingers on a hot cup. Real success was in finding an elegant approach to heat protection. This was more than outside-the-box thinking; it redefined the problem and yielded a simple, direct solution.[3]

Getting ideas to remain fixed—or stick—in people's minds is also key to effective leadership. In *Made to Stick*,[4] the authors posit that ideas adhere when they incorporate six characteristics: simplicity, unexpectedness, concreteness, credibility, emotions, and stories.

So how do you create and execute a BHAG for your company, division, or department?

Key Action Tips

1. Commit to keeping an open mind about doing something differently from the way you have been doing it.

2. Conceptualize your BHAG.
   a. Brainstorm and conceptualize a goal that changes your business.
   b. Allow your creativity and imagination to take charge. Know no limits.

3. Test your BHAG for the following qualities.
   a. Long-term, taking seven to fifteen years to achieve.
   b. Addresses a need.
   c. Exciting, compelling, life-changing.
   d. More than difficult; it seems unattainable.
   e. Follows Concept Modeling principles: redefine the problem to yield an "out-of-box," simple, direct solution.

4. Create an easy-to-understand message.
   a. Something you can articulate so people will understand it, even if they don't believe it can be achieved.
   b. Relate the new concept to an existing concept people already understand and accept.
   c. Use seven to ten words to describe.
   d. Employ the *Made to Stick* six 'SUCCESS" characteristics: simplicity, unexpectedness, concreteness, credibility, emotions, and stories.

5. Commit to and plan for your BHAG.
   a. Write down your commitment.
   b. Break your BHAG into a project plan, with measurable goals and time frames.
   c. Review your progress on a regular basis, whether monthly or quarterly.

d. Communicate progress, challenges, and opportunities.
e. Revise plans as needed.
f. Remember: failure is not an option.[5]

36

Stay Current, Identify Trends

The only interesting answers are those which destroy the questions.

Susan Sontag, literary icon

Bill Gates is known for going into seclusion for two "Think Weeks" each year. Everyone is banned from his retreats, including his family. During this time, Gates reads data from Microsoft associates on trends, from the future of technology to the next hot products. Mark Zuckerberg has similar retreats. So did Steve Jobs.

You should consider these people as role models for innovation. Why? Innovation is risky. It depends on identifying emerging trends three to five years in advance. Effective leaders do this by maintaining a solid understanding of their industry, emerging growth industries, and global economies. This takes a commitment to learning about advances and new technology within and across industries.

To succeed, today's leaders must marshal time away from the job. "Leaders need to create times for reflection and ask their staffs to do it individually," notes Margaret Wheatley, management professor and author of *Leadership and the New Science*. "Distraction is overwhelming. You can't connect the dots when you're stressed."[1]

What are you doing to learn about emerging trends?

In my career, I had the luxury of taking a few years off from the corporate world. After CardioDynamics sold, I took time to travel and then started a life sciences consulting company that exposed me to a broad range of medical technologies and industry trends. The confluence of the passage (and subsequent US Supreme Court upholding) of the Affordable Care Act, overwhelming financial pressures in healthcare, and emerging trends in the study of genes and proteins (referred to as genomics and proteomics, respectively) all directed my next career choice away from capital-intensive medical devices and toward less expensive, blood-based, cardiac protein biomarker tests.

Peter Schwartz, president of the Global Business Network and author of *The Art of the Long View*, is considered by many to be the world's leading futurist. His take: "A deep and realistic confidence is built on insight into the possible outcomes of our choices ... To act with confidence, one must be willing to look ahead and consider uncertainties: 'What challenges could the world present me? How might others respond to my actions?' Rather than asking such questions, too many people react to uncertainty with denial ... Not having tried to foresee surprising events, they are at a loss for ways to act when upheaval continues. They create blind spots for themselves."[2]

What are you doing to be knowledgeable about emerging trends? How much time do you spend thinking about ways to integrate emerging trends into your business model and career?

Key Action Tips

To navigate your career and business according to emerging *market trends:*

1. Devote at least two hours per week to staying current about *trends in your industry,* emerging trends in *other* industries, and global influences.

2. Facilitate quarterly one-day (or longer) *company retreats* for your department or team to consider industry trends, emerging trends, and global influences.

3. Create your own *Think Week,* or at least your own Think Week*end,* to consider your career and business.

4. During *Think Week,* assess current trends on a large scale. Ask:
   a. What changes are occurring in the economic and political landscape?
   b. How do these affect our industry?
   c. What technologies are being developed or are in their infancy? How do they affect my company or industry?
   d. What changes are occurring in various industries?
   e. What trends are emerging or have recently emerged? How can we capitalize on these?

5. Also during *Think Week,* consider current cultural trends on a small scale. Ask:

a. What is popular with the do-it-yourself crowd? This will help you identify currently emerging trends.
b. What is happening in different subcultures? Talk to young people or innovative customers who are involved in the subculture of interest and ask what they think is up-and-coming.

6. Examine the *large-scale and small-scale trends* side-by-side to identify parallels. Small-scale trends may become large scale.

7. Read industry and business publications, such as the *Wall Street Journal,* and pay attention to articles on the economy and economic trends.

37

Love Thy Dissenters

Nurturing diversity of thought builds a culture of inclusion. An inclusive environment prizes uniqueness over conformity and facilitates innovation—a profound basis upon which to build a successful business and career.

—Jennifer B. Rubin, national diversity chair,
Mintz Levin Cohn Ferris Glovsky
and Popeo PC

When someone disagrees with you or challenges your recommendations, how do you feel? Threatened? Minimized? Inferior? Firmer in your resolve that you are correct, and that your idea is the best one?

It's human nature to want people to agree with our opinions, ideas, and actions. This is particularly true for women, who are socialized to seek consensus and avoid conflict. We want to be liked. But if we are to succeed in business, there is something more important than having the best idea or being right.

While the traditional feminine approach is appropriate in many circumstances, it's not the best way to build strong teams, create innovative products, or lead successful companies. Dissent, more productively referred to as "diversity of thought," is essential. Dissenters foster discussion, facilitate better decision making, contribute positively to your company's bottom line, and offer you the opportunity to demonstrate your respect for different opinions. They may also point out something you hadn't considered, a perspective that, if you're open, may make your solution more robust. Showing respect for ideas that challenge your own demonstrates to your team that their input is valuable. It also contributes to a stronger solution that will have the entire team's buy-in and support.

Having worked in the largely male-dominated medical device industry, I have had plenty of experience with dissenters: inventors, researchers, engineers, marketers, physicians, regulators, and others, each of whom thought he knew more than I did. Was it because I was a woman? Perhaps. Did that matter? Not at all. I came to appreciate being challenged by someone coming from a perspective other than my own. I was not a PhD or engineer; I was not the physician treating patients; I was not the technical service person talking daily with customers and hearing their concerns about our product. On the other hand, I possessed knowledge and experience that my dissenters didn't have—early stage company experience, strategic planning, clinical application, reimbursement, concept selling, marketing, and finance/investor relations. But in each situation, listening to my colleagues' objections and concerns allowed us to develop a more effective strategy.

I was challenged repeatedly by one particular company vice president—yes, he was male. He insisted we couldn't do certain things I proposed, such as providing reimbursement coverage wording and medical diagnosis codes to Medicare, instituting workflow tools to enhance physician usage of our medical device, or conducting a meta-analysis of clinical studies.

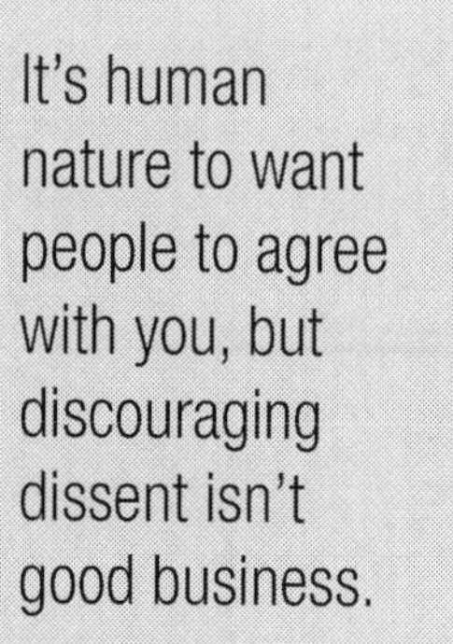

It's human nature to want people to agree with you, but discouraging dissent isn't good business.

At first I thought he objected to being told what to do by a female superior. After paying attention to the nature of his disagreement, I came to understand that he objected to pursuing most any strategy that wasn't his own. The solution was simple to understand, but more difficult to implement. I asked questions; I let him demonstrate—to me and to the team—what he knew that I didn't. I validated his concerns, and I responded in ways that demonstrated I understood his objections. I also engaged him in the visioning process so he would have a vested interest in the strategy's success. It didn't matter whether it was "his idea" or "my idea" that prevailed. What mattered was that I now had a strong ally. As a result of listening to him and engaging him in defining the approach, he developed a sense of ownership concerning the plan, and would thus work to ensure its success.

On another occasion, I nearly overlooked the importance of thought diversity. A particularly creative salesperson suggested that we sell our flagship product with a prepackaged five-year warranty instead of a standard one-year warranty. This was unheard of in the medical device industry. Although management was leery, we maintained an open attitude and investigated the possibility. We evaluated the costs, confirmed the accounting, and worked with marketing to roll out a nationwide offering. The program was a tremendous success, both for our customers and company. Customers primarily opted for a five-year equipment lease, and by selling five-year warranties and capturing nearly 100 percent of revenue up front, we immediately added millions of dollars to our company's net profit. Additionally, customers had the security of service and equipment software upgrades over the life of their lease. Had I not embraced thought diversity, I would have kept the company from considering, and ultimately embracing, an idea that benefitted everyone. The greatest testament to the success of our salesperson's idea was that other companies in our industry later copied this approach.

According to Drs. Claudia Fernandez and Edward Baker, management and public health experts, "Thought diversity allows for differing perspectives on ideas and unique insights into problems. It creates opportunities for innovation, entrepreneurship, and partnerships in unexpected places. It allows you to take a 'reality check' before plunging into new activities."[1] Creating a work culture that embraces diversity of thought also helps prevent *groupthink*, in which a few people or personality styles dominate a culture so completely that there is no room for differing ideas.

In embracing diversity of ideas, it's critical to make sure your team ultimately unifies behind decisions, processes, and strategies. "Indeed, one of the crucial elements in taking a company from good to great is somewhat paradoxical," points out Jim Collins, author of *Good to Great*. "You need executives, on one hand, who argue and debate—sometimes violently—in pursuit of the best answers, yet, on the other hand, who unify behind a decision regardless of parochial interests."[2]

If you wish to gain access to the corner office, I encourage you to lead by example and demonstrate support and respect for diversity of thought.

Key Action Tips

1. Use the following approach for problem solving, brainstorming, or discussing new initiatives.
   a. Encourage open discussion. Don't state your opinions or expectations, and don't control discussions. Emphasize that the goal is to examine problems and understand ideas. Don't allow criticism of ideas.
   b. List known facts about the situation. What can be learned? What relevant experiences do others have?
   c. Explore themes emerging from the facts. These help everyone to understand the bigger picture and identify alternative strategies.
   d. Chart pros and cons for each option. Don't allow the most logical solution to dominate the process.
   e. Let go of ownership of your ideas. The goal is to arrive at the best solution. Focus on what will achieve the overall goal, not on who arrived at the solution.
   f. Encourage and praise those who speak out against group consensus.
   g. Assign a devil's advocate. This person serves as a reality check by asking questions: What if current conditions change? Are we using the right metrics to measure success? What are the undesirable impacts? What if we fail?
   h. Remind employees that the process is not about people, but about ideas. Everyone needs to depersonalize any criticisms. The interactions are meant to strengthen and develop ideas.

i. Bring new perspectives to the discussion. If you're not making progress or you want more inclusion, invite a broader audience, possibly from different departments or levels of your company.
j. Take time to reflect and revisit tough decisions. Difficult or strategic decisions warrant time for reflection and review.

2. Create a corporate and/or department culture that values respect, diversity of thought, and mutual exploration of ideas.

3. Review your hiring process to ensure that you're hiring candidates who have diversity of profile, thought, and experience.

PART III

Ignite Your Management

Management and leadership are complementary, but they're also distinct and different. A manager administers and maintains standards, whereas a leader innovates and inspires. As Peter Drucker said, "Management is doing things right; leadership is doing the right things."[1]

As we ascend in our careers, we need to develop and appreciate the art of *both* leadership and management—and deploy each at the right time. Although it's ideal to develop these skills in parallel, the ability to manage is a precursor to attaining formal leadership positions.

Part III of *Keys to the Corner Office* provides key insights that will help you ignite your management skills.

38

Trust—Vital As Air

Responsibility and Trust—these two are like Yin and Yang, together perfectly complete, and each one requiring the presence of the other.

—Vera Nazarian, Armenian-Russian author

Trust is critical to healthy relationships and effective management. Trust goes both ways, but must be driven by the manager. Employees won't trust their manager until their manager shows trust in them. Without mutual trust, a constructive and productive relationship is impossible. Warren Buffet says it well: "Trust is like the air we breathe. When it's present, nobody really notices. But when it's absent, everybody notices."[1]

Trust takes considerable time to build, yet can be lost in a fleeting moment. Every word and action, or lack thereof, counts. When there is high trust, communication and joint decisions are easier. Interactions are fluid, open, productive, and easy to manage. When trust is low, progress and productivity are impeded. People are guarded, controlled, and defensive. It's difficult to give feedback. In short, it's like pulling teeth.

Trust also affects profitability. According to Towers

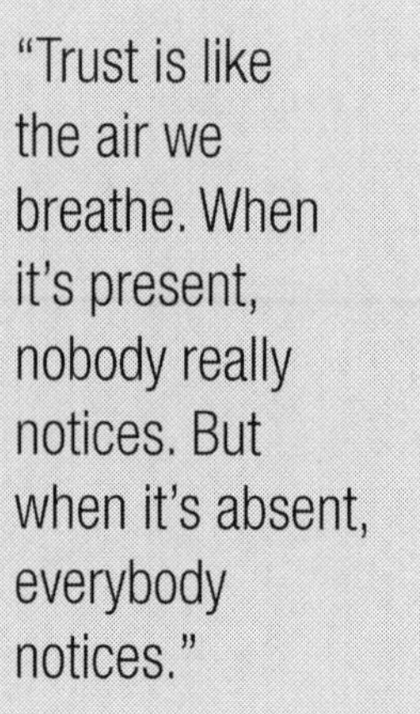
"Trust is like the air we breathe. When it's present, nobody really notices. But when it's absent, everybody notices."
—Warren Buffet

Watson, a leading global professional services firm, companies that develop high levels of trust generate shareholder returns three times that of companies with low levels of trust. The improvements in returns are largely attributed to trusting relationships within the company—between management, staff, and teams—as well as with customers and other stakeholders.[2]

This is one area in which women may have an advantage. According to Vanessa Hall, author of *The Truth About Trust in Business*, "What female leaders seem to have to their advantage is a much more intuitive response to trust and an openness to change. There are certainly exceptions, but in my experience, women understand how important trust is, are prepared to do what it takes to build trust, and are far more careful to ensure it isn't broken."[3]

How can we develop trust? In my experience, we can build considerable credibility with employees, customers, and prospective customers by having management meet face-to-face with them, hearing their concerns, and delivering on promises made.

Key Action Tips

To enhance the trustworthiness of your relationships:

1. Develop a model of trust similar to the following:
   a. *Understand the expectations* and *needs of others*

(employees, shareholders, customers, etc.) and share your own expectations and needs for your relationships with them. By defining and fulfilling basic needs and higher-level expectations, leaders can build and maintain trusting relationships.

b. *Commit to clearly defined corporate values, objectives, and promises,* then *communicate* on a regular basis the progress against these values, objectives, and promises.
   i. *Values.* By defining values, everyone will understand the rules of engagement. Behavior and actions can be measured against this standard. There should be corporate-wide involvement in the initial definition of values, and you should revisit those values on an annual basis. They should not change significantly, but the exercise allows time for reengagement and a reminder of the corporate values.
   ii. *Objectives.* Through quarterly objectives, establish short-term priorities and help employees understand what is expected of them.
   iii. *Communicate.* Establish a regular time to meet to communicate progress against agreed-upon goals and discuss challenges and new strategies for overcoming any roadblocks. Communication needs to be honest; in challenging or critical times, meetings need to be more frequent. Fulfillment of promises is essential to building and maintaining trust.

c. *Deliver results* and allow time for rejoicing and reflection. Results need to be compared against the objectives in a timely manner. I always advocate rejoicing over achievements and reflecting on what went right and where we can improve prior to setting the next round of objectives.

d. As a result of these regularly occurring actions and continuous cycles, employee and customer *retention and results* will be ongoing and improving.

2. Adhere to the following pearls:
   a. Extend trust.
   b. Be sincere and transparent.
   c. Listen first and practice active listening and paraphrasing.
   d. Make eye contact when communicating.
   e. Control facial expressions and body language.
   f. Be cautious of reactive verbal communication; respond thoughtfully.
   g. Accept feedback with openness and grace.
   h. Seek employee suggestions and make changes based on employee input.
   i. Treat employees consistently, fairly, and with respect.
   j. Be careful how you talk about underperforming or annoying employees behind their backs. The people you're talking to will wonder whether you speak the same way about them.
   k. Be objective and don't jump to conclusions. Listen to all sides before passing judgment.
   l. Hold employees, and yourself, accountable.
   m. Address poor performers, bad hires, and employees with negative attitudes.
   n. Hire secure, confident people.
   o. Act in the best interest of employees, the

company, and customers instead of acting in your own self-interest.

p. Understand that corporate tone is set from the top. Leaders need to lead in word, attitude, and actions. Every move will be scrutinized, so you need to be positive and confident.

q. Follow up and honor commitments.

r. Always communicate in an honest, candid manner. If you don't know the answer to a question, be honest and say you'll communicate when new information is available.

s. Hold regular department-wide or company-wide meetings to provide corporate updates and highlight individual and departmental contributions.

39

The Platinum Rule—Know Personality Styles

The most important single ingredient in the formula of success is knowing how to get along with people.

—Theodore Roosevelt,
twenty-sixth US president

Have you ever wondered why you get along effortlessly with one person, yet you continually clash with another? Chances are it has to do with differences in your behavioral styles. Following the Golden Rule—treating others as *you* would like to be treated—is often *not* the right approach to getting along with others. It's time to learn the Platinum Rule: treat others as *they* would like to be treated.

In *The Platinum Rule,* Drs. Tony Alessandra and Michael J. O'Conner describe four behavioral styles and their prescriptions for compatibility.[1,2] These include:

1. Relater
   a. Strengths: listening, loyal, diplomatic
   b. Seeks: acceptance, friendships, stability, personal assurances, regular contact

c. Desired behavior style from others: be pleasant, personal, friendly
d. What irritates: insensitivity
e. Weaknesses: indecisive, timid, submissive under stress, less assertive, hurt feelings
f. Typical job: customer service, human resources, clinical care (e.g., nursing)

2. Thinker
    a. Strengths: planning, problem solving
    b. Seeks: precision, thoroughness, accuracy, data, specific timetables, identifiable endpoints
    c. Desired behavior style from others: be precise, serious, detailed, organized
    d. What irritates: unpredictability
    e. Weaknesses: perfectionist, critical, withdrawn under stress, less assertive, guarded
    f. Typical job: finance, accounting, marketing, engineering

3. Director
    a. Strengths: leading, enjoys change
    b. Seeks: productivity, control, options with analysis, resolution of problems
    c. Desired behavior style from others: business-like, concise, focused
    d. What irritates: indecision, weakness
    e. Weaknesses: impatient, dictatorial under stress, overly assertive, guarded
    f. Typical job: CEO, president, sales leader

4. Socializer
    a. Strengths: persuading, highly intuitive
    b. Seeks: attention, approval, recognition, incentives/contests, regular contact

c. Desired behavior style from others: be stimulating, enthusiastic, playful
d. What irritates: routine
e. Weaknesses: disorganized, not detail-oriented, sarcastic under stress, overly assertive
f. Typical job: sales

The US population is evenly divided among the four styles,[3] and each of us has a dominant style. Further, each style represents critical functions within companies. I've found that amiable, Relater-style customer service personnel are fearful of the hard-charging, Director-style executives who communicate too directly and may not take time to ask, "How's your day is going?" The process-oriented, Thinker-style finance professional loathes the disorganized, overly assertive, Socializer-style salespeople for not dotting *i*'s and crossing *t*'s; conversely, the sales department feels as though finance is the "sales prevention department." And who could like the analytical, Thinker-style marketers and engineers who act like they know everything!

The truth is it takes all four behavioral styles—as well as respect for each style—to build a successful company. No company can succeed without research and development, engineering, product development, marketing, sales, customer service, and finance.

Effective leaders identify the behavioral styles of other people and adapt accordingly. As simple as this sounds, it takes analysis, diligence, and persistence to adapt your behavioral style and avoid reverting back to your dominant style. But if you persevere, you'll be amazed at how well this technique works and how much it can improve your relationships.

I used the Platinum Rule framework when we needed to hire sales representatives for an innovative new cardiovascular technology at CardioDynamics. Our CEO wanted to hire a former colleague—a Relater—who sold commodity medical technology to hospitals. The Relater's commodity sales, however, didn't require educating physician office customers about unfamiliar technology, and his sales cycle typically lasted one year. As a relationship-oriented, amiable, slower-paced individual, the hospital representative was perfect where he was. We needed a Socializer—a high-energy, persuasive, extroverted salesperson who could generate enthusiasm when speaking with physician end-users and quickly close a physician office sale. With the Platinum Rule framework, it was easier to explain why the Relater hospital sales rep would most likely not be effective in this role.

> You get along with only 25 percent of the population if you don't learn to relate with people who aren't like you.

Key Action Tips

To apply the Platinum Rule:

1. Understand your dominant behavioral style. You can go online to take a self-assessment test (www.platinumrule.com) or you can purchase a book that includes self-assessments.

2. Learn about the three other behavioral styles. Memorize how to identify and communicate with people who have different behavioral styles.

3. Begin each interaction by identifying the other person's behavioral style and adjust your behavior accordingly.

4. Hire a certified trainer to educate your team and employees on the Platinum Rule and make it part of your departmental or corporate culture.

5. Be an example by showing respect for all behavioral styles and talking about the importance of the different styles.

40

Motivational Management—One Style Doesn't Fit All

At Facebook, we try to be a strengths-based organization, which means we try to make jobs fit around people rather than make people fit around jobs. We focus on what people's natural strengths are and spend our management time trying to find ways for them to use those strengths every day.

—Sheryl Sandberg, COO, Facebook

If you want to enhance productivity, improve employee motivation, and retain talent, *motivational management* is ideal. Motivational management recognizes that there is no single best style of managing. Effective managers must adapt according to employees' ability and attitude.

Similar models date back to the 1980s, including that of *situational leadership*. According to Ken Blanchard, Patricia Zigarmi, and Drea Zigarmi, who popularized the model, situational leadership customizes styles of "leadership" based on an employee's competence and commitment.[1] While their emphasis on adaptation is highly useful, it's been my experience that there are significant differences between

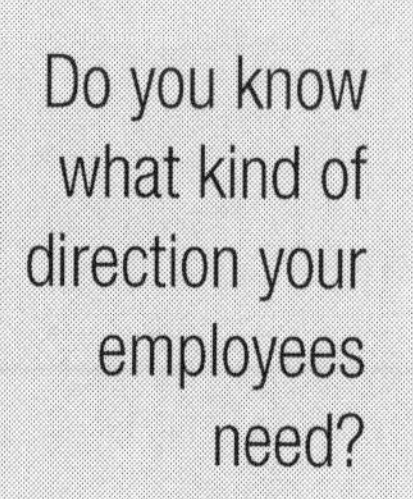
Do you know what kind of direction your employees need?

leadership and management. Effective management must be customized to the needs of a particular employee, whereas effective leadership is largely geared toward the needs of the company, division, or department.

I developed my own employee management model, motivational management, with four employee levels and corresponding management styles.

Ideally, a manager develops an employee's ability and attitude to encourage self-motivation rather than dependence on the manager's direction. Since many employees are more developed in some functions of their job than in others, it's important to assess an employee's level according to the objective or goal at hand and adjust management style accordingly.

I've found that younger, inexperienced new hires, often recent college graduates, fit in E1—low ability, high attitude. With specific education and encouragement, they excel. Without this support from managers, they struggle, fail, or quit. In various companies where I worked, we often started this level of employee in customer service. As they developed their ability and gained knowledge, entering the E2 to E3 category, we promoted them to support roles in more strategic departments, such as medical reimbursement. As we continued to reclassify their ability and attitude, we employed appropriate management styles—and they excelled. Our vice president of sales was a perfect example. He started in customer service, progressed to reimbursement, and was promoted to territory salesperson, then regional sales manager, and finally vice president of sales. Due, in part, to proper motivational management,

Employee Levels (E_1–E_4)		Management (M_1–M_4)	
E_1	Low ability, high attitude (Enthusiastic beginner; eager beaver)	M_1	EDUCATING—high education and encouragement. Respectfully explain the task/project and provide the how, why, what, when, and where.
E_2	Some ability, low to moderate attitude (Disillusioned learner)	M_2	ENCOURAGING— moderate education, high encouragement. Provide education, but also allow employee's involvement in decision making to garner buy-in, positive attitude, and development of employee's self-esteem.
E_3	Moderate to high ability, variable attitude (Capable yet cautious performer)	M_3	EMPOWERING— moderate education, high encouragement. Provide limited education but encourage employee to build motivation, commitment, and confidence.
E_4	High ability, high attitude (High achiever)	M_4	ENTRUSTING—low education, moderate encouragement. Co-establish objectives, but entrust the process and responsibility to employee. Allow employee to have autonomy and to engage in leadership and management of other employees and programs.

his advancement to an executive position only took seven years.

Key Action Tips

To enhance your proficiency in motivational management:

1. Examine the table in this chapter and read *Leadership and the One Minute Manager Updated Ed: Increasing Effectiveness Through Situational Leadership II.*

2. Identify employees at each development level. Evaluate whether you or their managers are managing them appropriately and make adjustments if necessary.

3. Share the principles of motivational management with colleagues. Seek their feedback and encourage them to use and refine it.

41

Goals, Execution, and Teamwork Will Get You Where You Need to Go

Turnaround or growth, it's getting your people focused on the goal that is still the job of leadership.

—Anne M. Mulcahy, former
Xerox Chairman and CEO

A company may have a visionary leader, but its success depends on management and employees. Management directs the strategy, objectives, and specific goals supporting the vision. Employees execute those goals as a team.

At all levels within an organization, employees need to have goals. Goals specify the expected outcome, enabling employees to understand how they should prioritize and how their managers will be evaluating their performance. Employees also need to understand how their goals align with the company's overall strategy. Think about how good you feel when you accomplish a worthwhile goal. Don't all your employees deserve the opportunity to feel that sense of accomplishment?

To set effective goals for those you manage, use the

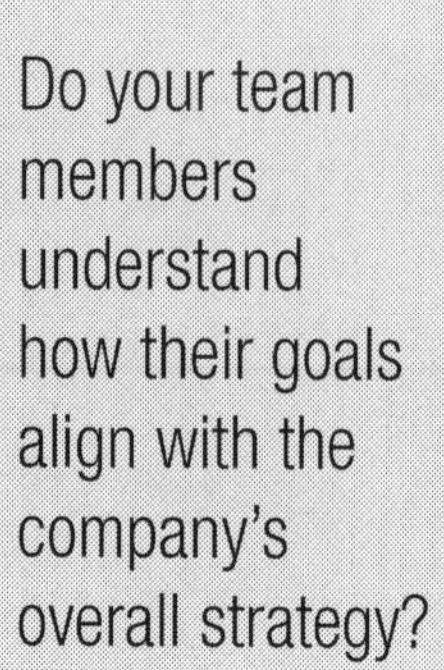
Do your team members understand how their goals align with the company's overall strategy?

SMARTER method—that is, make the goals specific, measurable, attainable, relevant, time-bound, evaluated, and rewarded. Write them in a worksheet so you can follow up and document progress. Regularly scheduled follow-up through one-on-one meetings enhances the probability of success while minimizing the perception of micromanagement.

"A routine weekly meeting is a very powerful, but often underutilized, tool," says Celine Peters, vice president of CRISI Medical Systems. "Besides communicating about goal progress, it demonstrates respect for your employees, shows interest in optimizing their success, and allows your staff to learn from you."

Though goals are essential, they're nothing without execution. Execution is the great unaddressed issue in the business world today. Its absence is the single biggest obstacle to success and the cause of most disappointments, which tend to be misattributed to other causes.[1] Building a team with experience, expertise, and a history of executing and accomplishing goals is critical. Insist on employees who thrive when stretched beyond their comfort zones and know how to work as a team.

Karin Eastham, board director and author of *Cook the Part: Delicious, Interactive and Fun Team Cooking,* advocates cooking together as an effective means of team building. "Through the cooking process, teams learn the importance of communication, delegation, goals, execution, and teamwork," explains Eastham. "Cooking is a metaphor for corporate life—you set goals and work within time constraints. Every member has an important role to play.

Interpersonal relationships can change dramatically in this comfortable setting, especially with good wines and a warm ambiance. Over dinner, members readily discuss team dynamics, means of improving interactions, new-found respect, and how to bring some of this fun into the daily work routine."

Just as you enjoy a wonderful dinner at the end of a team cooking event, celebrate your success and share credit with the entire team when major corporate milestones are achieved. This will motivate your employees to achieve higher goals and build loyalty beyond your wildest dreams.

Key Action Tips

1. *Set SMARTER goals.* Once your broad objectives are established, achieve them by making detailed goals that are specific, measurable, attainable, relevant, time-bound, evaluated, and rewarded. Limit your focus to three to five top-priority goals.

2. *Focus time and resources.* Time is a limited resource, so prioritize high-impact activities that contribute the most toward achieving the goal. Don't get lost in the daily urgent-but-unimportant tasks and communications.

3. *Keep score.* Set realistic deadlines, monitor progress, and hold yourself and others accountable to those deadlines. Make goals public so everyone understands the individual and team contributions required to achieve the overall corporate objectives. Provide coaching and resources when targets are in jeopardy or are not met.

4. *Regularly evaluate.* Set aside time on a regular basis, preferably monthly or quarterly, to assess goals, evaluate progress, and set new goals.

5. *Acknowledge and reward.* Share credit, acknowledge success, and reward success via monetary and/or nonmonetary means. See HR World[2] for twenty-five ways to reward employees without spending a dime.

6. *Build a strong team.* Recruit people with industry expertise, a history of accomplishing goals, and working as a team. Make sure team members thrive on being stretched beyond their comfort zones and achieving the impossible.

42

The Gift of Coaching

As you grow older, you will discover that you have two hands, one for helping yourself, the other for helping others.

—Audrey Hepburn,
British actress, humanitarian

Coaching helps people unlock their potential. It helps them understand their strengths and areas for improvement. Just as important, it encourages them to commit to improving their performance. As managers, we need to be proficient at coaching; as professionals, we need to be coachable.

Many times, I've hired people with "high potential"—the ability to perform, but not the experience or credentials. They had drive, intellect, and a desire to be coached. They repaid the opportunity with incredible loyalty and above-and-beyond results. One of my high-potential hires was a woman with only a high school diploma. I hired her as an executive assistant and then promoted her to office manager. We discussed her strengths, and I coached her on the areas she needed to develop. In this process, I encouraged her to complete her bachelor's degree in business, which she

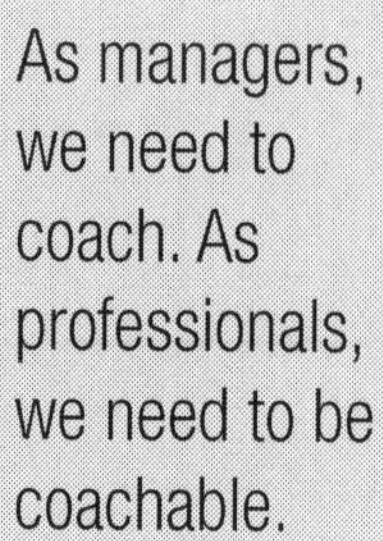

did. Her degree positioned her for promotion to investor relations manager, then to investor relations director, and eventually to a vice president role outside our company. My ability to coach, and her willingness to be coached, resulted in a win-win relationship.

Susan Heathfield, human resource expert, encourages employers to use coaching to improve employee performance. "Coaching often provides positive feedback about employee contributions. At the same time, regular coaching brings performance issues to an employee's attention when they are minor, and assists the employee [in] correct[ing] them."[1]

Topgrading,[2] an outstanding book on hiring and coaching, identifies four key components of coaching:

1. *Counseling:* improving self-awareness and changing points of view.

2. *Mentoring:* sharing sage advice to help become more proficient in corporate culture, networking, and career planning.

3. *Teaching:* instructing to improve expertise.

4. *Confronting:* addressing nonperformance to help achieve goals or accept the necessity of redeployment.

According to *Topgrading*, a super coach has ten characteristics:

1. *Partner:* willing to work with coachee and is interested, engaged, and respectful.

2. *Promotes autonomy:* assists coachee in independently diagnosing problems and considering solutions; makes informed choices regarding development.

3. *Positive:* supportive, builds confidence, and is an enthusiastic motivator; uses praise and recognition for progress; never ridicules.

4. *Trustworthy:* honest, open, maintains confidences; admits when wrong.

5. *Caring:* compassionate, empathetic, sincere.

6. *Patient:* understands how hard it is to change; tolerant; reasonable.

7. *Results-oriented:* focuses only on important issues; proactive, infectiously committed to helping coachee perform; follows through on promises.

8. *Perceptive:* understands coachee's strengths, shortcomings, goals, and needs.

9. *Authoritative:* knowledgeable, wise; clear and specific in feedback; has common sense; uses valid measures of improvement.

10. *Active listener:* repeats what the coachee has said, describing the coachee's underlying feelings; summarizes; clarifies.

Topgrading encourages coaches to help their coachees understand the seven psychological stages in change:

1. Awareness
2. Rational acceptance
3. Emotional commitment
4. Individual development plan
5. Reinforcement
6. Monitoring progress
7. Conclusion

As the coach, you need to eliminate the excuse of not having enough time. You and your coachee must commit to taking time for coaching, being coached, and following through on a development plan. Coaching is truly the best gift you can give your employees—and yourself.

Key Action Tips

1. Read a coaching book, such as *Topgrading,* and make a commitment to becoming a better coach. Develop a framework for coaching. Identify an exemplary coaching mentor to assist in your development.

2. Establish a regular time to meet with each of your employees—at least one hour per week. Allocate a certain amount of time to reviewing work objectives as well as to coaching.

3. Identify areas your coachees need to work on and communicate them. Utilize the *Topgrading* framework to help each of your employees develop.

43

Praise in Public, Criticize in Private

There are two things people want more than sex and money—recognition and praise.

—Mary Kay Ash, founder of Mary Kay Cosmetics

Recognition and praise are not just things to give in passing. They're critical tools. A survey of more than four million employees worldwide found that employees who received regular recognition and praise were more productive, more engaged with their colleagues, and more likely to stay with their company.[1] They also received higher loyalty and satisfaction scores from customers.

Dr. Kathy Johanson, CEO of ReJuVey, says that the best advice she ever received on how to reward employees came from the employees themselves. "In a weekly staff meeting, I asked each of them to send me an email describing the type of 'recognition' that would truly inspire them to do more and better," she recounts. "Interestingly, 90 percent expressed a desire for public praise for a job well done."[2] In other words, a simple thank-you in front of peers and leaders was all they wanted.

> Praise should highlight how an achievement contributes to the success of the company.

Catherine the Great is famously quoted as saying, "I praise loudly. I blame softly."[3] The longest-ruling Empress of Russia (1762–1796) was highly successful in creating economic development, border expansion, and diplomacy. She knew she needed the support of others to effectively lead—and what better way to create followers than with the use of public praise.

At one of my companies, we did just that. Each quarter, we asked employees to nominate other employees or themselves for outstanding contributions toward the achievement of corporate objectives. We created an employee committee that would discuss and vote on the nominees. During quarterly all-hands meetings, we recognized and awarded the winners. This recognition and praise inspired employees and focused them towards corporate goals.

"Blaming softly" is just as important as praising loudly. Reprimands and criticism must be offered, but they must be delivered privately. A leader who criticizes an employee in public loses the respect and loyalty of that employee, as well as that of other employees, peers, and superiors who fear the same could happen to them. Employees who are publicly humiliated are more prone to becoming disengaged, which destroys corporate profits. The *Gallup Business Journal* reported that actively disengaged employees cost the American economy up to $300 billion annually in lost productivity.[4] No company can afford this loss.

In the spirit of "praise in public, criticize in private" is a related rule: "Teams get credit for success; a boss gets the blame for failure." When a leader gets praise for performance, they should give credit to the team. Likewise, a leader should accept responsibility for any of their team's failures.

Key Action Tips

1. Make your praise (and criticism) effective. It should be:
   a. *Objective.* Establish criteria for what constitutes rewardable (or unacceptable) behavior or actions.
   b. *Relevant.* Ensure feedback is applicable to the person's career, objectives, or goals.
   c. *Specific.* Make feedback specific to an action.
   d. *Timely.* Provide feedback as close to the time of performance as possible. Timeliness enhances the likelihood that praised behavior will be repeated and criticized behavior will not.
   e. *Accurate.* If not accurate, it may be viewed as insincere.
   f. *Genuine.* For praise, put feeling in your tone of voice, emphasizing your gratitude. For criticism, make it less personal, and aim your comments at the person's behavior but still demonstrate your desire to see the person improve.
   g. *Proper place.* Praise can be offered publicly or privately. Criticism should always be given in private. If you do criticize an employee publicly, apologize. Make your apology timely, specific, and genuine.

2. Develop a corporate culture of recognition and praise.
   a. Have human resources work with team leaders and managers to ensure that they consistently

praise and recognize their team members when appropriate.

b. Develop a system to ensure that recognition and praise are balanced between employees, departments, and business units.
c. Share best practices across departments, divisions, or business units.
d. Pay close attention to employee surveys to determine whether specific departments are not feeling valued or equally treated.

3. Change your recognition programs to reflect the times and employee sentiments.
    a. Review recognition programs on an annual basis.
    b. Have human resources form a cross-functional team to seek employee input.

44

Be Friendly—Not Friends

Never make close friendships at work, or show favoritism toward employees. Fair and consistent treatment is my motto.

—Kathy Johanson, CEO of ReJuVey

A manager-subordinate relationship is a balancing act. On one hand, it should be authentic, caring, friendly, and hopefully fun. It also needs to remain professional. The main objective is not the relationship itself, but accomplishing the work.

Confusing friendship with professional trust and respect is a tragic downfall for some managers. And it's even more unsettling for female leaders. Is this because women are driven more by an innate need to be liked? Because women are socialized to focus on building personal relationships?

Whatever the reason, close personal ties with subordinates threaten your managerial effectiveness. They make it more difficult to evaluate personnel objectively and provide timely feedback. By maintaining those ties, you also run the risk of other employees feeling you are neither fair nor transparent. All of this is detrimental to morale.

I've had extensive experience in failing to follow the

Friendships with
subordinates
make it more
difficult to
evaluate them
objectively.

"don't be friends" rule. It was easy to fall into the trap of befriending people I spent a lot of time with. This was especially true in start-up companies, where everyone was working extraordinary hours and shared a passion for making the enterprise a success. Although a few invaluable friendships have outlasted the business relationships—and I am thankful for them—there was a price to pay. Other employees felt that my friends were treated preferentially and had easier access to promotion. Though I held anyone who shared a personal relationship with me to the same standards as everyone else, that didn't change the perception of favoritism. Not only did people harbor resentment against me and the company, but they also minimized the accomplishments of the "friend" employees, who lost out on well-deserved peer recognition.

As a manager, it's your responsibility to build the right kind of relationships. The workplace is not about friendships; it's about hiring competent people who can work as a team toward the achievement of your company's objectives. Does that mean friendships should never grow out of work relationships? Alia McKee, principal of Sea Change Strategies and cofounder of Lifeboat, offers a dissenting view: "The question isn't really should we mix friends and work. That's inevitable. The question is how do we get it right." McKee argues that the concept of a work-life division is eroding; as employees spend more time working—in the office and at home—their colleagues become their only social option.[1] Close friendships at work can also have business advantages, including increased productivity, employee retention, and competitive hiring advantages.[2]

All in all, I think the best advice for managers is to allow your employees to form strong, productive relationships, but to keep more of a professional distance yourself.

Key Action Tips

To be friendly without establishing personal friendships:

1. Critically evaluate your emotions and management. Are you treating some employees preferentially or more critically than others? If so, make a plan to change that.

2. Hold all employees accountable to the same standards.

3. Proactively evaluate your subordinates and challenge each of them to stretch goals. No employee should be allowed to skate by.

4. Limit social interactions, and keep your out-of-office meetings evenly balanced among your direct reports.

45

Your Personal Life Is Personal—Keep *Most of It* That Way

One of the real misses of our society is that social life doesn't affect professional life. It does.

—Nancy Rothbard, professor,
Wharton Business School

Do you share a lot of personal information at work? Disclosing too much can negatively affect your relationships with coworkers, as well as your career. Topics you need to be careful about include your family difficulties, health challenges, emotional problems, religion, political beliefs, career aspirations, and sex life.

Keeping our personal and professional lives separate, however, may be easier said than done. They overlap, especially in the age of social media. We inhabit a culture of oversharing and may actually derive the same level of intrinsic pleasure from sharing personal information as we do from food and sex. Recent surveys of social media indicate that approximately 80 percent of posts consist of announcements about one's immediate experiences.[1]

To complicate matters, sharing *some* personal information is acceptable, even critical, when building professional

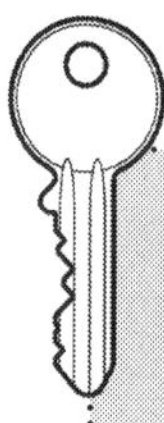
Err on the side of discretion.

relationships with amiable people. Sharing *limited* personal information can help build trust and make leaders appear more real and assessable.

So how do you figure out what to share and what not to share? It's best to err on the side of discretion. This is true even when you think you're being careful about whom you tell. For the most part, I have found that it's human nature for people to share what they've been told. We have all said or heard, "I'm not supposed to tell you, but . . ."

My advice—only disclose what you would tell a reporter who intends to print your story on the front page of the *New York Times*. Tough medicine to implement, but essential to maintaining your professional identity.

Key Action Tips

1. Do not discuss the following topics:
   a. *Family difficulties.* Talking about challenges with your spouse, children, or parents may raise questions about your ability to focus and do your job.
   b. *Health challenges and emotional issues.* People may question your ability to do your job. If you must disclose, keep it brief and generic. If pushed for more details, defer the conversation by saying you can (not will) go into details at a later time.
   c. *Religion and politics.* These are both very personal and sensitive subjects in which people have strong convictions. You have little to gain by discussing these topics and may run into legal issues with religion.
   d. *Career aspirations.* If you're interested in being

promoted, then do your current job well, offer to take on additional responsibilities, and let your direct superior and human resource department know about your aspirations. If you're interested in changing companies, don't discuss it with your coworkers or subordinates. Talking about moving to another company will make employees question your commitment and loyalty.

   e. *Sex life.* This is no one's business. Talking about this may make people feel uncomfortable and put you at risk for claims of sexual harassment.

2. The following topics are okay to share:
   a. *Hobbies and interests.* These are areas that can help build professional relationships. Talking about sports, movies, reading, art, music, and pop culture can help bridge differences in work style and personality.
   b. *Weekend activities and vacations.* This shows the human side of you. Everyone needs a break from work; talking about non-work activities demonstrates balance and gives your employees permission to lead a balanced life, as well.
   c. *Family.* So long as what you say is positive, this reveals another dimension of you and encourages your employees to do the same.

3. Social media and online tips:
   a. Assume your employer and prospective employers are privy to anything you post online. Be professional and positive. Never post disparaging or negative things about others, especially your employer or coworkers. Use the *New York Times* test (don't say anything you wouldn't

want to see on the front page of the *New York Times*).

b. Use different sites for different purposes. Some people use LinkedIn for business and Facebook for personal communication. Familiarize yourself with the privacy settings on each site. While Facebook allows you to select which group of friends can see certain information, I still strongly recommend the *New York Times* test.

46

Slow to Hire, Quick to Fire

History repeats itself. Only hire "A" players.

—Stephanie Pliha, clinical sales manager, Intuitive Surgical

Do you have an objective, thorough hiring process? Do you use multiple interviewers? Do you correct hiring mistakes quickly? Do have a productive team that makes the journey worthwhile? Your success as a leader depends on hiring the right people and firing the ones who don't perform, including those you mistakenly hired.

Hiring takes time, diligence, and skill. "Often hiring is done with little more than a passing thought to the skills, abilities, and knowledge needed for a position," says Carole Martin, author of *Boost Your Hiring I.Q.* "Your job in the interview is to ask the questions that will bring out the skills, abilities, traits, and past behaviors of the candidate so that you can get as 'clear' a picture of that person in a short amount of time."[1]

Companies and their new hires regret hiring decisions 50 percent of the time. Astounding, but that's what Recruiting Roundtable found when they studied more than 8,500 hiring managers and 19,000 of their most recent hires.[2]

> "It appears that there is a competition going on as to who can be more effective at interviewing—the interviewer or the candidate."
>
> —Carole Martin, *Boost Your Hiring I.Q.*

Hiring mistakes cost the average organization millions of dollars due to lower performance, less engaged new hires, and higher turnover.

Employee turnover is also one of the largest underreported costs in business. The average cost of mis-hiring is approximately fifteen times base salary, or $1.5 million for mid-managers with base salaries in the $100,000 range.[3] Mis-promoting internally is about as costly as mis-hiring external candidates. Further, these costs don't take into account the disruptions to other employees. One bad hire can bring down group performance by 30 to 40 percent.[4] That's a lot of lost productivity and profit.

Important reasons that companies fail to consistently hire high-quality candidates include overreliance on candidates' descriptions of themselves; not following a consistent, evidence-based decision process; and neglecting to provide candidates with enough information about what the job is really like.[5] Ensuring a good match with corporate culture is also a factor.

After we experienced unacceptably high turnover in our sales department at one of my companies, we incorporated skills and personality testing as well as an interviewer scorecard with objective, weighted measurements. This process helped us retain the people we hired.

"Just as interviewing for the job as a candidate is a learned skill," says Carole Martin, "so is hiring a learned skill."[6] However time-consuming, it's worth your while to work with your human resource personnel to refine your hiring skills and optimize the process.

Likewise, letting people go can be difficult, but it's your duty to do it when it becomes necessary. If you've coached, counseled, documented, and determined that your employee is still not meeting expectations, firing is the only reasonable option. Just make sure you dot the *i*'s and cross the *t*'s. Teresa Daggett, founder of Quantum Law, advises, "Prior to firing an employee, review documents signed by the employee upon hiring. There may be considerations of severance pay, noncompete, and return of company equipment. You'll want to take these factors into account during the termination process."[7]

When the time finally comes, don't forget to address the person you're letting go with compassion and empathy, preserving their dignity as best you can.

Key Action Tips

To enhance your hiring effectiveness:

1. Identify benchmarks for the position and establish a consistent, evidence-based selection process with objective, weighted assessment tools.

2. Give hiring the time and attention it deserves. For key hires, understand that it may take up to three months or more to find the right person. Have candidates interview with their potential boss, boss's boss, peers, subordinates, and outside people whose opinion you value. Establish cross-departmental involvement for every hire. Get executives involved, especially in organizations of less than three hundred people.

3. Ask why the candidate is looking for a new position and what the three most important elements are in his or her next career move. Discuss your company's ability to meet those elements.

4. Ensure that the candidate understands your corporate culture and verify there is a good fit.

5. When searching for senior personnel, consider working with an executive recruiter and meet the applicant's spouse in a social setting to ensure their support.

6. Look for happy, well-balanced, goal-oriented, well-adjusted people who enjoy life and have a good sense of humor.

7. Become a student and master of smart hiring. Routinely read about best hiring practices. Ask for advice from executives of well-staffed teams.

To enhance your firing effectiveness:

1. Whatever your position, understand that you are only as strong as your team. If you have unproductive personnel, your team and company cannot reach its potential—and you may get fired yourself. Furthermore, by keeping underperformers, you damage the productivity and morale of your other employees, and may lose your "A" players.

2. Ask your human resource personnel for assistance.

3. Don't allow firing to come as a surprise to employees. They should be well apprised of their under-

performance, the actions they need to take to keep their job, and the amount of time they will be given to improve. Only fire somebody suddenly and unexpectedly if fraud or unprofessional conduct is involved.

4. Remember that everyone will be watching—other employees as well as senior management. Your actions can have long-term consequences about how others perceive you. Observers will most likely be thinking, *Is this how I'd want to be treated if I were being fired?*

5. It's your duty to ensure that the termination is done with compassion and empathy, preserving the dignity of the person being fired.

6. In a professional manner, communicate with affected personnel that the fired person is no longer with the company. Explain how the responsibilities will be covered until a replacement is found.

7. Refrain from speaking disparagingly about departed former employees.

47

Delegate, Empower—Then Get out of the Way

Never do things others can do and will do if there are things others cannot do or will not do.

—Amelia Earhart, American aviation pioneer and author

Successful management starts with intelligent delegation. Too many talented managers fail because they don't feel anyone can do the job as well as they can, or because it takes too much time to train someone. Consequently, they don't meet deadlines and leave subordinates feeling incompetent, unvalued, and unmotivated.

In my earlier years of management, I found that my lack of delegation created tremendous challenges for both me and my subordinates. The more I trusted and delegated, the better employees performed.

When delegating, every manager must decide how much latitude to give direct reports. It runs the gamut from no direction to micromanagement. Neither extreme is ideal. Lack of direction leaves many employees feeling unsupported and oftentimes overwhelmed, whereas micromanagement demeans and frustrates competent people. Intelligent delegation falls somewhere in between and depends on the subordinate's level of experience, confidence, and competence. Use motivational management principles (see chapter 40, "Motivational Management—One Style Doesn't Fit All") to determine the optimal balance between delegation and direction.

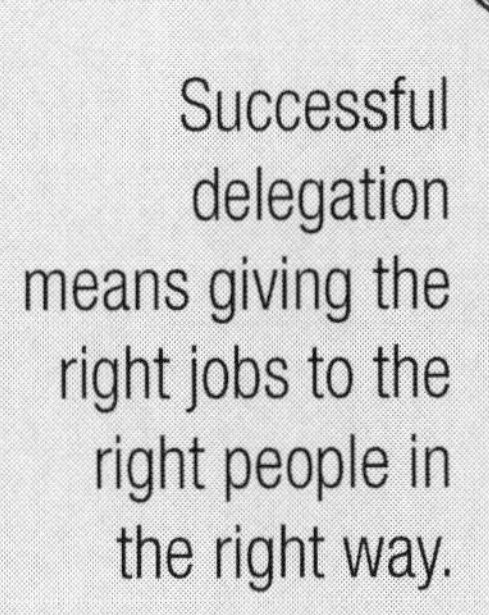
Successful delegation means giving the right jobs to the right people in the right way.

Intelligent delegation begets employee empowerment, demonstrating your trust and respect for your subordinates. That said, delegation is not just about making others feel valued; it is critical to your own success. Besides developing your employees' capabilities, confidence, and commitment, it gives you more time for strategic thinking, managing, and working on the more critical projects that only you can accomplish.

Successful delegation means giving the right jobs to the right people in the right way. This involves choosing appropriately skilled employees, communicating a set of standards, and defining the "what, by when" instead of the "how." Define and reach mutual agreement on goals, milestones, time frames, frequency of progress, follow-up, and required support. Then get out of the way!

Key Action Tips

To enhance your delegation and empowerment skills:

1. Develop the attitude that you should not be doing anything that one of your employees has the ability to accomplish. Although this is an exaggeration, it's a good mindset to adopt. Reserve your time for:

a. Mentoring
b. Developing and managing your employees
c. Strategic thinking and planning
d. Dealing with employee issues
e. Accomplishing those projects that require your expertise

2. Employ motivational management to create delegation plans that depend on employees' competence and confidence.

3. Define objectives, standards, milestones, and timeline. Reach a mutual agreement with employees on these things. Capture the information in a document. Discuss how the objectives fit into a larger project, vision, or corporate objective.

4. Determine what additional resources are available for the project in terms of other departments, personnel, and money. Share this information with other employees or departments should their participation be required.

5. Discuss the level of initiative you expect and the frequency of progress reporting throughout the project.

6. Discuss any concerns and confirm employees' understanding of the project's elements. Say that you're available for consultation throughout the project and suggest that they not only come to you with challenges and suggested resolutions, but also successes. Discuss rewards for good performance and consequences for failure.

7. Get out of the way. Let your employees unleash their creative talents. Stick to your periodic progress checks and ask your employees what decisions they feel they could make, but are not allowed to. Then, if appropriate, remove whatever inhibits their ability to make decisions.

8. After completing a project, set up a time for you and your employee to review the quality of the results, what went well, and what could be done differently next time.

9. Publicly praise your employees for their results and contributions to the company.

48

Crying—Best Left for Weddings and Funerals

To wear your heart on your sleeve isn't a very good plan; you should wear it inside, where it functions best.

—Margaret Thatcher,
British prime minister, 1979–1990

Is crying at work a "thou shall not" rule carved in stone? Most professional women say yes. Yet many women fail to follow this rule. Research suggests that when women cry on the job, it's because they feel helpless, lack control over their work, or feel they have been treated unfairly.[1] But no one is immune to these unpleasant workplace experiences. So why do men and women react differently?

According to Kim Elsbach, professor of management at the University of California, Davis, women are much more likely to cry at work, and elsewhere, due to socialization. Boys are taught not to cry, and thus holding back tears is a reflex. "Because women aren't socialized like men," Elsbach says, "they carry an extra burden of emotional labor."[2] And the consequences can be harsh. Crying in public leads to loss of respect and promotions.

In *Through the Labyrinth: The Truth About How Women Become Leaders,* Alice Eagly and Linda Carli stress that "nothing reinforces the negative stereotype of women being ruled by emotions rather than professionalism like a crying woman professional." The more male-dominated the field, the greater the damage.[3]

Why would crying be more damaging in male-dominated fields? "Testosterone is a key power hormone that gets corporate executives in warrior mode," explains Judith Orloff, psychiatrist and author of *Emotional Freedom.* When a woman cries in the presence of a male colleague, "it's threatening hormonally [to males]. Studies have associated lower testosterone levels in men with feelings of failure."[4]

Regardless of the reasons, a reputation for being overly emotional—or even emotional— almost always results in disparagement, damage to your professional status, and other undesirable consequences. Stephanie Pliha, clinical sales manager of Intuitive Surgical, advises, "There's no room in business for emotion. If you need to cry, go outside."[5]

Early in my career, I worked under intense conditions for more than a year to secure a new account. At the last minute, the account pulled the purchase order and was going to give it to our competitor, all because I'd said that our company would be releasing a new system in the next few months, and I wanted to ensure that they got the latest system. A newly hired department head (who purportedly did not like women) felt I was trying to gouge the account for a higher sales amount, which was not the case. I felt unfairly treated and broke down and cried to one of the account's decision makers. Luckily for me, he was an empathetic, father-like physician who became a mentor.[6] He advised me on how best to recapture the sale, and—just as importantly—gently counseled me against crying in business. I have shared the same advice with my fellow female colleagues.

Some female executives argue that crying is acceptable at work. Elbach's research suggests that crying due to a loss, like death or divorce, is acceptable if it only happens once, but crying in a public meeting or because of work-related stress is considered disruptive and weak.[7]

To minimize the risk of damage, do your best to prevent tears from flowing and emotions from flaring. And demonstrate empathy, care, and respect with others who haven't yet mastered the art of emotional control.

Key Action Tips

To improve your emotional control:

1. Anticipate situations. In order to unlearn, relearn, and strengthen your emotional and behavioral repertoires, take time outside the office to think of work situations likely to make you react emotionally and prepare in advance by planning calm, unemotional reactions. Write your plans down in a journal. As Louis Pasteur said, "fortune favors the prepared mind."[8] In essence, you'll be socializing yourself not to cry.

2. Increase self-awareness. Make a conscious effort to think before you speak, especially when you're upset. To control your emotions, focus on identifying what is causing them, and then think of solutions. Looking at the cause of your emotions as a problem to solve can help you head off tears. Also acknowledge that tears will not resolve the problem. Whatever the issue, try not to let it show, reassuring yourself that, given time, there will be a solution.

3. Think positively. Remind yourself that everything works out. I always say, what's the worst that can happen—I'll get fired and find a better job! Seek the perspective of mentors, coaches, or professional friends.

4. Depersonalize and compartmentalize. Don't lose your temper when something upsets you. Understand that it may actually have little to do with you, especially as a person. Being objective usually requires taking time away from the situation. If you can compartmentalize—put negative emotions in a "box"—you can learn not to react immediately on the basis of feelings, but instead take time to properly respond.

5. Buy time. If you cannot be objective at the moment and tears are imminent, delay the conversation. Say you would like to think about the issue, or simply try to excuse yourself (for instance, claim you need to use the restroom), and find a private place to vent and gain control of your emotions.

6. Learn persistence. When something doesn't work, try, try, try again.

To productively deal with an emotional employee:

1. Think of tears as an emotional reaction to an issue and handle them the same way you would if the person used words to express their anger, frustration, or sadness.

2. If there are other people around or you're in a public area, try to invite the person into your office

or another private place. Keep tissues in a handy place in your office.

3. Stay calm and be respectful. Tell the employee you understand the issue is very important to them and ask for further explanation or ask whether they want to schedule another time to meet. Listen and don't immediately try to solve the problem. Once they have clearly identified and explained the source of their distress, ask for solutions. Suggest that you meet in the next twenty-four to forty-eight hours to further discuss and address the matter.

4. Never discuss the emotional response with other employees.

5. If you're unable to take time to deal with an emotional employee, let them know the matter is important to you, but you need to schedule a meeting to address it.

6. Briefly listen, but limit the amount of time you allow an employee to vent regarding non-work matters, including significant others and family. Counsel them to seek assistance outside the company.

49

Roosters Crow, Hens Deliver—Successful Women Do Both

It is the rooster that crows, but it's the hen who delivers the goods.

—Ann Richards, former governor of Texas

Women consistently deliver, but we often don't take credit or effectively communicate our contributions. Even worse, we consistently downplay our accomplishments. Someone asks what we do, or compliments us on an achievement, and we blush and self-deprecate. "I just started my company, and it's small." "I just manage a small group in a large organization." "Oh, it was really nothing." Ugh!

These statements are self-minimizing at best and self-destructive at worst. Certainly they're not an effective way to market yourself!

I hate to admit it, but in spite of my admonishments to other women about this, I am also an offender. We just don't seem comfortable taking credit or accepting a compliment. We minimize our roles and accomplishments so as not to appear boastful—a factor to which our male counterparts rarely give a second thought.

Recognition doesn't happen automatically.

You may trust, as many women do, that if you do a good job and become an exemplary corporate citizen, you will be recognized and rewarded. This doesn't happen, especially when you have roosters crowing all around you. You need to not only deliver results, but also bring attention to your contributions and share the importance of your position.

Increasingly, professionals are creating elevator pitches—concise, eloquent descriptions of their experience and value. They're also developing, delivering, and advertising individual brand taglines, much like companies advertise their brands. Imagine if your brand tagline were as strong as some of the corporate brands'. Think of Nike's "Just do it," or Apple's "Think different." If you don't market yourself with an effective elevator pitch and brand, other people won't understand your professional value and won't market you.

Key Action Tips

1. Develop an elevator pitch highlighting your position, accomplishments, and strengths, and memorize it. Practice delivering it in a natural style and tone. For example:
   "I drive disruptive medical technologies to standard of care. As vice president of sales and marketing for QualMed, I've driven a fivefold increase in sales over three years. We have 20 percent market penetration and are establishing our product as a standard of care."

2. Develop a personal brand tagline consisting of five to seven words that succinctly describe your value. See chapter 2, "Brand Yourself—Unique, Memorable, and Authentic." Use it when you meet people, and also put it on your business cards and in your email signature line. Examples include:
   a. Leading start-ups to commercial success (Rebecca Boudreaux, entrepreneur and president of Oberon Fuels)
   b. Finding people who make a difference (Robin Toft, president and CEO of Sanford Rose Associates, an executive recruiting firm)
   c. Brand accelerator, strategist, connector (Deborah Jondall, branding entrepreneur)

3. When you receive a compliment, look the person in the eye and sincerely and humbly say "thank you."

4. Eliminate the phrase "It was nothing." Every accomplishment takes time, effort, and perseverance!

5. Keep a record of your quarterly accomplishments, awards, special assignments, etc. Quantify your accomplishments. Use these to update your elevator pitch and resume, and share them with your business associates.

50

MEN—THRIVING AMONGST DIFFERENCES

Don't treat men as the enemy. Become part of their informal network, positioning yourself for new opportunities, special assignments, and promotions.
—Jennifer Crittenden, Author

John Gray's bestselling book *Men Are from Mars, Women Are from Venus* couldn't have been more aptly titled. Simply put, men and women are as different as aliens. In general, we look, think, feel, speak, and act differently. Differences can create discomfort, tension, and conflict. So how can women not only work with men but thrive amongst them and the differences? Let's focus on three major areas of difference: thinking, communication, and approaches to work.

Why do women and men think differently? Some researchers[1,2] attribute the differences, in part, to women being more right-brain dominant while men are more left-brain dominant. In general, the left side of the brain processes information in a linear, sequential, and logical manner. Left-brained people have little trouble expressing

To talk so men
will listen, be
concise.

themselves in words. They like checklists, master schedules, daily planning, knowing rules, and following them. Are you envisioning male colleagues, significant others, or husbands? Conversely, right-brain-dominant people are considered more intuitive, thoughtful, and subjective. Sounds a lot like the innate skills of a woman.

It's also been reported that women have a more developed corpus callosum, the band of neural fibers separating the left and right sides of the brain. Researchers attribute a woman's ability to transition more quickly between the hemispheres of the brain to this advanced development.[3] Possibly, this is why women are reported to be better multitaskers than our male counterparts.

How about different communication styles? How do they affect workplace success?

According to Claire Damken Brown and Audrey Nelson, authors of *Code Switching: How to Talk So Men Will Listen*, "Men and women often talk a different language in the workplace. And if you're not speaking the same language, your ideas don't get heard and you don't get the respect you deserve."[4]

In general, women tend to speak in long sentences, write long email messages, and tell the whole story, whereas men are brief and largely focused on a message's content. To talk so men will listen, the authors advocate code switching, the practice of shifting the way you express yourself in your conversations. Women need to adopt some of the more masculine styles of communicating to successfully communicate with men in business—in short, women need to be more concise!

Women also hold themselves back when they emphasize subjective feelings, and couch opinions with phrases such as "kind of," "sort of," and "maybe." Jennifer Crittenden, author of *The Discreet Guide for Executive Women,* warns, "Be careful not to weaken your comments by using a hedge, such as 'This might be a bad idea, but…' or 'I know I'm new, but…' You rarely hear men use such hedges because they know it detracts from the importance of their message."[5]

Women and men also take different approaches to work. Studies consistently find that men embrace competition while women are raised to get along and be peacemakers. According to a study on nearly seven thousand job seekers from sixteen large US cities, men are 94 percent more likely than women to apply for a job with a salary potential dependent on outperforming their colleagues. The study concluded, "Women shy away from competitive workplaces whereas men covet, and even thrive in, competitive environments."[6] Don't take it personally if male colleagues competitively challenge you—it's in their DNA! It may partially explain why women earn, on average, 81 percent of what men earn.[7]

Key Action Tips

To thrive alongside men:

1. Be direct, objective, and calm. When presenting a proposal or plan of action, talk less about the problem and more about the solution. Men are solution-oriented. Minimize feelings (e.g., "I feel…"), emotion (high-pitched tone of voice, anger, tears), filler words ("just," "kind of," "sort of," "well," "gee," "maybe," "little bit") and skip to the solution or point of the discussion. Your goal is to get to the point and, to a lesser extent, humanize

the content of your message. Avoid phrases like "It's not fair" and "He isn't doing his job."

2. Be concise. Since women use up to two times as many words as men, this is critical. I have long favored the "rule of three," which is a framework for structuring your message and limiting it to the three most important points. You'll begin to notice that many sentences use the rule of three: structure your message so that it has an introduction, middle, and close. See chapter 28, "And Then There's Public Speaking."

3. Don't apologize or say "please" or "thank you" as much as you're inclined to.

4. Don't be overly eager or reassuring. Make men earn your agreement and support.

5. Take your turn at being the first to speak. This commands attention and allows you to set the tone.

6. Take a few seconds to respond when a question is directed at you. It enhances the perception that you are an intelligent, thoughtful communicator.

7. Don't take anything personally. Men tend to let things roll off their backs; conversely, women internalize and analyze—over and over—what is said and done by others. We can't seem to let incidents go as easily as men, which results in frustration and other unproductive emotions.

8. Don't worry if a man interrupts you. This is how many men communicate. You can keep talking or

redirect the discussion back to your topic. (Don't interrupt unless you absolutely need to, however, as women who interrupt are perceived more negatively than men.)

9. Don't sit around and complain about something if you don't have a reasonable solution to propose. Come up with a solution. It's acceptable to ask for support as long as you aren't complaining.

10. Proactively introduce yourself with a smile, direct eye contact, and a firm handshake. Don't wait to be introduced; stand up and be counted.

11. Don't let profanity creep its way into your vocabulary. Standards are different for men and women. You will never be criticized for *not* cussing, but you open the door to criticism if you use colorful language.

12. Give credit and recognition. It's always appreciated.

13. Be respectful when expressing viewpoints. If you're expressing a difference of opinion, try the following: "I understand," "That's true," or "We could also look at it from a second perspective…"

14. Don't ask men how they feel about something. Men tend to prefer logic to feelings. Ask what he thinks.

15. Don't let them see you stress out. And don't let men know when you know they're stressed. Men want to believe you have confidence in them. They love the phrase "I'm confident you can handle it."

16. Project confidence and optimism. Assure colleagues that there is a solution to all challenges and engage teamwork in working through to success. Display your awards, certifications, and degrees in your office. Display pictures of yourself with successful people or working on different projects. If a male colleague displays interest, describe your success with a tone of confidence.

17. If you're in a supportive role, ask in a friendly tone, "Would you like me to do X?" This ensures awareness, and hopefully recognition, of your contributions.

18. Be clear about the projects you want. Men respect clarity and a willingness to make reasonable compromises.

19. When you have a differing opinion in a multi-person meeting, be objective and non-emotionally deliver your arguments.

20. Men don't like being told what to do, especially by women. Minimize tension and ask, "Is this a good time to review some changes?" or "Let's schedule a time when we can talk, as I have some changes to discuss."

51

Angels and Demons—Make That Demonettes

There is a special place in hell for women who do not help other women.

—Madeleine Albright, first female US Secretary of State

Discussions of glass ceilings largely focus on the biases and actions of men. But what about the role women play in the advancement of other women? It's an important, but frequently overlooked factor.

Women have a responsibility to support, mentor, and sponsor other women. To do otherwise works against everything women have fought for. Gail Evans, CNN's first female executive vice president and author of *She Wins, You Win,* declares, "Every time a woman succeeds in business, every other woman's chance of succeeding in business increases. Every time a woman fails in business, every other woman's chance of failure increases."[1]

That makes it all the more tragic to consider that approximately 40 percent of workplace bullies are women. According to a Workplace Bullying Institute survey, "at least the male bullies take an egalitarian approach, mowing down men and women pretty much in equal measure. The women appear to prefer their own kind, choosing women as targets more than 70 percent of the time."[2]

> Women have enough obstacles without other women sabotaging them.

There's a difference between a bully and someone who's just having a difficult day. Bullying happens on a regular basis and includes yelling, intimidating, or humiliating behaviors; vicious gossip; lying; and taking credit for others' work.

On a more positive note, there are certainly female leaders who provide guidance, support, and sponsorship. Although most of my mentors and sponsors have been men, two women have been especially supportive in my career: Patricia A. Reno, senior vice president of RBC Wealth Management, and Karin Eastham, life sciences executive, board director, and author. Patricia promoted and nominated me for Ernst & Young's Entrepreneur of the Year award, which I won in 2003. Karin has been a mentor, sponsor, publishing partner, and friend, and she has promoted my advancement in serving as a director on corporate boards. I encourage you to find women like Pat and Karin if you haven't already.

Let us be grateful and thank the female angels who provide encouragement, mentoring, and wind beneath our wings. Let's emulate their actions and support others, especially women, in the same manner.

Key Action Tips

To enhance your survival in the midst of demonettes (or demons):

1. *Know the difference* between a bully and a coworker having a difficult day.
   a. Is the behavior happening regularly?
   b. Does it involve yelling, intimidating, or humiliating behaviors; vicious gossip; lying; or taking credit for your work?
   c. If the answer to these questions is yes, then admit there is a problem and develop a plan to address the situation.

2. *Be proactive.* If you anticipate that your boss or coworker is having "one of those days," approach a meeting or interaction with a positive attitude. Maintain your composure and confidence. Don't allow your boss or anyone else to intimidate you. Likewise, be positive and reinforce the good things your boss does. Compliment your boss when you feel a meeting has gone well. Everyone needs positive reinforcement, and it may help in the long run.

3. *Prepare and role-play how you'll respond.* Preparation will minimize your frustration, paralysis of thought, and emotional response. Use the tried and true "When you do X, I feel Y." This is one of the few times I recommend using the word "feel." It helps you avoid being accusatory. Your initial conversation may best be conducted in private.

4. *Take it public.* If the private conversation does not improve the situation, then deal with it publicly. Raise your voice slightly and be firm. Tell your boss you feel they're treating you unprofessionally and describe the abusive or unacceptable behavior. This may help temporarily. Be sure to be consistent in addressing your boss's unacceptable behaviors.

5. *Excuse yourself.* If you're in a bullying situation and have addressed it or aren't ready to address it, excuse yourself by saying you need to use the restroom or have another appointment. Suggest the conversation be continued at a later time.

6. *Keep documentation.* Maintain a file documenting the times, situations, and names of witnesses when you feel you're being bullied. Even though I strongly recommend against lawsuits, it's important to document and be objective about the occurrences. Teasing, sarcasm, and silent treatment are all considered forms of bullying.

7. *Take time to consider your options.* Take a day off or use the weekend to objectively assess your situation. Question whether this is a situation that will resolve with time, how long you wish to deal with it, and what your options are. Consult your employee handbook. Write down your options, and the pros and cons of each one. Whether to consult your human resource department is a tricky question. In general, I recommend you consult them, but the degree of support and the outcome will largely depend on your company's culture. If necessary, engage an outside professional to assist you in assessing the situation.

8. *Make a plan.* Once you have identified and weighed your options, decide on a plan. This will allow you to feel in control and help you move forward. I have been in situations where I had to stop an incompetent boss from cheating me out of an opportunity. In each case, I made a plan, rode out the situation, and lasted longer than the boss. Conversely, I have left companies when I decided my colleagues were not worth my time and damage to my emotional health.

PART IV

Transform Your Life

Life can be hectic, so much so that we fail to find time for ourselves and our loved ones. The fact is, we could work 24/7 and still not get everything done. And what kind of life would all work and no play be? Finding *some semblance* of a work-life balance is more challenging than ever—but also more important than ever.

As we ascend in our careers, we need to take control, find peace, and minimize life's chaos. If we don't take control, life controls us—and that does not lead to an empowered, happy, successful life.

Part IV of *Keys to the Corner Office* provides insights into the key elements you need to transform your life.

52

Be Balanced—Physically, Mentally, and Spiritually

Everything in moderation.

—Aristotle, Greek philosopher

In our 24/7, wired, data-overloaded work culture, it's nearly impossible to imagine a balanced life. But the sobering truth is that we could work twenty-four hours a day and still not get everything done. Furthermore, balance is critical for our long-term physical, mental, and spiritual health. If you don't integrate some semblance of balance into your life, the imbalance may eventually lead to poorer quality of life, or possibly even a physical or mental disorder. Then where will you be?

Prioritization and, as Aristotle said, moderation are the keys to finding balance. Depending on what stage you're at in life, your priorities will be different. Once you decide what is important, establish realistic boundaries. Unless there are extraordinary circumstances at work or home, your goal should be to achieve a balance among work, family, and friends, devoting enough time to the physical, mental, and spiritual realms.

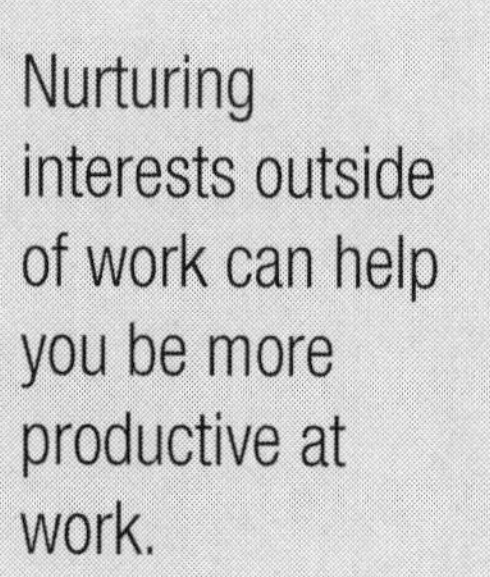

Nurturing interests outside of work can help you be more productive at work.

In your quest for balance, remember that time spent in one area can have positive effects in other areas. For instance, frequent exercise reportedly boosts wages, and the increase is more pronounced for women than for men. Researcher Vasilios Kosteas found that "women who exercise frequently earn 11.9 percent more, on average, than women who don't—a premium that's approximately equal to the effect of 1.8 additional years' schooling. For men, the wage benefit of frequent exercise is 6.7 percent, equivalent to about 1.3 years more school. The findings are consistent with the hypothesis that beauty and fitness matter more for women's wages than for men's."[1]

"Even when my professional life consumes a majority of my time, I am happiest and most productive at work when I am involved in a hobby," says Krista Dalton, Pacific Northwest marketing and sales leader for PwC. "Interests outside of the office are essential to personal well-being, and they help you recharge and connect with new communities. Whether it's physically intense, like sailboat racing, or less so, like participating in a book club, find something that can offer balance to a demanding work life. While it might be difficult initially to create balance, once you have incorporated an activity into your schedule, you will actually become more productive!"[2]

In my own life, when I take time away from work to do an unrelated activity, I often come up with ingenious solutions to work problems in the process. It's a win-win situation.

Key Action Tips

To achieve a healthy life balance:

1. *Define your values, goals, priorities, and boundaries.* Evaluate your values. Think about your short-term and long-term SMARTER (specific, measurable, attainable, relevant, time-bound, evaluated, and rewarded) goals. Based on your values and goals, prioritize and document your goals on a worksheet. Make a specific and realistic daily, weekly, and monthly plan. Consult your goals worksheet daily and evaluate your progress against goals at least weekly. You'll need to establish boundaries and limit commitments in order to achieve your goals.

2. *Nurture yourself.* Get a minimum of seven hours of sleep daily, exercise three times a week, and eat properly. You can only function for so long on inadequate sleep, little exercise, and junk food. You'll be amazed at how much better you feel with sleep, exercise, and healthy eating. Make sure to include these on your goals worksheet.

3. *Plan for success.* On Sundays, take time to review the previous week and assess the week ahead. Create a to-do list and prioritize tasks into critical, nice-to-accomplish, and not-so-important categories. Calendar time for the critical things that need to be accomplished. Don't forget to balance the professional with the personal, and include time for family, spiritual growth, mental growth, and physical activities.

4. *Be flexible.* You've established a plan. Acknowledge that things go awry. Readjust your plan if necessary, keep life in perspective, and remind yourself that you have the critical things covered. Not every week will be balanced.

5. *Reevaluate your values, priorities, and goals on an annual basis.* Let's face it: we change and our lives change. It's healthy to regularly evaluate what you identified as important and confirm that's still the case. If you can, get away. Go to a retreat. Take time to truly reflect on yourself and your life. Enjoy!

53

Ingratitude and Injustice

People are often unreasonable, irrational, and self-centered. Forgive them anyway.

—Mother Teresa, Indian Roman Catholic religious sister, Nobel Peace Prize recipient

The world is filled with ungrateful people and unjust situations. Successful people don't take it personally. You must train yourself to depersonalize ingratitude and injustice. If you do, you'll be less disappointed when an employee, friend, or family member lets you down, disrespects you, lies, or sues you for some unfounded claim. Should this happen—and it will—realize it has little to do with you and much to do with the other person or situation.

The best—or worst—example of this in my own life happened when I broke one of the *Keys to the Corner Office* rules: be friendly, not friends. In the early stages of my tenure at one company, I took a woman under my mentorship, sponsorship, and friendship, and promoted her through the ranks. Initially, she was unwavering in her corporate dedication and commitment. Increases in title, pay, and privilege followed, but so did her feelings of entitlement and ingratitude. When corporate times got tough and

> Successful people don't take things personally.

we needed employees to focus on the things that mattered—at that time, driving revenue—she felt she was above certain requests, even though they were professional and reasonable. As layoffs ensued, she was on the list. Complaints and legalities followed, and, of course, I was the target. I wager that no person had ever—or will ever—support this person the way I had, both professionally and personally. But truly, I took my own advice. I depersonalized the situation and forgave her anyway.

By depersonalizing, you will not waste further time and emotional energy wondering how a person could repay you so poorly for your support.

Key Action Tips

1. Depersonalize incidents. Remind yourself that the situation has little to do with you. Be objective. Identify the potential underlying reasons for the other person's actions. Remind yourself that the person is probably hurting, not taking responsibility, and looking to blame someone other than him- or herself.

2. Talk to the person. Try to understand his or her position and emotions. As illogical as the perspective may be, listen, paraphrase back what you hear, and empathize. It's hard to argue with someone who is just listening.

3. Forgive the person. Regardless of what happens, it's always best to seek to understand and then forgive the person. If you don't, anger and resentment can eat you alive. It's truly not worth your peace of mind. You don't have to forget what happened or trust the person in the future, but you can still forgive.

4. Move on and focus on the future. It's impossible to change the past. Make it as much of a learning experience as possible and move on. Focus on the future and what you'll do differently. Focus on the positives in your life.

5. The exemplary verses below were reportedly written by Mother Teresa on her bedroom wall in her home for children in Calcutta, India. It may help put the rest of this chapter into perspective. It was given to me by a colleague who said that she thought of me when she read it. Thank you, Ashlee! I have it posted in my office and read it daily. Do the same.

Do It Anyway

People are often unreasonable, irrational and self-centered.

Forgive them anyway.

If you are kind, people may accuse you of selfish, ulterior motives.

Be kind anyway.

If you are successful, you will win some unfaithful friends and some genuine enemies.

Succeed anyway.

If you are honest and sincere, people may deceive you.

Be honest and sincere anyway.

What you spend years creating, others could destroy overnight.

Create anyway.

If you find serenity and happiness, some may be jealous.

Be happy anyway.

The good you do today, will often be forgotten.

Do good anyway.

Give the best you have, and it will never be enough.

Give your best anyway.

In the final analysis, it is between you and God.

It was never between you and them anyway.

54

No Room for Drama (Queens)

Leave the drama where it belongs—in the theater.

—Peter C. Rosvall, chairman
and CEO of Dynamic Strategies

Some years ago, I had a friend whose entire life was built on drama. It seemed exciting at the time. She always had something interesting and crazy to talk about. The fun part was the storytelling, which is an important skill in business. The downside was the emotional and productivity drain, not only on her, but also on those who lived through the drama with her.

To excel in both your personal and professional lives, you must learn to control the drama. Though all of us have the raw material for a dramatic life, we also possess the power to compartmentalize it—put it in a box. If it's personal drama, don't bring it into work. If you do, everyone suffers, and it will be your career that suffers the most!

Once you've taken charge and compartmentalized your own personal issues, you then need to take steps to corral the professional ones. As we have all experienced, the office is loaded with drama, from rumor mills to backstabbers to office cliques to romantic indiscretions. It's fertile ground

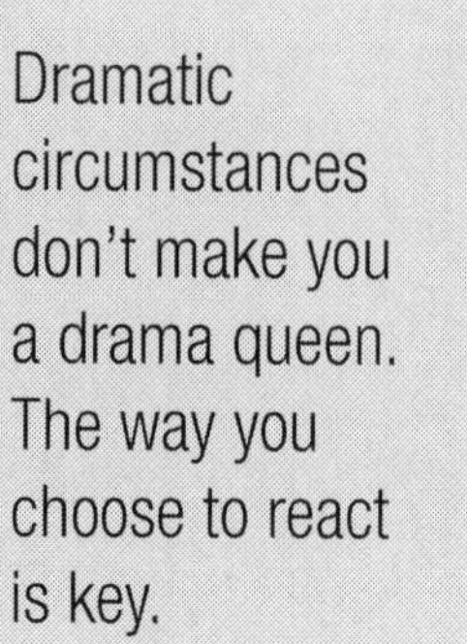

Dramatic circumstances don't make you a drama queen. The way you choose to react is key.

to get sucked into. Don't! Nothing productive comes from talking about others or getting involved in nonproductive relationships. The problems—and solutions—begin with each of us. Your life at work should revolve around solving problems, exceeding goals, and fulfilling your company's mission. If you stay focused on what's good for your company, good things will happen.

To avoid contributing to workplace drama, thoughtfully analyze and respond to others rather than reacting to them. For instance, a mild but still detrimental form of drama is overreacting to criticism, offhanded comments, rudeness, and confrontations. You have a choice about how you deal with these commonplace issues. You control how you respond, how you interact with others, and how you spend your time in the office. When you take charge and de-dramatize your life, you make an important contribution toward creating a drama-free workplace.

Key Action Tips

To leave the drama where it belongs:

1. Be self-aware. Analyze your own personal and professional life and see if you're contributing to the chaos. If you are, make a robust plan to cease. Make a conscious effort to think before you speak, especially when you're upset.

2. Stay away from people who talk about others, spread rumors, or are negative unless they're a direct report or someone you can influence.

3. If someone in your area of influence is creating drama, consider what type of person they are. If they're controlling or cynical, having a direct conversation and setting boundaries may work best; if they're a caretaker or complainer, showing appreciation and encouragement may work best.

4. If you are the target of the office drama, decide whether to rise above it, ignore it, or take action. Consider whether the situation warrants your time and effort. If it does require action, take time prior to responding if you can. Gain control of your emotions, find time to process, and determine the best response. For direct conversations with the perpetrator, remain unemotional, clearly and concisely state your perception of the facts, and (if you must) clearly and concisely describe any emotions you've experienced. Explain how you contributed to the situation and conclude with a specific request. Allow for discussion and hopefully end with a commitment and go-forward plan.

5. Let your work do the talking. So long as you're not mowing down people as you achieve your goals, there's merit in rising above the fray, whenever possible.

55

Multiply Success—Share Your Goals

Nothing is impossible, the word itself says "I'm possible."

—Audrey Hepburn, British actress and humanitarian

It's critical to communicate corporate goals at the office, but it's equally important to communicate your personal and professional goals with appropriate people you encounter elsewhere. There's no more powerful engine driving a person toward excellence and success than realistic, worthwhile goals that are widely shared.

Some argue for concealing one's goals to avoid the negative effects of naysayers, as psychological research indicates that telling someone your goals makes them less likely to happen.[1] I, however, recommend making your goals public—and here's why.

1. *Clarity.* Each time you share your goals, you'll get questions about them. The questions will give insight, make you think the goals through, and help you refine your vision and plans.

2. *Emotional connection.* When you share your goals, or someone trusts you and cares about you enough to share their aspirations with you, there is more transparency in the relationship and a greater emotional connection.

3. *Accountability.* When you go public with a goal, you can bet you'll feel more pressure to make progress and achieve the goal, especially when you'll be seeing the person you told in the near future.

4. *Motivation.* As your goal takes on more clarity and visibility through sharing with others, it will naturally become more motivating.

5. *Assistance.* I believe that people truly want to help others achieve their goals. In sharing your goals, you'll find numerous people who have great ideas or know other people who can help you.

Writing *Keys to the Corner Office* offered many opportunities to share my authorship goals, which enabled me to multiply my successes. It was amazing how many people I met who were also writing books. Through talking about my goal, I got clarity, emotional connections, a heightened sense of accountability, motivation boosts, progress checks, and assistance. Two women I connected with were Bryna Kranzler and Karin Eastham, who eventually became dear friends—and my publishing company partners. They contributed significantly to my book writing success. How blessed I am to have shared my goals with them!

Key Action Tips

To make your goal sharing more effective:

1. Develop SMARTER (specific, measurable, attainable, relevant, time-bound, evaluated, and rewarded) goals.

2. Decide which goals are appropriate to share with different sets of people. Some personal goals, such as those related to family, weight loss, or religion, may be better reserved for those closest to you, whereas many others are fine to share with a broader audience.

3. Be enthusiastic and confident when you share your goals.

4. Be prepared to have those you previously shared your goals with ask about your progress the next time you speak with them. Give truthful yet optimistic updates.

5. Be respectful of advice, observations, and criticism. Follow up on all referrals for assistance. Demonstrate your appreciation for people's follow-up and interest.

56

PERFECTION IMPEDES PROGRESS

Done is better than perfect.

—Sheryl Sandberg, chief operating officer of Facebook, author

The chapter title says it all. To make progress, heed the law of diminishing returns. There comes a point where more effort will not produce significant gains. The key is knowing when a project, plan, or idea is good enough.

Many of us have insisted on obtaining more data or waiting for the "right time" before acting. Unfortunately, the time never seems right, conditions are never perfect, and opportunities pass us by. Most likely, the root of our need for perfection resides in fear of failure, resistance to change, or obsessive-compulsive behavior. Inaction stemming from any of these sources leads to stagnation, which eventually leads to a different kind of failure or a life of boredom.

"Since perfection is impossible, seeking it keeps you focused on what you cannot achieve . . . and will therefore make you constantly feel like a failure," advises Cate Goethals, professor in Women's Leadership at the University of Washington Foster School of Business. "Most people have had the experience of being micromanaged by others—be-

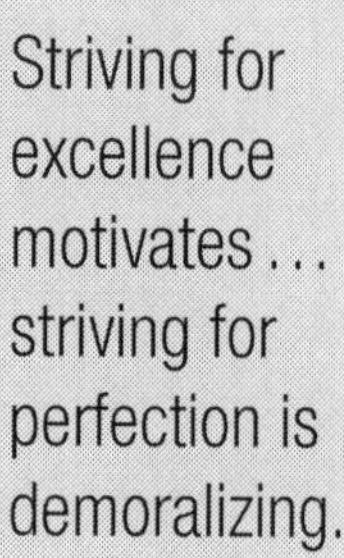
Striving for excellence motivates . . . striving for perfection is demoralizing.
—Harriet Braiker, author

ing directed to do something 'just so,' with no room for creativity. Seeking perfection is the same thing, only the micromanager is internal, keeping you poring over less important details. Just like a bad boss, you're tyrannized by a voice in your head that is impossible to please."[1] It's equally damaging to demand perfection from ourselves—or from those around us—as human beings. A "nothing is quite good enough" attitude is demoralizing and destructive. It borders on obsessive-compulsive behavior. It's the opposite of great leadership. Perfectionism robs you of peace of mind, self-esteem, and health. It can literally lead to physical and mental ailments.

A former colleague used to tease me because I had an issue with the way documents were stapled. It drove me crazy to see "improperly placed staples." Is there a manual on how to properly staple? I certainly thought so. I inherited the perfectionist trait from my father, and tragically, perfectionism led to his suicide. Luckily, I can now report that I am a "reformed" perfectionist.

We perfectionists should replace our quest for perfection with the pursuit of excellence. Unlike perfection, excellence actually exists. The trick is to identify when we are giving too much attention to things that don't matter and ensure that we are giving extra attention to things that do. Let's strive for our actions and attitudes to inspire us and others to dream more, learn more, do more, and become more.[2] After you've collaborated on research for a project, involve others in the planning, and then take action—even if it's a small action. You can always retool the plan if your first assumptions were off the mark. If you never act, you'll never know how (im)perfect your plan really is.

Letting go of perfectionism allows you to avoid getting mired in the details. According to Goethals. "Inspirational CEOs have the ability to look at the big picture, to see beyond the edges of the task at hand to what is important for themselves and for their companies."[3]

Just remember—you can insist on perfection when you're building an airplane or a bridge. Otherwise, just do your best, strive for excellence, and keep things in perspective.

Key Action Tips

1. *Make a cost-benefit analysis.* Take inventory of how perfectionism is impeding progress, hurting you, and hurting those around you. Does this list outweigh the benefits?

2. *Identify the positive.* You probably have a tendency to see what's wrong, what's missing, and what's imperfect. Stop and force yourself to identify what's right, what's present, and what's excellent. Strive for five to ten things that are right for every one you want to correct. This will help balance your critical focus.

3. *Alter critical self-talk.* Interrupt critical, negative thoughts in your head. Force yourself to think of five positive things about an idea, plan, or project before you think about what you or others could be doing better.

4. *Implement pilot programs.* To overcome action anxiety, test programs on a small scale while collecting additional data. This iterative process generally results in a better program than originally planned.

5. *Set realistic goals.* Setting realistic goals for yourself and your team allows your team members to feel goals are achievable and makes the process positive. Sure, you can have stretch goals, but don't make them so improbable that your members feel defeated at the outset.

6. *Focus on results and celebrate wins.* Engage your team's efforts in setting the goals and evaluating results. Allow them to decide what went well and what they would do differently next time. Then celebrate the wins!

57

Say No with Yes

The art of leadership is saying no, not saying yes. It is very easy to say yes.

—Tony Blair, British prime minister, 1997–2007

As you're rushing to finish a meeting so you can be on time for your next meeting, your direct report says, "Our department wants to have an offsite celebration for the product launch. It's okay, right?" Do you immediately say yes or no without any discussion of location, budget, entertainment, or risk?

How many times have you agreed to or declined a request, and then wished you'd given it thorough consideration prior to answering? How many times have you reacted emotionally or jumped to conclusions, only to later regret it? Wouldn't it be great to stop angering, alienating, and discouraging other people with reactive responses?

A key component to taking charge of your life, both personally and professionally, is the ability to identify, assess, and control your emotions. Once you have completed this process, you can then more productively respond to requests.

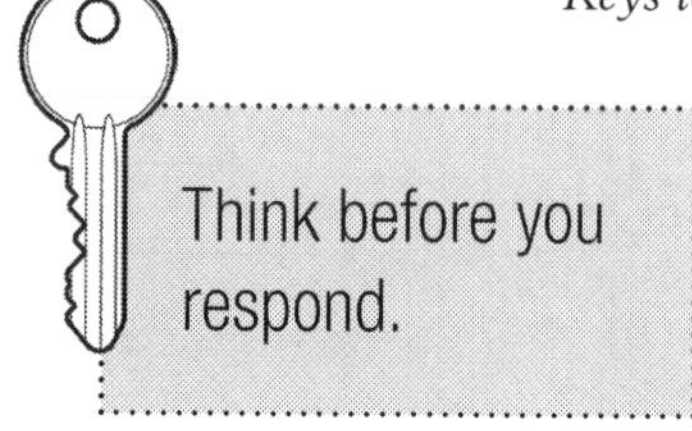
Think before you respond.

Our reactions are often based on guilt, anger, or fear. After time has passed, we often wish we'd taken time to think and responded more appropriately. Just remember—time is on your side. If you're unsure, or even if you think you're sure, take time to think through your response prior to delivering it. Taking time allows you to identify your emotions and formulate the best response. The major difference between reacting and responding is time, whether it's a few seconds, minutes, hours, days, or weeks. The outcome at stake is your happiness and, frankly, the happiness of those around you.

"We accommodate out of fear and guilt," says William Ury, cofounder of Harvard's Program on Negotiation and author of *The Power of a Positive No*. "We attack out of anger. We avoid out of fear. To get ourselves out of this three-A trap, we need to become proactive, forward-looking, and purposeful."[1]

I could not agree more. As women, it seems we have a gene that wants to please everyone, and we're raised with the idea that we need to accommodate, support, and help everyone. We are rewarded for being "nice." We say yes—even when we want to say no. Although this chapter focuses on being proactive and purposeful with our responses, its most important application is our biggest challenge—how to gracefully say no and not feel guilty. Imagine how wonderful life will be when you start making people feel positive, even when your answer is no. Dr. Thema Bryant-Davis, psychologist and associate professor at Pepperdine University, sagely advises, "Have the clarity and courage to not enter every door and to not accept every invitation. Protect your peace."[2]

Key Action Tips

1. Always be sincere, appreciative, and enthusiastic in your response.

2. For your initial response, combine one of the following "Positive, Noncommittal" phrases in column A with one of the "Buy Yourself Time" or "No Way, No How" phrases in column B. This will provide you additional time to answer in a manner you won't regret. And practice, practice, practice until it naturally flows.

A **Positive, Noncommittal**	**B** **Buy Yourself Time or No Way, No How**
That's interesting . . .	. . . Let me check my schedule and get back to you.
That sounds fascinating . . .	. . . Let me check with my spouse (my significant other, team, human resource department, boss, another higher authority) and get back to you.
I would absolutely love to help . . .	. . . I promised to get this important project completed by the end of today. Could I do it for you tomorrow?
I'd love more information . . .	. . . I look forward to receiving it and will give your project serious consideration.

A Positive, Noncommittal	B Buy Yourself Time or No Way, No How
What a great opportunity . . .	. . . Let me review my current commitments and get back to you.
I was really looking forward to lunch . . .	. . . Unfortunately, I can't make it. I find myself inundated with future, foreseeable commitments and [optional: at this time] cannot reschedule. Thank you very much for understanding, and I wish you much success in your quest.
Thank you for your suggestion of getting together. Your background [cause, etc.] is very interesting and I know we share much in common . . .	. . . Unfortunately, I find myself inundated with present commitments and can't commit to additional meetings. Thank you very much for understanding, and I wish you much success [in your quest].

For example,
"That's interesting; let me check my schedule and I'll get back to you."
"I would absolutely love to help. I promised to get this important project completed by the end of today. Could I do it for you tomorrow?"

3. Before you provide a definitive answer, identify your emotions and assess whether your inclination is being influenced by guilt, anger, or fear.

4. In response to an email or phone message, where you have time to reflect on your answer, try the following: "What a great opportunity. I would really

enjoy participating; unfortunately, I have another commitment. I look forward to another opportunity."

5. If you decline, acknowledge the thoughtful invitation or suggestion, emphasize your regret over your "missed opportunity," and always be authentic.

58

You're No Dog—Bitch's New Paradigm

Laugh, and the world laughs with you; Weep, and you weep alone.

—Ella Wheeler Wilcox,
American author and poet

I venture to say that many of us have been called a bitch at least one time in our lives—if not, you aren't too far along in your career. I bet the reference hurt. You may have even shed a few tears. Just remember, there's a very fine line between what is and is not considered acceptable for a woman leader. The "bitch" label is easily obtained and hard to shed.

For now, let's face it—the term won't be eliminated from other people's vocabulary anytime soon. So take control and plan for the day somebody bestows this title on you. The *Key Action Tips* offer a creative, productive, and new paradigm for "bitch."

I like to remind myself and others not to take mean things that people say too seriously. Criticism is the price we pay for success. Three of my favorite quotes:

"I'm tough, I'm ambitious, and I know exactly what I want. If that makes me a bitch, okay." —Madonna Ciccone[1]

"To escape criticism, do nothing, say nothing, be nothing." —Elbert Hubbard[2]

"Why is it that men can be bastards and women must wear pearls and smile?"—Lynn Hecht Schafren[3]

Key Action Tips

1. Accept the things you cannot immediately change, including people's past impressions and biases, and focus on the present and future. While you're developing respect-centric leadership and a tough skin, be like a stereotypical man and let it roll off your back. Don't allow criticism or the bitch label to consume you. Most men certainly wouldn't give a second thought to being called a bastard—they would just laugh about it. If we are to succeed in this male-dominated business world, we need to take a page or two from their book.

2. Take a look at yourself and seek confidential feedback from people who have historically been candid with you. Each of us has areas we need to improve, and I have found for the most part that there is at least a small grain of truth in all comments about you. Once you have feedback, identify the most critical areas you need to address and get going. Most likely you can identify and implement short-term, easy-to-take steps. As importantly,

make action plans for addressing areas that require longer-term development.

3. Lastly, explore a new definition of "bitch." Try to have fun and create your own acronym. The first (or next) time you're called a bitch (probably behind your back), consider the following response: "If they mean that I am bold, intelligent, talented, creative, and hard-working, then yes I am, and very proud of it." Commit it to memory and practice it so it rolls off your tongue! Say it with confidence, yet lightheartedly. Just remember: laugh, and the world laughs with you; cry, and you cry alone![4]

Parting Thoughts

59

Put It All Together—Know Your Value

The way you treat yourself sets the standard for others.

—Sonya Friedman, *New York Times* bestselling author

One of the cornerstones of *Keys to the Corner Office* is helping women realize their value. Simply put, in order to be recognized, promoted, and fairly compensated, you must know your value. If you don't declare your value, the world will—and most likely it will be less than you're worth!

So what is value? Value starts from within and moves outward: how you feel about yourself, how you carry yourself, and how you're received. Fortunately—or not—you largely determine how you feel about yourself. Self-image is one of life's most important ingredients for happiness and success. Some say self-image is all. It's not only the little voice you allow yourself to hear every day; it's the loud voice that you project to the outside world. The world can sense your self-worth through your presence, dress, energy, voice, and attitude. By and large, your self-image significantly affects the way the world perceives and responds to you.

The subject of self-image reminds me of a significant loss in the music world. Whitney Houston was the most awarded female artist of all time—415 career awards, including six Grammies and thirty Billboard Music Awards. Yet Houston tragically descended into a world of alcohol and drugs, ultimately leading to her premature death at forty-eight. At her funeral, Kevin Costner eloquently recalled Houston's audition for her debut movie, *The Bodyguard.* "Whitney was scared ... She seemed so small and sad ... Call it doubt, call it fear. The Whitney I knew, despite her success and worldwide fame, still wondered, 'Am I good enough?' 'Am I pretty enough?' 'Will they like me?' It was the burden that made her great and the part that caused her to stumble in the end."[1] What a tragedy for someone who possessed such undeniable talent and beauty.

Houston was a classic example of a person with low self-esteem. Paradoxically, the world valued her more than she valued herself. For most of us, that won't happen. If we doubt ourselves, the world doubts us more.

Houston wasn't alone. In general, women tend to undervalue themselves. This transfers to the way we communicate about ourselves. To compound the issue, women are raised not to be boastful. For men, it's very much the opposite. Men talk up their value and accomplishments. Catherine Birndorf, clinical professor of psychiatry at New York-Presbyterian Hospital/Weill Cornell Medical Center points out that "Society teaches men that it's OK, even beneficial, to think more of themselves, while women are raised to be collaborative and primarily concerned with other people."[2]

While improving your self-worth, develop a strong brand and deliver an articulate elevator pitch, highlighting your accomplishments and goals.

A professional branding and resume writer can significantly enhance the packaging of your professional experience, your elevator pitch, and the value you bring to an employer. "Because we live in an attention-deficit business world, you need to quickly and effectively communicate your value to others. Why should someone hire you, promote you, or invite you to a board? Many people have a hard time articulating an answer to such questions," observes Mary Schumacher, principal of Career Frames. "A professional resume writer can give you the message and content that crisply demonstrates how you can solve a company's urgent problems now. Investing in professional services pays off not only in documents but in self-knowledge of your value."[3]

> If you don't declare your value, the world will—and most likely it will be less than you're worth!

In essence, talk yourself up—just like a man! The catch, as you already know, is that women who do what men do aren't always treated the way men are. So let's face it: as women, we have higher bars and heavier burdens than men. We need to be humble, but forthright. We need to balance our collaborative nature with a healthy competitive disposition. We need to respect others as well as ourselves. We need to balance our duties at home with our business duties.

To demonstrate self-respect, proactively manage your personal life and career. Give yourself praise and self-awards for accomplishments. Regularly assess how your current and previous companies are valuing your skills and experience. Armed with this data, objectively justify pay increases, promotions, or your next job. Seek companies that recognize your contributions and fairly compensate.

In all, we must know our value, communicate our worth, and secure equitable titles and compensation. This chapter's *Key Action Tips* may seem repetitive, as they've been covered in other chapters, but the tips are reemphasized because of their importance.

Key Action Tips

1. *Do things to maintain a positive attitude and positive self-image.* Don't allow the little voice in your head to minimize yourself. Remember, your thoughts become your words, and your words become your actions. Read blogs and books, and attend seminars that help you maintain your positivity. My mother—my role model and the person who instilled in me a positive self-image—swore that *Pyscho-Cybernetics*,[4] a renowned self-image book, saved her life.

2. *If you don't like the way you look, get professional advice and a makeover.* There are an amazing array of options to improve your appearance. And doing so may help improve your outlook, professional success, and income.

3. *Seek outside counsel on describing your accomplishments.* When I hired a professional resume writer, I became more impressed with myself. She took my achievements and packaged them in a way that I was unable to do for myself.

4. *Be forthright and acknowledge your accomplishments, interests, and goals.* When paid a compliment, a simple "thank you" will do. Don't minimize your achievements!

5. *Figure out who you are (your brand), what you want, and what your elevator pitch is.* Be ready to share, even if you haven't been asked yet. Read chapter 2, "Brand Yourself—Unique, Memorable, and Authentic," and chapter 49, "Roosters Crow, Hens Deliver—Successful Women Do Both."

6. *Surround yourself with encouragers, empowerers, and people who are making it happen.* It's enlightening and motivating to be around productive and supportive people. The more you are, the more likely you'll become the same.

7. *Cast a wide net.* Spend time with people who have earned your respect and achieved executive success in any arena, particularly one that interests you. Take risks; every month, contact one person you would like to meet. Make a goal of getting one or two referrals from everyone you meet. Knowing the right people will open up additional career opportunities.

8. *Find professional sponsors and mentors.* A sponsor not only provides advice, but actually champions you in your organization by publicly advocating for more responsibilities and recognition. Read chapter 4, "Sponsors and Mentors."

9. *Demonstrate a warm, enthusiastic, and positive attitude.* Be an encouraging person filled with love, kindness, hope, and faith. If you exude these qualities, you'll feel better about yourself and set yourself apart from others. It will be one of your biggest assets.

10. *Treat your career like a public relations campaign.* While remaining authentic, try to get people to

respect and like you. However, don't trade being liked for being respected. It's a delicate balance, but respect is more critical to your success. Sincerely treat everyone with kindness, empathy, and respect. Offer to help people to a degree that allows balance in your life. These actions will immeasurably enhance your career and make you feel valued.

11. *Ask for what you want and deserve.* Too often women assume good works are automatically recognized and rewarded. In reality, awards and promotions often go to the ones who talk up their accomplishments and ask for recognition.

12. *Regularly update your online presence, especially on LinkedIn.* Add highlights when you achieve quarterly goals and receive professional recognition. Your contacts will receive notice of your updates.

13. *Update relevant recruiters and executive search firms.* Make sure you target national and regional firms, including Korn/Ferry, Heidrick & Struggles, Spencer Stuart, Russell Reynolds, Berkhemer Clayton, Sanford Rose, the Domann Organization, and Kazan International.

14. *Source your worth annually by searching job sites.* You'll become more knowledgeable about current job opportunities and how other companies value experience and skills similar to your own. Use this information to negotiate as a powerful woman with your current or future company. Actualize your full worth!

60

Lastly, Lighten Up—Be a Fun, Fabulous Person!

Put on your dream hat and dance all the way to success!

—Terri Guillemets, creator of the Quote Garden

Early in my career, I felt I had to be serious to be respected. As a result, I was too intense and too serious. Too much work, too little play, fun, and laughter.

Along the way, I learned a life-changing lesson from several highly successful people: I could be more successful in both my personal and professional lives by having fun, developing hobbies, and exploring varied interests. In doing so, I better connected with people in my professional life, and it did not detract from my professionalism.

Look around at the successful people you know personally. Chances are they are multidimensional and amazing. They're fun, they don't take themselves too seriously, and they help others approach life with that attitude.

You need to have fun at work also. Enjoyment of work plays an important role in workplace attitude and success

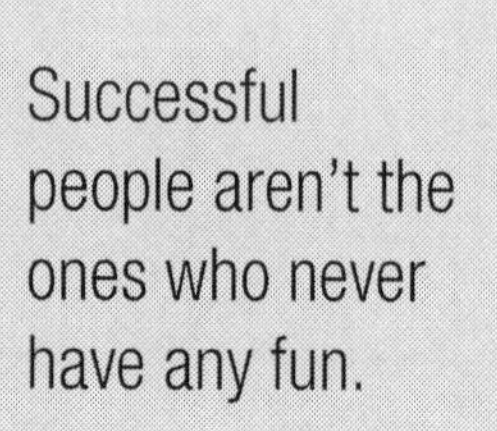
Successful people aren't the ones who never have any fun.

as a leader. Successful CEOs believe that work should be inherently enjoyable.[1]

"The happier your employees are at work, the more productive they will be," declares Angela Huffmon, keynote speaker and corporate trainer. "In order to create a more cheerful atmosphere, you must integrate fun into the whole culture of the company. This isn't something that occurs only once at the company picnic and then expect the good feeling to last all year. You must encourage light heartedness into the day-to-day operations of the business while still upholding high standards of work performance."[2]

One of the fascinating, fun, and empowering things I've learned is champagne sabering—using a sharp knife to slice the neck and cork off of a champagne bottle. When I demonstrate it, people are intrigued and want to try it. It's fun for dinner parties, team-building, and corporate celebrations. We even used it in corporate sales training as an analogy for sales perseverance: if you don't succeed (saber, or close a sale) on your first attempt—try, try, try again!

Developing a fun personal life and corporate culture helps maintain energy and keeps things in perspective, especially during stressful times. So wherever you are on the spectrum, keep striving to incorporate fun into your personal and professional life. Develop hobbies, seek interesting life experiences, and lighten up to be the fun, fabulous person you're meant to be!

Key Action Tips

1. Assess your life. Are you fun and energizing to be with? Are you involved in joyful, interesting, and rewarding activities outside of your professional life?

2. Develop a bucket list of activities and hobbies. Make a plan to achieve them. Make a goal of doing one to two—or more—of these activities each year.

3. Pursue a hobby or goal a few times a week during your lunch hour. It can be anything—a yoga class, a run, reading a book, writing a letter, or sharing a meal with a friend or colleague.

4. Inventory what you're doing to make your work life and corporate culture more enjoyable. Make a monthly or quarterly goal of doing a team-building and/or fun activity with your department, company, or colleagues. Plan a fun activity after meeting a project or corporate deadline.

5. Take time to be balanced—physically, mentally, and spiritually. Read chapter 52, "Be Balanced—Physically, Mentally, and Spiritually."

Appendix

Glass Ceilings

Glass ceilings have little or nothing to do with education, experience, and skills. Why, then, do they exist? Here's a top ten list.

1. *Upbringing.* Girls and young women are taught to get along and find consensus whereas boys and young men are generally taught to be competitive and take risks. This likely contributes to the reason women measure success differently than men. Women place higher value on interpersonal relationships with colleagues and community service; men tend to measure success by high salaries, promotional opportunities, and important job titles. Additionally, women tend not to request higher salaries or negotiate as well, at times due to perceived lack of qualifications, which rarely, if ever, stops a man.

2. *Double standards.* Men and women are judged differently for the same behavior. For instance, a man who is confident and direct may be praised for his leadership qualities, while a confident, direct woman may be considered difficult and a poor

leader. A Carnegie Mellon and Harvard study gave participants descriptions of female and male job applicants with equivalent qualifications. When examining the candidates who negotiated for a higher salary, the participants found fault with the women twice as often as they did with the men.[1]

3. *Communication style.* Given innate gender differences, communication styles between men and women are naturally different. Women generally use more words and more emotionally based language. Compounding this, women are expected to stay within a narrower band of "acceptable" communication.

4. *Ingrained bias about women's roles, abilities, commitment, and leadership style.* Examples include colleagues and customers frequently not seeing women as equal to men; (mis)perceptions about women's abilities and willingness to assume responsibilities; and counterproductive behavior of male colleagues, which includes attributing women's success to tokenism and minimizing their effectiveness and leadership ("she tries hard, she works hard"). A 2012 Yale study[2] gave participants application materials for a lab manager, who was randomly assigned either a male or female name. Subjects rated the male applicant as significantly more competent and hirable than the (identical) female applicant. The hiring participants also selected a higher starting salary and offered more career mentoring to the male applicant. Further, the hiring participants' gender did not affect responses—women and men were equally likely to exhibit bias against the female applicant.

5. *Sexual harassment.* Women too frequently experience inappropriate sexual remarks or sexual advances that place them in uncomfortable positions. This often affects their reputation and professional advancement more negatively than it does the offenders'.

6. *Traditional jobs that don't lead to management positions.* Women tend not to work in jobs that lead to management positions. This has been referred to as the "sticky floor." Sticky-floor positions include clerical work, as well as less strategic functions such as human resources and finance. Companies are sometimes also resistant to women transferring to other departments; this has been referred to as "glass walls."

7. *Lack of career and succession planning.* Companies delay succession planning because there are often higher-priority items to deal with, and it does not appear to be a value-adding task. It's also often reserved only for the highest-level leadership positions. Because not as many women have high-profile jobs or solid financial backgrounds, they're often overlooked even if the company has succession planning and career development programs.

8. *Corporate culture.* Many corporate environments are not conducive to women excelling. Factors include lack of role models, mentors, or sponsors at the highest levels; lack of flexibility in work schedules; lack of access to management training and executive education; and/or lack of opportunities for management, revenue-producing jobs, and profit and loss (P&L) responsibilities.

9. *Commitment and family responsibility.* Some women choose to spend more time on family. They dedicate less time to their career while they're employed or have career gaps due to taking time off for children.

10. *Exclusionism: Socialization and informal networks.* Women are often excluded from informal networks and communication channels where important information on organizational politics and decision making is shared. The "good old boy" network is still alive.

Recommended Reading

Chapter 1: Your Career—Care the Most

The Board Game: How Smart Women Become Corporate Directors, Betsy Berkhemer-Credaire

Career Development and Planning: A Comprehensive Approach, Robert C. Reardon, Janet G. Lenz, James P. Sampson, and Gary W. Peterson

Getting to the Top: Strategies for Career Success, Kathy Ullrich

Going to the Top: A Road Map for Success from America's Leading Women Executives, Carol A. Gallagher and Susan K. Golant

Managing Your Career (Lessons Learned), Fifty Lessons

Now Discover Your Strengths, Marcus Buckingham and Donald O. Clifton

Strengths Finder 2.0, Tom Rath

The Truth About Managing Your Career, Karen L. Otazo

Your Road Map for Success: You Can Get There from Here, John C. Maxwell

Chapter 2: Brand Yourself—Unique, Memorable, and Authentic

BrandingPays: The Five-Step System to Reinvent Your Personal Brand, Karen Kang

The Brand You 50: Fifty Ways to Transform Yourself from an "Employee" into a Brand That Shouts Distinction, Commitment, and Passion!, Tom Peters

Make a Name for Yourself: 8 Steps Every Woman Needs to Create a Personal Brand Strategy for Success, Robin Fisher Roffer

Promote Yourself: The New Rules for Career Success, Dan Schawbel

You Are a Brand!: How Smart People Brand Themselves for Business Success, Catherine Kaputa

Chapter 3: Executive Presence

Executive Presence: The Art of Commanding Respect Like a CEO, Harrison Monarth

The Hidden Factor: Executive Presence, Sally Williamson

Leadership Presence, Kathy Lubar and Belle Linda Halpern

The Power of Presence: Unlock Your Potential to Influence and Engage Others, Kristi Hedges

Seeing Yourself as Others Do: Authentic Executive Presence at Any Stage of Your Career, Carol Keers and Thomas Mungavan

Chapter 4: Sponsors and Mentors

Common Sense Mentoring, Larry Ambrose

Fostering Sponsorship Success Among High Performers and Leaders (available online), Catalyst.org

Maximizing Mentoring, and Securing Sponsorship (available online), Catalyst.org

The Mentee's Guide to Mentoring, Dr. Norman H. Cohen

So You Want to be Mentored, Stella Cowan

Unwritten Rules: What Women Need to Know About Leading in Today's Organizations, Lynn Harris

Chapter 5: Networking—Not a Dirty Word

Courting Your Career, Shawn Graham

From Business Cards to Business Relationships: Personal Branding and Profitable Networking Made Easy, 2nd edition, Allison Graham

How to Instantly Connect with Anyone, Leil Lowndes

Make Your Contacts Count, Lynne Waymon

The Start-up of You, Reid Hoffman and Ben Casnocha

Chapter 6: Talk—to Anyone, Anytime

The Complete Book of Questions: 1001 Conversation Starters for Any Occasion, Garry Poole

Confident Conversation: How to Communicate Successfully in Any Situation, Mike Bechtle

How to Instantly Connect with Anyone: 96 All-New Little Tricks for Big Success in Relationships, Leil Lowndes

How to Talk to People: The Shy Person's Guide to Confident Conversation, Kate Kennedy

How to Win Friends and Influence People, Dale Carnegie

How to Work a Room, Revised Edition: Your Essential Guide to Savvy Socializing, Susan RoAne

Just Listen: Discover the Secret to Getting Through to Absolutely Anyone, Mark Goulston, MD, and Keith Ferrazzi

Never Eat Alone, Keith Ferrazzi

Chapter 7: To Golf or Not to Golf—the Power of Informal Networks

Ben Hogan's Five Lessons: The Modern Fundamentals of Golf, Ben Hogan

A Golf Swing You Can Trust, John Hoskison

FINALLY: The Golf Swing's Simple Secret: A Revolutionary Method Proved for the Weekend Golfer to Significantly Improve Distance and Accuracy from Day One, J. F. Tamayo and J. Jaeckel

Game Time: Learn to Talk Sports in 5 Minutes a Day for Business, Jen Mueller

Golf Etiquette, Barbara Puett and Jim Apfelbaum

Playing Through: A Guide to the Unwritten Rules of Golf, Peter Post

Chapter 8: Fear—the Great Paralyzer

The Confident Woman: Start Today Living Boldly and Without Fear, Joyce Meyer

Courage: Overcoming Fear and Igniting Self-Confidence, Debbie Ford

Just Start: Take Action, Embrace Uncertainty, Create a Future, Leonard A. Schlesinger, Charles F. Kiefer, and Paul B. Brown

The Secret Thoughts of Successful Women: Why Capable People Suffer from the Imposter Syndrome and How to Thrive in Spite of It, Valerie Young, EdD

Chapter 9: *If You Don't Risk Anything, You Risk Everything*

Celebrating Failure: The Power of Taking Risks, Making Mistakes, and Thinking Big, Ralph Heath

Emotional Intelligence 2.0, Travis Bradberry and Jean Greaves

Managing the Dynamics of Change: The Fastest Path to Creating an Engaged and Productive Workplace, Jerald Jellison

Smart Women Take Risks: Six Steps for Conquering Your Fears and Making the Leap to Success, Helene Lerner

Taking Smart Risks: How Sharp Leaders Win When Stakes Are High, Doug Sundheim

Chapter 10: *Seek Revenue-Producing Jobs and Profit-and-Loss Responsibilities*

Company P&L Economics, William F. Christopher

Financial Intelligence, Revised Edition: A Manager's Guide to Knowing What the Numbers Really Mean, Karen Berman, Joe Knight, and John Case

The Sales Bible: The Ultimate Sales Resource, New Edition, Jeffrey Gitomer

Selling 101: What Every Successful Sales Professional Needs to Know, Zig Ziglar

The 25 Sales Habits of Highly Successful Salespeople, Stephan Schiffman

Chapter 11: *Know Thy Numbers*

Analysis of Financial Statements, Leopold Bernstein and John Wild

Finance and Accounting for Nonfinancial Managers: All the Basics You Need to Know, William G. Droms and Jay O. Wright

Financial Intelligence, Revised Edition: A Manager's Guide to Knowing What the Numbers Really Mean, Karen Berman, Joe Knight, and John Case

The McGraw-Hill 36-Hour Course: Finance for Non-Financial

Managers, third edition, H. George Shoffner, Susan Shelly, and Robert Cooke

Chapter 12: Ongoing Education—Invest in You

The Best Book on Top Ten MBA Admissions, David Santos, Frank Tobler, James Hu, and Jessica Wang

The Best Business Schools' Admission Secrets: A Former Harvard Business School Administration Board Member Reveals the Insider Keys to Getting In, Chioma Isiadinso

Great Applications for Business School, second edition, Paul Bodine

MBA Admissions Strategy: From Profile Building to Essay Writing, Avi Gordon

Your MBA Game Plan, Third Edition: Proven Strategies for Getting into the Top Business Schools, Omari Bouknight and Scott Shrum

Chapter 13: Loyalty—a Two-Way Street

The 5 Patterns of Extraordinary Careers: The Guide for Achieving Success and Satisfaction, James M. Citrin and Richard Smith

Getting to the Top: Strategies for Career Success, Kathy Ullrich

Great Work, Great Career, Stephen R. Covey and Jennifer Colosimo

The Leap: How 3 Simple Changes Can Propel Your Career from Good to Great, Rick Smith

The Truth About Managing Your Career, Karen L. Otazo

Chapter 14: Never Pass on New Jobs Because of "Inexperience"

Fearless Interviewing: How to Win the Job by Communicating with Confidence, Marky Stein

"Headhunter" Hiring Secrets: The Rules of the Hiring Game Have Changed... Forever!

Skip Freeman

How to Interview Like a Pro: Forty-Three Rules for Getting Your Next Job, Mary Greenwood, JD, LLM

Interview Skills: How to Get Hired NOW! Quick Job Interview Success Tips, Angela Massey

Chapter 15: Recruiters—Yes, Return All Calls

The Board Game: How Smart Women Become Corporate Directors, Betsy Berkhemer-Credaire

Directory of Executive & Professional Recruiters (Directory of Executive Recruiters), Kennedy Information BNA Subsidiaries

Guerrilla Marketing for Job Hunters 2.0: 1,001 Unconventional Tips, Tricks, and Tactics for Landing Your Dream Job, Jay Conrad and David E. Perry

"Headhunter" Hiring Secrets: The Rules of the Hiring Game Have Changed . . . Forever!, Skip Freeman and Michael Garee

Chapter 16: The Job Search—Maximize Success Through Due Diligence

The First 90 Days: Critical Success Strategies for New Leaders at All Levels, Michael Watkins

The New Leader's 100-Day Action Plan: How to Take Charge, Build Your Team, and Get Immediate Results, George B. Bradt, Jayme A. Check, and Jorge Pedraza

You're in Charge—Now What?: The 8 Point Plan, Thomas J. Neff and James, M. Citrin

Your Next Move: The Leader's Guide to Navigating Major Career Transitions, Michael Watkins

Chapter 17: Mission: Interview—Get the Offer

Competency-Based Interviews, Revised Edition: How to Master the Tough Interview Style Used by the Fortune 500s, Robin Kessler

Interview Skills: How to Get Hired NOW!: Quick Job Interview Success Tips, Angela Massey

Land That Job! The ULTIMATE Guide to Answering Interview Questions (Landing Your Job Series), Stacy Michelle

101 *Great Answers to the Toughest Interview Questions, Sixth Edition,* Ron Fry

The Quintessential Guide to Behavioral Interviewing, Katharine Hansen

60 *Seconds & You're Hired!,* Robin Ryan

What Does Somebody Have to Do to Get a Job Around Here?, Cynthia Shapiro

Chapter 18: Dare to Ask—Negotiate for Pay Raises, Promotions, and New Jobs

Dare to Ask! A Woman's Guidebook to Successful Negotiation, Cait Clarke

Getting More: How to Negotiate to Achieve Your Goals in the Real World, Stuart Diamond

Negotiating Your Salary: How to Make $1000 a Minute, Jack Chapman

Secrets of Power Negotiating, 15th Anniversary Edition: Inside Secrets from a Master Negotiator, Roger Dawson

Women Don't Ask: Negotiation and the Gender Divide, Linda Babcock and Sara Laschever

Chapter 19: First Ninety Days—Critical Success Strategies

The First 90 Days: Critical Success Strategies for New Leaders at All Levels, Michael Watkins

The Five Dysfunctions of a Team, Patrick Lencioni

The New Leader's 100-Day Action Plan: How to Take Charge, Build Your Team, and Get Immediate Results, George Bradt, Jayme A. Check, and Jorge Pedraza

You're in Charge—Now What?: The 8 Point Plan, Thomas J. Neff and James M. Citrin

Chapter 20: Marriage, Motherhood, Career Advancement—a Perfect Storm?

High-Octane Women: How Superachievers Can Avoid Burnout, Sherrie Bourg Carter

Mothers on the Fast Track: How a New Generation Can Balance Family and Career, Mary Ann Mason and Eve Mason Ekman

Telling Tales: Kids, Husbands, Career... It Can Be a Mother of a Tale, Becky Andrews and Angel Kane

Tweak It: Make What Matters to You Happen Every Day, Cali Williams Yost

What Successful People Do Before Breakfast: A Short Guide to Making Over Your Mornings—and Life, Laura Vanderkam

Chapter 21: Sexual Harassment

Back Off!: How to Confront and Stop Sexual Harassment and Harassers, Martha J. Langelan
The Sexual Harassment Handbook, Linda Gordon Howard
Sexual Harassment in the Workplace, Mary L. Boland

Chapter 22: "Fair" Is Where You Go on Rides and Eat Cotton Candy

The Glass Castle: A Memoir, Jeanette Walls
The Last Lecture, Randy Pausch and Jeffrey Zaslow
Life's Not Fair but God Is Good, Robert Schuller
Man's Search for Meaning, Viktor Frankl
What Would Lincoln Do?: Lincoln's Most Inspired Solutions to Challenging Problems and Difficult Situations, David Acord

Chapter 23: Refine Your Leadership—Before It Defines You

The Center for Creative Leadership Handbook of Leadership Development, Ellen Van Velsor, Cynthia D. McCauley, Marian N. Riderman
Climbing the Ladder in Stilettos, Lynette Lewis
Developing the Leader Within You, John C. Maxwell
How to Grow Leaders: The Seven Key Principles of Effective Development, John Eric Adair
Leading So People Will Follow, Erika Andersen
The 360 Degree Leader: Developing Your Influence from Anywhere in the Organization, John C. Maxwell

Chapter 24: Servant Leadership—It's About Others

If I Knew Then: How to Take Control of Your Career and Build the Lifestyle You Deserve, Bill. J. Bonnstetter
Leading at a Higher Level, Revised and Expanded Edition: Blanchard on Leadership and Creating High Performing Organizations, Ken Blanchard
The Servant as Leader, Robert Greenleaf
The Servant Leader, Ken Blanchard and Phil Hodges

Chapter 25: Primal Leadership

Emotional Intelligence: Why It Can Matter More Than IQ, Daniel Goleman

Enlightened Leadership: Getting to the Heart of Change, Ed Oakley and Don Krug

The EQ Edge: Emotional Intelligence and Your Success, Steven J. Stein and Howard E. Book

The Heart of Leadership: Influencing by Design: How to Inspire, Encourage and Motivate People to Follow You, Elizabeth Jeffries

Primal Leadership, Daniel Goleman, Richard E. Boyatzis, and Annie McKee

Chapter 26: Respect-Centric Leadership

Cook the Part: Delicious, Interactive and Fun Team Cooking, Karin Eastham

Harvard Business Review on Leadership, Harvard Business School Press

Helping People Win at Work, Ken Blanchard and Garry Ridge

How to Win Friends and Influence People, Dale Carnegie

Leadership & Vision: 25 Keys to Motivation, Ramon Aldag, PhD, and Buck Joseph, EdD

The 21 Irrefutable Laws of Leadership: Follow Them and People Will Follow You, John C. Maxwell

Chapter 27: Communication—More Important Than Ever

Communication: The Key to Effective Leadership, Judith Ann Pauley and Joseph F. Pauley

Communication: Principles for a Lifetime, 4th Edition, Steven A. Beebe, Susan J. Beebe, and Diana K. Ivy

Great Communication Secrets of Great Leaders, John Baldoni

Leadership: A Communication Perspective, Michael Z. Hackman and Craig E. Johnson

Speaking As a Leader: How to Lead Every Time You Speak... From Board Room to Meeting Rooms, From Town Halls to Phone Calls, Judith Humphrey

Chapter 28: *And Then There's Public Speaking*

Presenting to Win, Jerry Weissman

The Quick and Easy Way to Effective Speaking, Dale Carnegie

slide:ology: The Art and Science of Creating Great Presentations, Nancy Duarte

Speaking as a Leader: How to Lead Every Time You Speak—From Board Room to Meeting Rooms, From Town Halls to Phone Calls, Judith Humphrey

Speak Like Churchill, Stand Like Lincoln: 21 Powerful Secrets of History's Greatest Speakers, James C. Humes

10 Days to More Confident Public Speaking, Lenny Laskowski

The Well-Spoken Woman: Your Guide to Looking and Sounding Your Best, Christine K. Jahnke

Chapter 29: *Just Do It—with Confidence, Passion, and Sensitivity*

How to Develop Self-Confidence and Influence People by Public Speaking, Dale Carnegie

100 Ways to Boost Your Self-Confidence: Believe in Yourself and Others Will Too, Barton Goldsmith

Unstoppable Confidence: How to Use the Power of NLP to Be More Dynamic and Successful, Kent Sayre

What's Holding You Back?: 30 Days to Having the Courage and Confidence to Do What You Want, Meet Whom You Want, and Go Where You Want, Sam Horn

Chapter 30: *Perseverance Is King—Make That Queen!*

1001 Motivational Quotes for Success: Great Quotes from Great Minds, Thomas J. Vilord

Perseverance: Life Lessons on Leadership and Teamwork, Marc Trestman and Ross Bernstein

Unstoppable: 45 Powerful Stories of Perseverance and Triumph from People Just Like You, Cynthia Kersey

Chapter 31: Relativity Applies to Physics—Not Ethics

Business Ethics: Decision Making for Personal Integrity & Social Responsibility, Laura Hartman and Joseph DesJardins

Essentials of Business Ethics: Creating an Organization of High Integrity and Superior Performance (Essentials Series), Denis Collins

In Search of Ethics: Conversations with Men and Women of Character, Len Marrella

Chapter 32: Intelligence—IQ versus EQ

The Emotional Intelligence Activity Book: 50 Activities for Promoting EQ at Work, Adele B. Lynn

Emotional Intelligence: Why It Can Matter More Than IQ, Daniel Goleman

The EQ Edge: Emotional Intelligence and Your Success, Steven J. Stein and Howard E. Book

E-Q Equation: Develop Your Emotional Quotient and Lead a Balanced Life, Charlotte James

Chapter 33: In Piles of Crap ... Find the Pony

The Be (Happy) Attitudes: 8 Positive Attitudes That Can Transform Your Life, Robert Schuller

Breaking Murphy's Law: How Optimists Get What They Want from Life—and Pessimists Can Too, Susan Segerstrom

Little Gold Book of YES! Attitude: How to Find, Build and Keep a YES! Attitude for a Lifetime of SUCCESS, Jeffrey Gitomer

Three Complete Books: The Power of Positive Thinking; The Positive Principle Today; Enthusiasm Makes the Difference, Norman Vincent Peale

You Can If You Think You Can, Norman Vincent Peale

Chapter 34: To Lead, Inspire and Drive Change

Built to Last: Successful Habits of Visionary Companies, Jim Collins and Jerry I. Porras

Carrots and Sticks: Unlock the Power of Incentives to Get Things Done, Ian Ayres

The Change Masters, Rosabeth Moss Kanter

Managing the Dynamics of Change: The Fastest Path to Creating an Engaged and Productive Workforce, Jerald M. Jellison, PhD

Organizational Change: An Action-Oriented Toolkit, Thomas (Tupper) F. Cawsey, Gene Deszca, and Cynthia A. Ingols

Practically Radical: Not-So-Crazy Ways to Transform Your Company, Shake Up Your Industry, and Challenge Yourself, William C. Taylor

Switch: How to Change Things When Change is Hard, Chip Heath and Dan Heath

The Welch Way, Jack Welch and Suzy Welch

Chapter 35: Get Strategic—Think Big but Simplify Concepts

Blue Ocean Strategy, W. Chan Kim and Renée Mauborgne

Competitive Strategy, Michael Porter

Good to Great: Successful Habits of Visionary Companies, Jim Collins and Jerry I. Porras

Made to Stick: Why Some Ideas Survive and Other Die, Chip Heath and Dan Heath

Winning in FastTime, John A. Warden, III, and Leland A. Russell

Chapter 36: Stay Current, Identify Trends

The Art of the Long View: Planning for the Future in an Uncertain World, Peter Schwartz

Minitrends: How Innovators & Entrepreneurs Discover & Profit from Business & Technology Trends, John H. Vanston and Carrie Vanston

The Next Big Thing: Spotting and Forecasting Consumer Trends for Profit, William Higham

Trend Forecaster's Handbook, Martin Raymond

2012 *Industry Trends and Perspectives*, Booz and Company

Chapter 37: Love Thy Dissenters

The Cultural Intelligence Difference: Master the One Skill You Can't Do Without in Today's Global Economy, David Livermore, PhD

The Difference: How the Power of Diversity Creates Better Groups, Firms, Schools, and Societies (New Edition), Scott E. Page

The Five Dysfunctions of a Team: A Leadership Fable, Patrick Lencioni

Leveraging Diversity at Work: How to Hire, Retain and Inspire a Diverse Workforce for Peak Performance and Profit, Kim Olver and Sylvester Baugh

The Wisdom of Crowds, James Surowiecki

Y-Size Your Business: How Gen Y Employees Can Save You Money and Grow Your Business, Jason R. Dorsey

Chapter 38: Trust—Vital as Air

Jeffrey Gitomer's Little Teal Book of Trust: How to Earn It, Grow It, and Keep It to Become a Trusted Advisor in Sales, Business, and Life, Jeffrey H. Gitomer

The SPEED of Trust: The One Thing That Changes Everything, Stephen M. R. Covey and Rebecca R. Merrill

The Thin Book of Trust: An Essential Primer for Building Trust at Work, Charles Feltman and Sue Annis Hammond

The Truth About Trust in Business: How to Enrich the Bottom Line, Improve Retention, and Build Valuable Relationships for Success, Vanessa Hall

Chapter 39: The Platinum Rule—Know Personality Styles

People Styles at Work . . . and Beyond: Making Bad Relationships Good and Good Relationships Better, Robert Bolton and Dorothy Grover Bolton

The Platinum Rule: Discover the Four Basic Business Personalities and How They Can Lead You to Success, Tony Alessandra and Michael J. O'Connor

Power Genes: Understanding Your Power Persona—and How to Wield It at Work, Maggie Craddock

Chapter 40: Motivational Management—One Style Doesn't Fit All

Leadership and the One Minute Manager Updated Ed: Increasing Effectiveness Through Situational Leadership II, Ken Blanchard, Patricia Zigarmi, and Drea Zigarmi

Self Leadership and the One Minute Manager: Increasing Effectiveness Through Situational Self Leadership, Ken Blanchard, Susan Fowler, and Laurence Hawkins

Chapter 41: Goals, Execution, and Teamwork Will Get You Where You Need to Go

Closing the Execution Gap: How Great Leaders and Their Companies Get Results, Richard Lepsinger

Cook the Part: Delicious, Interactive and Fun Team Cooking, Karin Eastham

Execution: The Discipline of Getting Things Done, Larry Bossidy, Ram Charan, and Charles Burck

The 4 Disciplines of Execution: Achieving Your Wildly Important Goals, Chris McChesney, Sean Covey, and Jim Huling

Living in Your Top 1%: Nine Essential Rituals to Achieve Your Ultimate Life Goals, Alissa Finerman

The Other Side of Innovation: Solving the Execution Challenge, Vijay Govindarajan and Chris Trimble

Chapter 42: The Gift of Coaching

Coaching: Evoking Excellence in Others, James Flaherty

Coaching for Performance: GROWing Human Potential and Purpose—The Principles and Practice of Coaching and Leadership, Fourth Edition, John Whitmore

Coaching into Greatness: 4 Steps to Success in Business and Life, Kim George

A Manager's Guide to Coaching: Simple and Effective Ways to Get the Best from Your Employees, Anne Loehr and Brian Emerson

Topgrading: How Leading Companies Win by Hiring, Coaching, and Keeping the Best People, Bradford D. Smart, PhD

Chapter 43: Praise in Public, Criticize in Private

Carrot Tracker: The Ultimate Tool for Motivating Your Employees with Recognition, Adrian Gostick and Chester Elton

Drive: The Surprising Truth About What Motivates Us, Daniel H. Pink

Employee Engagement 2.0: How to Motivate Your Team for High Performance (A Real-World Guide for Busy Managers), Kevin Kruse

A Guide to Non-Cash Reward, Michael Rose

Make Their Day! Employee Recognition That Works—2nd Edition, Cindy Ventrice

Chapter 44: Be Friendly—Not Friends

Being the Boss: The 3 Imperatives for Becoming a Great Leader, Linda A. Hill and Kent Lineback

From Bud to Boss: Secrets to a Successful Transition to Remarkable Leadership, Kevin Eikenberry and Guy Harris

The Girl's Guide to Being a Boss (Without Being a Bitch): Valuable Lessons, Smart Suggestions, and True Stories for Succeeding as the Chick-in-Charge, Caitlin Friedman and Kimberly Yorio

Chapter 45: Your Personal Life Is Personal—Keep Most of It That Way

Fierce Conversations: Achieving Success at Work and in Life One Conversation at a Time, Susan Scott

Home and Work: Negotiating Boundaries through Everyday Life, Christena E. Nippert-Eng

Chapter 46: Slow to Hire, Quick to Fire

Boost Your Hiring I.Q., Carole Martin

From Hello to Goodbye: Proactive Tips for Maintaining Positive Employee Relations, Christine V. Walters

The Manager's Guide to HR: Hiring, Firing, Performance Evaluations, Documentation, Benefits, and Everything Else You Need to Know, Max Muller

Nuts!: Southwest Airlines' Crazy Recipe for Business and Personal Success, Kevin Freiberg, Jackie Freiberg

Topgrading, 3rd Edition: The Proven Hiring and Promoting Method That Turbocharges Company Performance, Bradford D. Smart, PhD

Chapter 47: Delegate, Empower—Then Get out of the Way

Delegating Work, Harvard Business School Press

How to Delegate, Robert Heller

151 Quick Ideas for Delegating and Decision Making, Robert E. Dittmer and Stephanie McFarland

Questions That Get Results: Innovative Ideas Managers Can Use to Improve Their Teams' Performance, Paul Cherry and Patrick Connor

Chapter 48: Crying—Best Left for Weddings and Funerals

Living Beyond Your Feelings: Controlling Emotions So They Don't Control You, Joyce Meyer

Overcoming the Seven Deadly Emotions, Michelle Borquez

There's No Crying in Business: How Women Can Succeed in Male-Dominated Industries, Roxanne Rivera

Chapter 49: Roosters Crow, Hens Deliver—Successful Women Do Both

Make a Name for Yourself: Eight Steps Every Woman Needs to Create a Personal Brand Strategy for Success, Robin Fisher Roffer

Me 2.0, Revised and Updated Edition: 4 Steps to Building Your Future, Dan Schwabel

Nice Girls Don't Get the Corner Office, Lois P. Frankel

The 10Ks of Personal Branding: Create a Better You, Kaplan Mobray

Chapter 50: Men—Thriving Amongst Differences

Break Your Own Rules: How to Change the Patterns of Thinking That Block Women's Path to Power, Mary Davis Holt

Code Switching: How to Talk So Men Will Listen, Claire Damken Brown, PhD, and Audrey Nelson, PhD

The Discreet Guide for Executive Women: How to Work Well with Men (and Other Difficulties), Jennifer K. Crittenden

How Men Think: The Seven Essential Rules for Making It in a Man's World, Adrienne Mendell, MA

The Male Mind at Work: A Woman's Guide to Working with Men, Deborah Swiss

Chapter 51: Angels and Demons—Make That Demonettes

The Bully at Work: What You Can Do to Stop the Hurt and Reclaim Your Dignity on the Job, Gary Namie and Ruth Namie

The Bully-Free Workplace: Stop Jerks, Weasels, and Snakes from Killing Your Organization, Gary Namie and Ruth F. Namie

Bullying Bosses: A Survivor's Guide, Robert Mueller

The Complete Guide to Understanding, Controlling, and Stopping Bullies and Bullying at Work: A Complete Guide for Managers, Supervisors, and Co-Workers, Margaret R. Kohut, MSW

She Wins, You Win: The Most Important Rule Every Businesswoman Needs to Know, Gail Evans

Chapter 52: Be Balanced—Physically, Mentally, and Spiritually

Balance Your Life, Balance the Scale: Ditch Dieting, Amp Up Your Energy, Feel Amazing, and Release the Weight, Jennifer Tuma-Young

Ignite Your Life!: How to Get from Where You Are to Where You Want to Be, Andrea Woolf

Life Matters: Creating a Dynamic Balance of Work, Family, Time, & Money, A. Roger Merrill and Rebecca Merrill

Off Balance: Getting Beyond the Work-Life Balance Myth to Personal and Professional Satisfaction, Matthew Kelly

Chapter 53: Ingratitude and Injustice

Life Is What You Make It: Find Your Own Path to Fulfillment, Peter Buffett

Life's Not Fair but God is Good, Robert Harold Schuller

Pay It Forward, Catherine Ryan Hyde

Tuesdays with Morrie, Mitch Albom

21 *Days of Gratitude Challenge: Finding Freedom from Self-Pity and a Negative Attitude (A Life of Gratitude),* Shelley Hitz

Chapter 54: No Room for Drama (Queens)

The Drama-Free Office: A Guide to Healthy Collaboration with Your Team, Coworkers, and Boss, Jim Warner and Kaley Klemp

The Drama-Free Workweek: How to Manage Difficult People for Workplace and Career Success, Treivor Branch

How to Reduce Workplace Conflict and Stress: How Leaders and Their Employees Can Protect Their Sanity and Productivity from Tension and Turf Wars, Anna Maravelas

The No Complaining Rule: Positive Ways to Deal with Negativity at Work, Jon Gordon

Stop Workplace Drama: Train Your Team to Have No Complaints, No Excuses, and No Regrets, Marlene Chism

Chapter 55: Multiply Success—Share Your Goals

Amazing Things Will Happen: A Real-World Guide on Achieving Success and Happiness, C.C. Chapman

Goals!: How to Get Everything You Want—Faster Than You Ever Thought Possible, Brian Tracy

Live Your Dreams: Powerful Strategies for Attaining Your Greatest Goals, Matt Byron

Smart Goal Setting: 92 Tips for Using Short Term Goals to Create a Great Life, Gary Vurnum

Chapter 56: Perfection Impedes Progress

The Effective Executive: The Definitive Guide to Getting the Right Things Done, Peter F. Drucker

Good Enough Is the New Perfect: Finding Happiness and Success in Modern Motherhood, Becky Beaupre Gillespie and Hollee Schwartz Temple

The Pursuit of Perfect: How to Stop Chasing Perfection and Start Living a Richer, Happier Life, Tal Ben-Shahar

Simply Effective: How to Cut Through Complexity in Your Organization and Get Things Done, Ron Ashkenas

Chapter 57: *Say No with Yes*

How to Say No Without Feeling Guilty: And Say Yes to More Time, More Joy, and What Matters Most to You, Patti Breitman and Connie Hatch

The Power of a Positive No: How to Say No and Still Get to Yes, William Ury

Too Nice for Your Own Good: How to Stop Making 9 Self-Sabotaging Mistakes, Duke Robinson

When I Say No, I Feel Guilty, Manuel J. Smith, PhD

"Yes" or "No": The Guide to Better Decisions, Spencer Johnson

Chapter 58: *You're No Dog—Bitch's New Paradigm*

Constructing Effective Criticism: How to Give, Receive, and Seek Productive and Constructive Criticism in Our Lives, Randy Garner, PhD

Don't Get Angry at Your Critics: 3 Techniques for Dealing with Unfair Criticism at Work and Elsewhere, Devon White

Toxic Criticism: Break the Cycle with Friends, Family, Coworkers, and Yourself, Eric Maisel

The Verbally Abusive Relationship: How to Recognize It and How to Respond, Patricia Evans

Chapter 59: *Put It All Together—Know Your Value*

Knowing Your Value: Women, Money, and Getting What You're Worth, Mika Brzezinski

Nice Girls Don't Get the Corner Office: 101 Unconscious Mistakes Women Make That Sabotage Their Careers, Lois P. Frankel, PhD

Psycho-Cybernetics, Maxwell Maltz

Women Don't Ask: The High Cost of Avoiding Negotiation—and Positive Strategies for Change, Linda Babcock and Sara Laschever

Chapter 60: *Lastly, Lighten Up—Be a Fun, Fabulous Person!*

Enjoy Life, Richard Pearce

Enjoy!: Stop Worrying and Love Life, June Saunders

The 52-Week Life Passion Project, Barrie Davenport

Fun Works: Creating Places Where People Love to Work, Leslie Yerkes and Jim Kouzes

Managing to Have Fun: How Fun at Work Can Motivate Your Employees, Inspire Your Coworkers, and Boost Your Bottom Line, Matt Weinstein

Notes

Part I: Turbocharge Your Career

Introduction

1. Marianne Schnall,"What Will It Take to Get a Women in the White House?" *The Daily Beast,* November 11, 2013, accessed November 11, 2013, http://www.thedailybeast.com/witw/articles/2013/11/11/what-will-it-take-to-make-a-woman-president.html.
2. Leslie Bennetts, "Women and the Leadership Gap," *Newsweek,* March 5, 2012, accessed August 3, 2013, http://www.thedailybeast.com/newsweek/2012/03/04/the-stubborn-gender-gap.html.
3. Melissa J. Anderson, "Three Ways Executive Search Firms Can Boost Women on Boards," TheGlassHammer.com, October 11, 2012, accessed December 12, 2012, www.theglasshammer.com/news/2012/11/three-ways-executive-search-firms-can-boost-women-on-boards.
4. US Bureau of Labor Statistics, "Highlights of Women's Earnings in 2012," October 2013, accessed November 10, 2013, http://www.bls.gov/cps/cpswom2012.pdf.
5. Paula Vasan, "Investors Fight for Women on Boards," February 6, 2013, accessed March 11, 2013, http://www.ai-cio.com/channel/NEWSMAKERS/Investors_FIght_for_Women_on_Boards.html.
6. Marilyn Nagel, "California Passes First Legislation to Encourage More Women on Boards," *Huffington Post,* August 28, 2013, accessed September 14, 2013, http://www.huffing-

tonpost.com/marilyn-nagel/california-passes-first-legistlation-to-encourage-more-women-on-boards_b_3831479.html?goback=%2Egde_3381466_member_271905069#21.

Chapter 1: Your Career—Care the Most

1. John Bussey, "How Women Can Get Ahead: Advice From Female CEOs," *Wall Street Journal,* May 18, 2012, accessed May 19, 2013, http://online.wsj.com/article/SB10001424052702303879604577410520511235252.html.

Chapter 2: Brand Yourself—Unique, Memorable, and Authentic

1. "Best Global Brands: The Top 100 List," 2013, accessed November 11, 2013, http://interbrand.com/en/best-global-brands/2013/top-100-list-view.aspx.
2. Dan Schawbel, "How to Brand Yourself: An Introduction," *Entrepreneur,* November 1, 2010, accessed September 1, 2013, http://www.entrepreneur.com/article/217481.
3. "Branding Expert Karen Kang Says Reinvent Your Brand in 2013 or Be Left behind," *Bellevue News,* January 10, 2013, accessed September 14, 2013, http://bellevuebusinessjournal.com/2013/01/10/branding-expert-karen-kang-says-reinvent-your-brand-2013-or-be-left-behind/.
4. Deborah Jondall, personal communication, February 1, 2012.
5. Mary Schumacher (http://www.careerframes.com), personal communication, September 23, 2013.

Chapter 3: Executive Presence

1. Jennifer K. Crittenden, "Creating Exceptional Presence: Excerpt from the Program Handbook," *The Discreet Guide for Executive Women,* accessed September 2, 2013, http://www.discreetguide.com/executive-presence/creating-executive-presence-an-excerpt-from-the-course-handbook/.
2. Vanessa Ko, "Deep-voiced bosses bring in the big bucks, says study," *CNN,* May 30, 2013, accessed September 7, 3013, http://edition.cnn.com/2013/05/29/business/ceo-deep-voice-more-money.
3. Amy Cuddy, "Your Body Language Shapes Who You Are," *Huffington Post,* January 11, 2013, accessed September 2,

2013, http://www.huffingtonpost.com/amy-cuddy/body-language_b_2451277.html?utm_hp_ref=email_share.

4. Cuddy, "Your Body Language Shapes Who You Are."
5. Ko, "Deep-voiced bosses bring in the big bucks, says study."
6. Deborah Jondall, personal communication, September 10, 2013.
7. Nancy L. Etcoff, Shannon Stock, Lauren E. Haley, Sarah A. Vickery, and David M. House, "Cosmetics as a Feature of the Extended Human Phenotype: Modulation of the Perception of Biologically Important Facial Signals," *PLOS ONE* 6(10) (2011): e25656. doi:10.1371/journal.pone.0025656, accessed September 7, 2013, http://www.plosone.org/article/info:doi%2F10.1371%2Fjournal.pone.0025656.

Chapter 4: Sponsors and Mentors

1. Melissa J. Anderson, "How Sponsorship Can Help Senior Women Break the Marzipan Ceiling," *The Glass Hammer,* January 19, 2011, accessed January 21, 2011, http://www.theglasshammer.com/news/2011/01/19/how-sponsorship-can-help-senior-women-break-the-marzipan-ceiling/.
2. Sylvia Ann Hewlett, "What Women Need to Advance: Sponsorship," *Forbes,* August 25, 2011, accessed November 30, 2013, http://www.forbes.com/sites/sylviaannhewlett/2011/08/25/what-women-need-to-advance-sponsorship/.
3. Anderson, "How Sponsorship Can Help Senior Women Break the Marzipan Ceiling."
4. Joanna Barsh and Lareina Yee, "Unlocking the full potential of women at work" (McKinsey & Company, 2012), accessed April 1, 2012, http://online.wsj.com/public/resources/documents/womenreportnew.pdf.

Chapter 5: Networking—Not a Dirty Word

1. "Networking and Pay," *The Economist,* November 12, 2011, accessed June 23, 2013, http://www.economist.com/node/21538162.
2. Kathryn Minshew, "Never Say No to Networking," *Harvard Business Review Blogs,* October 18, 2012, accessed October 19, 2012, http://blogs.hbr.org/2012/10/the-serendipitous-entrepreneur/.
3. Minshew, "Never Say No to Networking."

4. Todd Wasserman, "8 Job Search Tips From the Co-Founder of LinkedIn," *Mashable*, February 15, 2012, accessed February 16, 2012, http://mashable.com/2012/02/15/reid-hoffman-linkedin-job-tips/.
5. Lorraine Herr, personal communication, August 25, 2013.
6. Lauren Tanny, personal communication, April 10, 2013.

Chapter 6: Talk—to Anyone, Anytime

1. "12 tips for making small talk," *CNN.com*, March 4, 2005, accessed March 2, 2013, http://www.cnn.com/2005/US/Careers/03/03/small.talk/index.html.
2. Allison Graham, "Hate Small Talk? These 5 Questions Will Help You Work Any Room," *Fast Company*, July 27, 2012, accessed March 2, 2013, http://www.fastcompany.com/1843753/hate-small-talk-these-5-questions-will-help-you-work-any-room.
3. Maya Angelou said it best: "People will forget what you said. People will forget what you did. But people will never forget how you made them feel." *Goodreads*, accessed September 14, 2013, http://www.goodreads.com/quotes/5934-i-ve-learned-that-people-will-forget-what-you-said-people.
4. "12 tips for making small talk," *CNN.com*.

Chapter 7: To Golf or Not to Golf—the Power of Informal Networks

1. "Women On Top Interview," *Washington DC Women's Weekly*, April 29, 2012, accessed June 23, 2013, http://www.womensweekly-wdc.com/women-on-top/rose-harper/.
2. Jamie Rosvall Cantu, personal communication, April 1, 2013.

Chapter 8: Fear—the Great Paralyzer

1. *Goodreads.com*, accessed September 14, 2013, http://www.goodreads.com/quotes/73915-what-would-you-attempt-to-do-if-you-knew-you.
2. Modified from quote by Robert H. Schuller, *Thinkexist.com*, accessed December 27, 2013, http://thinkexist.com/quotation/if_you_listen_to_your_fears-you_will_die_never/14600.html.
3. Kimberly Ann Holle, "Fear: Mastering the negative end of the emotional continuum," *examiner.com*, April 19, 2013, accessed September 15, 2013, http://www.examiner.com/article/fear-mastering-the-negative-end-of-the-emotional-continuum/

4. Adam Bluestein, Leigh Buchanan, Issie Lapowsky, and Eric Schurenbery, "The Rules," *Inc.*, February 2013.
5. Ashlee Gora, personal communication, April 1, 2013.
6. Barbara Rocha, "What Dr. Michael Gervais told Misty May-Treanor and Kerri Walsh Jennings," *Getting Over Yourself*, August 7, 2012, accessed December 2, 2013, http://gettingoveryourself.wordpress.com/tag/olympics/.

Chapter 9: If You Don't Risk Anything, You Risk Everything

1. John Bussey, "How Women Can Get Ahead: Advice From Female CEOs," *Wall Street Journal*, May 18, 2012, accessed May 19, 2013, http://online.wsj.com/article/SB10001424052702303879604577410520511235252.html.
2. Cate Goethals, personal communication, September 1, 2013.
3. Catherine C. Eckel, "Men, Women and Risk Aversion: Experimental Evidence," accessed February 27, 2013, http://aysps.gsu.edu/sipfiles/ISP_Ind_3.pdf.
4. Julie A. Nelson, "Are Women Really More Risk-Averse than Men?" September 21, 2012, accessed February 27, 2013, https://papers.ssrn.com/sol3/papers.cfm?abstract_id=2158950.
5. Sheryl Ball, Catherine C. Eckel, and Maria Heracleous, "Risk aversion and physical prowess: Prediction, choice and bias," *Journal of Risk and Uncertainty* 41, no. 3 (2010): 167–193, accessed February 27, 2013, http://www.springerlink.com/index/10.1007/s11166-010-9105-x.
6. Friedrich Nietzsche, *Twilight of the Idols* (1888), quoted in *The Quotations Page*, accessed September 15, 2013, http://www.quotationspage.com/quote/38037.html.
7. Emilie Richards, "Sunday Inspiration: 'The danger lies in refusing to face the fear…,'" *Emilie Richards*, November 3, 2013, accessed December 2, 2013, http://www.emilierichards.com/blog/2013/11/sunday-inspriation-the-danger-lies-in-refusing-to-face-the-fear/.
8. Goodreads.com, accessed December 2, 2013, http://www.goodreads.com/quotes/tag/failure.
9. Baberuth.com, accessed September 15, 2013, http://www.baberuth.com/quotes/.
10. Brainyquote.com, accessed December 2, 2013, http://brainyquote.com/quotes/authors/b/brain_tracy.html.

Chapter 10: Seek Revenue-Producing Jobs and Profit-and-Loss Responsibilities

1. Acknowledgement and gratitude to Philip Press.
2. Michelle V. Stacy, "Stepping Back to Lead Better," *New York Times,* November 17, 2012, accessed December 16, 2012, http://www.nytimes.com/2012/11/18/jobs/keurigs-president-on-stepping-back-to-lead-better.html.

Chapter 11: Know Thy Numbers

1. Tara Siegel Bernard, "Financial Advice by Women for Women," *New York Times,* April 23, 2010, accessed February 22, 2013, http://www.nytimes.com/2010/04/24/your-money/24money.html?_r=0.

Chapter 12: Ongoing Education—Invest in You

1. "College Graduates Earn 84% More Than High School Grads, Study Says," *Huffington Post,* September 15, 2013, accessed September 15, 2013, http://www.huffingtonpost.com/2011/08/05/college-graduates-earn-84_n_919579.html.
2. Kent Hill, Dennis Hoffman, and Tom R. Rex, *The Value of Higher Education* (Tempe, Arizona: L.W. Seidman Research Institute and Arizona State University, 2005), accessed January 15, 2013, http://wpcarey.asu.edu/seidman/Reports/P3/ValueOfEducation_10-05.pdf.
3. Jana Morrelli, personal communication, December 1, 2013.
4. Hill, Hoffman, and Rex, *The Value of Higher Education.*
5. Jené Luciani, "28 Powerful Women Share Their Best Advice," *Shape,* August 13, 2013, accessed September 21, 2013, http://www.shape.com/celebrities/interviews/28-powerful-women-share-their-best-advice?page=17.

Chapter 13: Loyalty—a Two-Way Street

1. "Are women more loyal to employers than men?" *Financial Times,* July 27, 2011, accessed February 20, 2013, http://www.ft.com/cms/s/0/5e761258-b830-11e0-823-00144feabdc0.html.
2. J. Ricker, "Study dispels perception that women leave jobs more than men do," April 2002, accessed February 20, 2013, http://www.apa.org/monitor/apr02/ispels/aspx.
3. Lauren Tanny, personal communication, April 10, 2013.

Chapter 14: Never Pass on New Jobs Because of "Inexperience"

1. Laura Petrecca, "More women on tap to lead top companies," *USA Today*, October 26, 2011, accessed February 27, 2013, http://usatoday30.usatoday.com/MONEY/usaedition/2011-10-27-New-IBM-CEO-_ST_U.htm.
2. Melissa J. Anderson, "Voice of Experience: Lisa Sawicki, Partner, Assurance, PwC," *The Glass Hammer*, February 6, 2012, accessed February 24, 2013, http://www.theglasshammer.com/news/2012/02/06/voice-of-experience-lisa-sawicki-partner-assurance-pcw/.
3. Jessi Hempel, "IBM's Ginni Rometty: Growth and comfort do not coexist," *CNNMoney*, October 5, 2011, accessed February 27, 2013, http://management.fortune.cnn.com/2011/10/05/ibms-ginni-rometty-growth-and-comfort-do-not-coexist/.

Chapter 15: Recruiters—Yes, Return All Calls

1. Betsy Berkhemer-Credaire, personal communication, September 29, 2013.
2. Berkhemer-Credaire, personal communication.
3. Acknowledgement and gratitude to Betsy Berkhemer-Credaire for her contributions throughout this chapter.

Chapter 16: The Job Search—Maximize Success Through Due Diligence

1. George B. Bradt, Jayme A. Check, and Jorge E. Pedraza, *The New Leader's 100-Day Action Plan: How to Take Charge, Build Your team, and Get Immediate Results* (Hoboken, New Jersey: John Wiley & Sons, Inc., 2006), 31.

Chapter 17: Mission: Interview—Get the Offer

1. Carole Martin, "The Ultimate Secret of Acing Behavioral Interviews," *Hcareers*, accessed November 30, 2013, http://www.hcareers.com/us/resourcecenter/tabid/306/articleid/963/default.aspx.
2. Caroline Howard, "Best Questions to Ask in Your Job Interview," *HireStrategy*, accessed September 15, 2013, http://www.hirestrategy.com/articles/feature_content.asp?id=1123.
3. Joy Bridges, "How to Use Psychology to Ace the Interview,"

HCareers, accessed September 15, 2013, http://www.hcareers.com/us/resourcecenter/tabid/306/articleid/934/default.aspx.

Chapter 18: Dare to Ask—Negotiate for Pay Raises, Promotions, and New Jobs

1. Linda Babcock, Sara Laschever, Michele Gelfand, and Deborah Small, "Nice Girls Don't Ask," *Harvard Business Review*, October 2003, accessed September 15, 2013, http://hbr.org/2003/10/nice-girls-dont-ask/.
2. Babcock et al., "Nice Girls Don't Ask."
3. Patricia Sellers, "Will the next Facebook be founded by a woman?" *CNNMoney*, October 4, 2011, accessed November 5, 2011, http://postcards.blogs.fortune.cnn.com/2011/10/04/will-the-next-facebook-be-founded-by-a-woman/.
4. Peggy Klaus, "Neither Mice Nor Men," *New York Times*, March 6, 2010, accessed June 1, 2010, http://www.nytimes.com/2010/03/07/jobs/07preoccupations.html.
5. Heidi Grant Halvorson, "The One-Minute Trick to Negotiating Like a Boss," *Harvard Business Review Blogs*, June 11, 2013, accessed September 1, 2013, http://blogs.hbr.org/2013/06/the-1-minute-trick-to-negotiat/.
6. Valerie Carricaburu, personal communication, July 23, 2013.
7. "Interview with Author Cait Clark in Lawyer Magazine," *Women Negotiating*, December 20, 2010, accessed September 15, 2013, http://womennegotiating.com/2010/12/interview-with-author-cait-clarke-in-lawyer-magazine/.
8. Kelly Powers, personal communication, December 1, 2013.
9. Amanda Augustine, "How to Respond to the Question, 'What Are Your Salary Requirements?'" *The Ladders*, October 23, 2012, accessed September 15, 2013, http://info.theladders.com/blog/bid/161918/How-to-Respond-to-the-Question-What-Are-Your-Salary-Requirements-Ask-Amanda.

Chapter 19: First Ninety Days—Critical Success Strategies

1. Anne Fisher, "New job? Get a head start now," *CNNMoney*, February 17, 2012, accessed June 23, 2013. http://management.fortune.cnn.com/2012/02/17/new-job-head-start/.
2. Anne Fisher, "Ace your first 100 days in a new job," *CNNMoney*,

January 20, 2009, accessed February 24, 2013, http://money.cnn.com/2009/01/19/news/economy/start.job.fortune/index.htm.

3. Roz Walker, "Improve Your Chances of Being Hired with a 90-day Plan," *Yahoo Voices*, February 17, 2009, accessed September 16, 2013, http://voices.yahoo.com/improve-chances-being-hired-90-day-2628854.html.
4. "Business Prof's Research in *Wall Street Journal*," *Clarkson University*, March 30, 2011, accessed September 16, 2013, http://www.clarkson.edu/news/2011/news-release_2011-03-30-1.html.
5. Anne Fisher, "New job?"
6. Adapted from *The New Leader's 100-Day Action Plan* and *The First 90 Days.*

Chapter 20: Marriage, Motherhood, Career Advancement—a Perfect Storm?

1. Lucy Kellaway, "Breaking the glass ceiling at home," *Financial Times*, November 19, 2010, accessed February 17, 2013, http://www.ft.com/cms/s/0/ea15f318-f428-11df-89a6-00144feab49a.html#axzz2LDvcT4PP.
2. Sherrie Bourg Carter, "Motherhood versus Career: The Epic Battle that Need Not Be," *Psychology Today*, November 29, 2011, accessed September 15, 2013, http://www.psychologytoday.com/blog/high-octane-women/201111/motherhood-versus-career-the-epic-battle-need-not-be.
3. John Bussey, "How Women Can Get Ahead: Advice From Female CEOs," *Wall Street Journal*, May 18, 2012, accessed May 19, 2013, http://online.wsj.com/article/SB10001424052702303879604577410520511235252.html.
4. Celine Peters, personal communication, April 1, 2013.
5. Caroline Cox, "Print Pioneer in a Web World," *Little Pink Book*, May 20, 2013, accessed June 1, 2013, http://www.littlepinkbook.com/christine-osekoski-publisher-fast-company/.
6. Sherrie Bourg Carter, *High-Octane Women: How Superachievers Can Avoid Burnout* (New York: Prometheus Books, 2011), 70.

Chapter 21: Sexual Harassment

1. Hien DeYoung, personal communication, September 16, 2013.

Chapter 22: "Fair" Is Where You Go on Rides and Eat Cotton Candy

1. *Tiny Buddha,* accessed August 3, 2013, http://tinybuddha.com/wisdom-quotes/if-you-don-t-like-something-change-it-if-you-can-t-change-it-change-the-way-you-think-about-it/.
2. The chapter title and quote is attributed to my beloved niece, Shelby Lee Rhyne.

Part II: Unleash the Leader Within

Chapter 23: Refine Your Leadership—Before It Defines You

1. Nicholas Carlson, "The Truth About Marissa Mayer: She Has Two Contrasting Reputations," *Business Insider,* July 17, 2012, accessed August 1, 2012, http://www.businessinsider.com/the-truth-about-marissa-mayer-she-has-two-contrasting-reputations-2012-7.
2. Carlson, "The Truth About Marissa Mayer."
3. "How Can Young Women Develop a Leadership Style," *Wall Street Journal,* accessed February 24, 2013, http://guides.wsj.com/management/developing-a-leadership-style/how-can-young-women-develop-a-leadership-style/.
4. Mindy Bortness, personal communication, August 1, 2013.

Chapter 24: Servant Leadership—It's About Others

1. Robert Greenleaf, *The Servant as Leader,* accessed July 4, 2013, http://www.benning.army.mil/infantry/199th/ocs/content/pdf/The%20Servant%20as%20Leader.pdf?
2. Mindy Bortness, personal communication, August 1, 2013.

Chapter 25: Primal Leadership

1. Robert Safian, "The Secrets of Generation Flux Leader," *Fast Company,* November 2012, 9.
2. Safian, "The Secrets of Generation Flux Leader," 101.
3. "Leadership Styles," *Wall Street Journal,* adapted from Alan Mury, *Wall Street Journal Guide to management,*" accessed September 15, 2013, http://guides.wsj.com/management/developing-a-leadership-style/how-to-develop-a-leadership-style/.
4. Safian, "The Secrets of Generation Flux Leader," 101.

5. Adapted from *Primal Leadership*, Daniel Goleman, Annie McKee, and Richard E. Boyatzis.

Chapter 26: Respect-Centric Leadership

1. "Respect-centric leadership" was created and trademarked by Rhonda Rhyne.

Chapter 27: Communication—More Important Than Ever

1. Judith Humphrey, *Speaking as a Leader: How to Lead Every Time You Speak… From Boardrooms to Meeting Rooms, From Town Halls to Phone Calls* (Mississauga, Ontario: John Wiley & Sons Canada, Ltd., 2013), 2.
2. Tia Ghose, "People Prefer Female Leaders With Deeper Voices," *LiveScience*, December 12, 2012, accessed February 26, 2013, http://www.livescience.com/25485-people-prefer-manly-voiced-leaders.html.
3. Devonia Smith, "Kirsten Powers: Palin & Bachmann should 'Get voice coaches'—Hillary did," *Examiner.com*, April 19, 2011, accessed February 25, 2013, http://www.examiner.com/article/kirsten-powers-palin-bachmann-should-get-voice-coaches-hillary-did.
4. Kathy Johanson, personal communication, March 25, 2013.
5. Dr. Nicole Fitzhugh, "Leadership 101" excerpt from Hay Group survey (Lamb, McKee, 2004), accessed June 26, 2013, http://www.counselorleadership.wikispaces.com/file/view/2-Week2-Leadership.ppt.
6. "Summary: Great Communication Secrets of Great Leaders—John Baldoni," *Business News Publishing*, 2013, accessed September 16, 2013, http://books.google.com/books?id=Y_Spf59nirEC&pg=PT1&lpg=PT1&dq=John+Baldoni+Just+as+there+is+no+single+way+to+lead&source=bl&ots=huMitjJ4qG&sig=BhxHnRpqCrrx3i1y6EgxYQaHofM&hl=en&sa=X&ei=hMU3UpmOD5GYigLwrYHoDw&ved=0CDUQ6AEwAw#v=onepage&q=John%20Baldoni%20Just%20as%20there%20is%20no%20single%20way%20to%20lead&f=false.

Chapter 28: And Then There's Public Speaking

1. "Fear of Public Speaking Statistics—Staggering Numbers," accessed February 21, 2013, http://www.thefearofpublicspeaking.com/fear-of-public-speaking-statistics.html.

2. "Fear of Public Speaking Statistics."
3. Yale Law Women, *Yale Law School Faculty and Students Speak Up about Gender: Ten Years Later,* April 2012, accessed February 21, 2013, http://www.law.yale.edu/documents/pdf/Student_Organizations/YLW_SpeakUpStudy.pdf.
4. Christine Jahnke, *The Well-Spoken Woman: Your Guide to Looking and Sounding Your Best,* accessed September 16, 2013, http://books.google.com/books?id=UzspaAmh3gsC&pg=PT10&lpg=PT10&dq=Christine+Jahnke+The+glass+ceiling+is+cracked,+yet+women+still+wage+battles&source=bl&ots=Bgx8D60X6d&sig=yqP3BdK27JslrLMs9wIppyEmzqA&hl=en&sa=X&ei=VMs3Ur7CHuTAigKowoDwCA&ved=0CCsQ6AEwAA#v=onepage&q=Christine%20Jahnke%20The%20glass%20ceiling%20is%20cracked%2C%20yet%20women%20still%20wage%20battles&f=false.
5. Betty Sue Flowers, "Dividing Your Writing Project into Manageable Tasks," *Harvard Business Review,* February 4, 2013, accessed March 1, 2013, http://hbr.org/tip2013/02/04/divide-your-writing-project-into-manageable-tasks.

Chapter 29: Just Do It—with Confidence, Passion, and Sensitivity

1. Hannah Furness, "Key to career success is confidence, not talent," *The Telegraph,* August 14, 2012, accessed September 16, 2013, http://www.telegraph.co.uk/news/uknews/9474973/Key-to-career-success-is-confidence-not-talent.html.
2. Eleanor Roosevelt, *This Is My Story,* accessed July 20, 2013, http://www.goodreads.com/quotes/11035-no-one-can-make-you-feel-inferior-without-your-consent.

Chapter 30: Perseverance Is King—Make That Queen!

1. *Brainy Quote,* accessed September 16, 2013, http://www.brainyquote.com/quotes/quotes/c/calvincool414555.html.
2. *Brainy Quote,* access September 16, 2013, http://www.brainyquote.com/quotes/quotes/a/alberteins133991.html.
3. Gene Kranz, *Failure Is Not an Option* (New York: Simon & Schuster, 2000).
4. Thanks to Paul Jansen and Kevin Wagner.
5. *Fact Monster,* accessed July 13, 2013, http://www.factmonster.com/ipka/A0906931.html.

Chapter 31: Relativity Applies to Physics—Not Ethics

1. "Extra Thinking Time Leads to Ethical Decisions," *The Daily Stat,* January 31, 2012, accessed February 1, 2012, http://web.hbr.org/email/archive/dailystat.php?date=013112.
2. From a quote commonly attributed to Albert Einstein.

Chapter 32: Intelligence—IQ versus EQ

1. Lucia Moses, "Surprise: Male and Female Execs Are Held to Different Standards," February 27, 2013, accessed March 6, 2013, http://www.adweek.com/advertising-branding/surprise-male-and-female-execs-are-held-different-standards-147455.
2. "Beginning to Understand Our Emotional Intelligence," *UCSF Human Resources,* accessed September 16, 2013, http://ucsfhr.ucsf.edu/index.php/assist/article/beginning-to-understanding-our-emotional-intelligence/.

Chapter 33: In Piles of Crap … Find the Pony

1. Martha Mangelsdorf, "Why It Pays To Be An Optimist," *Forbes.com,* February 18, 2011, accessed March 3, 2013, http://www.forbes.com/2011/02/18/optimism-job-success-payleadership-careers-promotions.html.
2. Fiona Parashar, "Optimism and Pessimism," *Positive Psychology UK,* accessed March 4, 2013, http://www.positivepsychology.org.uk/pp-theory/optimism/98-optimism-and-pessimism.html.
3. Hannah Seligson, "Optimism Breeds Success," *Daily News,* May 7, 2008, accessed March 4, 2013, http://www.nydailynews.com/jobs/optimism-breeds-success-article-1.328859.
4. Parashar, "Optimism and Pessimism."
5. Daniel Goleman, "Research Affirms Power of Positive Thinking," *New York Times,* February 3, 1987, accessed March 4, 2013, http://www.nytimes.com/1987/02/03/science/research-affirms-power-of-psotive-thinking.html.
6. *Brainy Quote,* accessed January 12, 2014, http://www.brainyquote.com/quotes/quotes/n/normanvinc130593.html.

Chapter 34: To Lead, Inspire and Drive Change

1. Jack and Suzy Welch, "What Change Agents Are Made Of," *Bloomberg Businessweek Magazine,* October 8, 2008, accessed

September 16, 2013, http://www.businessweek.com/stories/2008-10-08/what-change-agents-are-made-of.

2. "Lessons for 2013," *Fast Company.com,* December 2012/January 2013, 89.
3. Jim Collins and Jerry I. Porras, *Built to Last: Successful Habits of Visionary Companies* (New York: HarperCollins, 2002).
4. Kathy Johanson, personal communication, March 20, 2013.
5. Rosabeth Moss Kanter, "Seven Truths about Change to Lead By and Live By," *HBR Blog Network,* August 23, 2010, accessed February 24, 2013, http://blogs.hbr.org/kanter/2010/08/seven-truths-about-change-to-l.html.
6. Jone Johnson Lewis, "Rosalynn Carter Quotes," *About.com,* accessed July 20, 2013, http://womenshistory.about.com/od/quotes/a/rosalynn_carter.htm.

Chapter 35: Get Strategic—Think Big but Simplify Concepts

1. Jim Collins and Jerry I. Porras, *Built to Last: Successful Habits of Visionary Companies* (New York: HarperCollins, 2002).
2. Winston Perez, *Concept Modeling,* accessed December 2, 2013, http://www.conceptmodeling.com/.
3. Michael Cieply, "Enough with the Elevator Pitch. What's the Concept?" *New York Times,* December 25, 2010, accessed January 9, 2013, http://www.nytimes.com/2010/12/26/business/26steal.html?_r=0.
4. Chip Heath and Dan Heath, *Made to Stick: Why Some Ideas Survive and Others Die* (New York: Random House, 2008).
5. Famously uttered by Gene Kranz, flight director of Apollo 13. *Goodreads,* accessed July 21, 2013, http://www.goodreads.com/author/quotes/81570.Gene_Kranz.

Chapter 36: Stay Current, Identify Trends

1. Robert Safian, "Secrets of the Flux Leader," *FastCompany,* November 2012, 136.
2. Peter Schwartz, "An excerpt from *The Art of the Long View: Planning for the Future in an Uncertain World,*" accessed July 20, 2013, http://www.wiley.com/legacy/wileychi/strat100/readingroom2.htm.

Chapter 37: Love Thy Dissenters

1. E. Baker and C. Fernandez, "The Management Moment: Creating Thought Diversity: The Antidote to Group Think," *Journal of Public Health Management & Practice* 13, no. 6 (December 2007): 670–671.
2. Randy Hain, "Diversity of Thought: The Next Frontier," *Inside NAPS*, October 2007, accessed September 16, 2013, http://www.belloaks.com/media/BAhbBlsHOgZmIkMyMDExL-zEyLzI4LzEyXzM5XzAyXzIyNV9EaXZlcnNpdHlfaW5zaW-RlX05BUFNfT2Nob2Jlcl8yMDA3LnBkZg.

Part III: Ignite Your Management

1. Peter F. Drucker, *The Essential Drucker: Management, the Individual and Society*, accessed June 23, 2013, http://www.goodreads.com/author/quotes/12008.Peter_F_Drucker.

Chapter 38: Trust—Vital as Air

1. Chris Sandlund, "Trust is a Must," *Entrepreneur*, September 30, 2002, accessed February 1, 2014, http://www.entrepreneur.com/article/55354#.
2. Vanessa Hall, "Why Women Are More Trusted Than Men and How to Use Trust to Our Advantage," *The Glass Hammer*, March 11, 2011, accessed April 1, 2011, http://www.theglasshammer.com/news/2011/03/11/why-women-are-more-trusted-than-men-and-how-to-use-trust-to-our-advantage/.
3. Hall, "Why Women Are More Trusted Than Men."

Chapter 39: The Platinum Rule—Know Personality Styles

1. Tony Alessandra, "The Platinum Rule," accessed September 19, 2013, http://www.mindperk.com/dvdnotes/PlatinumRuleGuide.pdf.
2. Tony Alessandra, "Behavioral Styles," accessed September 19, 2013, http://ver5.elliswyatt.com/RiteWay/menus/documents/behaviorstyles/behavioralstyles.ppt.
3. Robert Bolton and Dorothy Grover Bolton, *People Styles at Work and Beyond*, 2nd ed. (New York: AMACOM, 2009).

Chapter 40: Motivational Management—One Style Doesn't Fit All

1. K. Blanchard, P. Zigarmi, and D. Zigarmi, *Leadership and the One Minute Manager: Increasing Effectiveness Through Situational Leadership II* (New York: HarperCollins, 1985).

Chapter 41: Goals, Execution, and Teamwork Will Get You Where You Need to Go

1. Larry Bossidy, Ram Charan, and Charles Burck, *Execution: The Discipline of Getting Things Done.*
2. Dan Tynan, "25 Ways to Reward Employees (Without Spending a Dime)," *HR World,* accessed September 19, 2013, http://www.hrworld.com/features/25-employee-rewards/.

Chapter 42: The Gift of Coaching

1. Susan M. Heathfield, "Use Employee Coaching to Improve Performance," *About.com,* accessed February 22, 2013, http://www.humanresources.about.com/od/glossaryc/g/coaching.htm.
2. Bradford D. Smart, *Topgrading: How Leading Companies Win by Hiring, Coaching, and Keeping the Best People* (Prentice Hall Press, 1999).

Chapter 43: Praise in Public, Criticize in Private

1. Tom Rath and Donald O. Clifton, "The Power of Praise and Recognition," *Gallup Business Journal,* July 8, 2004, accessed August 1, 2011, http://businessjournal.gallup.com/content/12157/power-praise-recognition.aspx. Excerpted from *How Full Is Your Bucket,* Expanded Anniversary Edition (New York: Gallup Press, 2004, 2009).
2. Kathy Johanson, personal communication, April 2, 2013.
3. *Brainy Quote,* accessed September 21, 2013, http://www.brainyquote.com/quotes/c/catherinet108926.html.
4. Rath and Clifton, "The Power of Praise and Recognition."

Chapter 44: Be Friendly—Not Friends

1. Dorie Clark, "Debunking The 'No Friends At Work' Rule: Why Friend-Friendly Workplaces Are The Future," *Forbes,* May 21, 2013, accessed July 20, 2013, http://www.forbes.com/sites/

dorieclark/2013/05/21/debunking-the-no-friends-at-work-rule-why-friend-friendly-workplaces-are-the-future/.

2. Clark, "Debunking The 'No Friends At Work' Rule."

Chapter 45: Your Personal Life Is Personal—Keep Most of It That Way

1. Diana I. Tamir and Jason P. Mitchel, "Disclosing information about the self is intrinsically rewarding," *PNAS* 109, no. 21 (2012), accessed June 22, 2013, http://wjh.harvard.edu/~dtamir/Tamir-PNAS-2012.pdf.

Chapter 46: Slow to Hire, Quick to Fire

1. Carole Martin, "5 Hiring Rules," accessed September 21, 2013, http://www.boostyourhiringiq.com/become-an-interview-coach/.
2. Corporate executive board press release, "Hiring Decisions Miss the Mark 50% of the Time," accessed September 21, 2013, http://ir.executiveboard.com/phoenix.zhtml?c=113226&p=irol-newsArticle&ID=1205091&highlight=.
3. Bradford D. Smart, *Topgrading: How Leading Companies Win By Hiring, Coaching, and Keeping the Best People* (New York: Penguin, 2005), 44.
4. Robert Sutton, "How a Few Bad Apples Ruin Everything," *Wall Street Journal*, October 24, 2011, accessed July 20, 2013, http://online.wsj.com/article/SB10001424052970203499704576622550325233260.html.
5. Corporate executive board press release, "Hiring Decisions Miss the Mark 50% of the Time."
6. Carole Martin, "Boost Your Interview IQ," accessed December 2, 2013, http://boostyourhiringiq.com/.
7. Teresa Daggett, personal communication, July 19, 2013.

Chapter 48: Crying—Best Left for Weddings and Funerals

1. James Cunliffe, "Study reveals why women cry at work," *Bedfordshire News*, May 2, 2010, accessed June 1, 2010, http://www.bedfordshire-news.co.uk/Home/Study-reveals-why-women-cry-at-work-2.htm.
2. Jenna Goudreau, "Crying at Work, A Woman's Burden," *Forbes*, January 11, 2011, accessed February 1, 2011, http://www.forbes.com/sites/jennagoudreau/2011/01/11/crying-

at-work-a-womans-burden-study-men-sex-testosterone-tears-arousal/.
3. Audrey Nelson, "The Crying Game," *Psychology Today*, January 2, 2011, accessed February 1, 2011, http://www.psychologytoday.com/blog/he-speaks-she-speaks/201101/the-crying-game.
4. Goudreau, "Crying at Work, A Woman's Burden."
5. Stephanie Pliha, personal communication, July 19, 2013.
6. Thanks to Charles K. Guttas, MD.
7. Goudreau, "Crying at Work, A Woman's Burden."
8. *Brainy Quote*, accessed September 21, 2013, http://www.brainyquote.com/quotes/quotes/l/louispaste159478.html.

Chapter 50: Men—Thriving Amongst Differences

1. Bruce Holland, "Women Are Significantly More Right Brained Than Men," accessed September 22, 2013, http://www.virtual.co.nz/index.php?n=StrategicSnippets.WomenAreSignificantlyMoreRightBrainedThanMen.
2. Stephen Bavolek, "Male and Female Brain Functioning: Left Brain and Right Brain," accessed September 22, 2013, http://nurturingparenting.com/images/cmsfiles/maleandfemalebrainfunctioning2-23-2012-r3.pptx.
3. Bavolek, "Male and Female Brain Functioning."
4. Claire Damken Brown and Audrey Nelson, "10 Tips to Enhancing Women's Credibility," *Colorado SBDC Network*, accessed September 25, 2013, http://www.denversbdc.org/announcements/10-tips-to-enhancing-womens-credibility.
5. Jennifer Crittenden, personal communication, March 1, 2013.
6. Lee Dye, "Men Crave Competition, In Work and Play," *ABC News*, January 19, 2011, accessed September 24, 2013, http://abcnews.go.com/Technology/DyeHard/men-crave-competition-women-work-play/story?id=12641830.
7. US Bureau of Labor Statistics, "Highlights of Women's Earnings in 2012."

Chapter 51: Angels and Demons—Make That Demonettes

1. LPL Financial, lploceanave.com, accessed September 24, 2013, http://lploceanave.com/new/lploceanave/content.asp?contentid=2017655592.
2. Mickey Meece, "Backlash: Women Bullying Women at Work," *New York Times*, May 9, 2009, accessed June 1, 2009,

http://www.nytimes.com/2009/05/10/business/10women.html?pagewanted=all&_r=0.

Part IV: Transform Your Life

Chapter 52: Be Balanced—Physically, Mentally, and Spiritually

1. Vasilios D. Kosteas, "The Effect of Exercise on Earnings: Evidence from the NLSY," *Journal of Labor Research, Journal of Labor Research* (June 2012), http://dx.doi.org/10.2139/ssrn.1612384.
2. Krista Dalton, personal communication, April 24, 2013.

Chapter 55: Multiply Success—Share Your Goals

1. Peter M. Gollwitzer, Paschal Sheeran, Verena Michalski, and Andrea E. Seifert, "When Intentions Go Public: Does Social Reality Widen the Intention-Behavior Gap?" *Psychological Science,* Vol 20:5, 612–618, accessed November 10, 2013, http://www.psych.nyu.edu/gollwitzer/09_Gollwitzer_Sheeran_Seifert_Michalski_When_Intentions_.pdf.

Chapter 56: Perfection Impedes Progress

1. Cate Goethals, personal communication, September 1, 2013.
2. Adapted from a quote by Dolly Parton, accessed November 10, 2013, http://www.goodreads.com/author/quotes/144067.Dolly_Parton.
3. Cate Goethals, personal communication, September 1, 2013.

Chapter 57: Say No with Yes

1. "Learn to master 'The Power of a Positive No,'" *NBC News.com* video, March 5, 2008, accessed April 1, 2011, http://www.today.com/id/23466223/ns/today-today_books/t/learn-master-power-positive-no/.
2. Thema Bryant-Davis, tweet, September 28, 2012 (6:30 a.m.), accessed September 19, 2013, https://twitter.com/drthema/status/251675282086440960#.

Chapter 58: You're No Dog—Bitch's New Paradigm

1. *Goodreads,* accessed September 25, 2013, http://www.goodreads.com/author/quotes/104438.Madonna.

2. *Quoteworld.org,* accessed September 25, 2013, http://www.quoteworld.org/quotes/6825.
3. *Thinkexist.com,* accessed September 25, 2013, http://thinkexist.com/quotation/why_is_it_that_men_can_be_bastards_and_women_must/213491.html.
4. Adapted from a quote by Ella Wheeler Wilcox.

Chapter 59: Put It All Together—Know Your Value

1. Kevin Costner, "Kevin Costner's emotional speech in full at Whitney Houston's funeral," *The Showbiz 411,* YouTube video, February 18, 2012, accessed August 24, 2013, http://m.youtube.com/watch?v=2wjhoN1EzPI&desktop_uri=%2Fwatch%3Fv%3D2wjhoN1EzPI.
2. Margarie Ingall, "Know Your Worth & Get More of What You Deserve," *Self,* 2012, accessed September 25, 2013, http://www.self.com/health/2012/01/know-your-worth.
3. Mary Schumacher, personal communication, September 23, 2013.
4. Maxwell Maltz, *Psycho-Cybernetics* (New Jersey: Prentice-Hall, Inc., 1960).

Chapter 60: Lastly, Lighten Up—Be a Fun, Fabulous Person!

1. Geoffrey James, "8 Core Beliefs of Extraordinary Bosses," *Inc.,* accessed February 24, 2013, http://www.inc.com/geoffrey-james/8-core-beliefs-of-extraordinary-bosses.html.
2. Angela Huffmon, "Fun at Work Increases Productivity," *Angela Huffmon Presents* blog, March 1, 2011, accessed July 14, 2013, http://www.angelahuffmon.biz/blog/?id=29&showEntry=1.

Appendix: Glass Ceilings

1. Peggy Klaus, "Neither Mice Nor Men," *The New York Times,* March 6, 2010, accessed June 1, 2010, http://www.nytimes.com/2010/03/07/jobs/07preoccupations.html."
2. Corinne A. Moss-Racusin, John F. Dovidio, Vitoria L. Brescoll, et al., "Science faculty's subtle gender biases favor male students," *Proceedings from the National Academy of Sciences of the United States of America* 109, no. 41 (2012): 16474–16479, accessed May 22, 2013, doi:10.1073/iti4112109, http://www.pnas.org/content/109/41/16474.short.